UNDER THE AUSPICES OF CRYSTALS

Ellen Tewkesbury

ATHENA PRESS
LONDON

UNDER THE AUSPICES OF CRYSTALS
Copyright © Ellen Tewkesbury 2005

All Rights Reserved

No part of this book may be reproduced in any form
by photocopying or by any electronic or mechanical means,
including information storage or retrieval systems,
without permission in writing from both the copyright
owner and the publisher of this book.

ISBN 1 84401 433 9

First Published 2005
ATHENA PRESS
Queen's House, 2 Holly Road
Twickenham TW1 4EG
United Kingdom

Printed for Athena Press

UNDER THE AUSPICES OF CRYSTALS

*To dearest Debbie,
with much love
from the author,
Andrea
December 2005*

For my sister

The myth is not my own, I had it from my mother.
					Euripides

Contents

Part I
The Threshold   9

Part II
The Reign of the Belvedere Apollo   101

Part III
The Inextinguishable Myth   189

Part I

The Threshold

Something is happening in me; a subtle change is occurring: a pause in my life. I arrive at a cleared space, a place without clutter. I am earthed to the colour green. I tell myself that I must rest here in coolness before I do anything. I must learn to breathe differently. The book I am holding falls from my hands, the voice of the narrator fades to a faint murmur. I close my eyes and allow myself to sink into a misty distance. My own voice floats from a far location. I speak as a writer speaks, and yet I scarcely know what that is, myself as creator, expressing words, extracting essence. Oh, I know the voice of other writers. I have, in my life, read hundreds of books, for experience moulded me to the role of the hearer, never the speaker. I sat in receptive silence and listened. I have observed the behaviour and heard the words of so many creative people, praising their gifts, living their particular delights, grateful for the experience. Having seen and having heard, honouring books as sacred objects, I now wish to speak. I am charged with the responsibilities of the oracle; not voice of everyday communication, the stories of today, but *vox* from somewhere within an imagined antiquity. I would like to relinquish English for Latin, but I cannot. I am not a scholar. The feeling is so deep, so remote that I can only grope with fragments of language, fitting words to feeling, testing the validity of my discoveries as I go along. Is this *locus* in me, this rare and wondrous place, a seat of learning, a site of ancient memory lifted into the present, inviting me to return to origins? I do not know. Only exploration will tell. I give myself to these very words, here on the page, in a way I have never given myself to words before. I enter darkness. The page is blank and without any visible boundaries: a beckoning space. I begin to fall into the abyss, away from outer reality, falling through a small earthy opening that upon the instant becomes a watery stream of feeling, a racing dream. My fall is this, nothing but a single question: what will happen if I live my life, my life of feeling and experience, under the auspices of crystals? I must admit that I am in the thrall of these words, 'under the auspices'. As I hear them whispered in me, a mantle of the arcane falls upon my shoulders. The phrase arches softly in the air and then floats down, folding in winged movement around me. From now on, the spirit speaks. I ask myself, what will arise in me if I submit my entire being, moment by moment, to the power and influence of stones? Why do these crystalline creatures of the earth disturb me? I know that something darkly beautiful calls, something absolute in its insistence, an elemental energy, arising to meet me from the earth. All my imaginings now are of stones, in the spirit of beautiful visitations. I inhale the colour green. The question is asked over and over again: what will happen to me? What will happen? I place a hand upon my heart. The sensation in my body is the pull of gravity, a plunge to earth and water, a compulsive, heavy feeling that suddenly, and at the last moment, gives way to the joys of height. Cast into darkness, I am elated. I anticipate great feeling, delightful discoveries still to come, if they may come. I do not know what they will be. All I do know is that I want to experience everything that arises in me under the auspices of crystals, giving voice to every single event, every nuance, here in written words that are oracular, living things, as vibrant as crystals themselves.

I begin with the word, *auspex*: a Latin word that governs the phrase and opens the door to the past. Language shifts to the present tense. In ancient Roman civilisation, an auspex is a birdseer: someone who contemplates the flight, singing or feeding of birds and from their observed behaviour predicts future events. The gaze is ever upwards to the skies. How does the crow fly, and from which direction? Is there meaning in his call? An auspex is an augur, a seeker and a seer of good omens. I do not know why I like this idea so much. Perhaps it is because there are no such auspices in our modern society, our superstitions having changed. We have only the remnant of meaning in the idea of patronage or protection. The power of the auspex has departed. The word has only the faintest vibration. Who today would go to receive the auspices before embarking on a journey or rush outside to observe the flight of birds? I have never heard anyone say, *as the crow does not cry, I cannot go*. We have our rituals, but there are no auspices. Our rational minds would condemn such weakness. But if the truth is to be told, the voice of the oracle may still be called upon to speak, to utter deeply. She comes in many guises, and I need not name them here. Compelled to give voice to the auspex in me, I must lean into the space softly, in order to modify the thrust of gravity. If I can break my fall to earth with some magic that comes to me, a relic of antiquity, I will do so. I can do nothing more than say, I study the flight of birds within the mystery of the crystal. This, I believe, is already a good omen.

At the moment my feeling is very soft, but at the same time I am aware of an unwelcome presence, a lurking shadow with power to turn softness into a stone wall. How will I negotiate the coming difficulties and penetrate barriers? Will someone forbid me to speak of subtleties? Will something prevent me from using the tools of psychic insight? I hold to my fear. Perhaps old obscurities will return. First of all, I must be attentive to each and every moment. I must feel. Everything relies on the refinement of seeing and hearing.

For the whole day I have been preoccupied with my inclinations. From waking, I have become aware of the depth of my breathing, and how breath carries me to another location. I am holding in my left hand a tapered natural crystal with a clear point, its rough root speaking of a rude birth into this world. Its irruption into air after countless ages underground is much of the mystery. I observe mineral transformations, absorbing them as my own experience, sensing a hidden activity. Now a crystal destiny touches something in me. Breathing green, I am stimulated by the vibrations of silicon quartz lying in my hand. How I love it. I regret its wrenching from the matrix. I am sorry it had to be flung from a southern pole to a northern home, but at the same time I am grateful to it for the feeling it brings me. It comes into my life for the purposes of teaching. I will hear it and I will see it, even more, oh, far, far more, than I am doing now. This is merely a beginning. I know through feeling that I am an initiate of the mysteries of the auspex. I wish to speak.

What occurs in me? Holding a crystal, I return to music. Music emerges as a model of origins, but my origins are already given a distinct shape. Sonata form occurs. In this, I become a lover of art. I hear a particular mode of music, a composition for the piano. I receive the sonata, not as I imagine a musician might receive it, with acquired knowledge. I receive it in the manner of an enthused hearer, as if I have nothing but ears. It moves in the imagination as pure, ordered vibration. Although I am aware of the principles of sonata form, the earthy perfection of the quartz crystal presents again the classical sonata to me. It is the sonata as archetype, a primal integration of seeing and hearing. Somewhere within me, the sonatas of Haydn, Mozart and early Beethoven are uncovered in a manner that is more than mere memory. I ask myself as I stroke the crystal, 'Is this thing of beauty a quartz sonata?' The question sounds ridiculous, but I have promised myself to write everything that occurs, no matter how awkward it seems. Before my eyes alighted upon clear quartz, sonata form acted upon my mind in the same way that clear quartz now draws my attention to the subtleties of nature's shapes. My ear knows and loves the sonata; the root of its meaning deep in the Latin *sonus*, sound. I see it, resting upon the palm of my hand. In the depths of being, where turbulence occurs, the crystal vibrates as music, recalling origins, an ancient memory of the heart. And without the active ear and music in my life, it is unlikely that I would be declaring in these pages that clear quartz is an earthy mutation of sonata form. I hear it.

In my childhood, born into patriarchal Protestantism in Tasmania, into the extremities of religion and its shadowy associate, alcohol, music was the only integrating influence that life provided. It offered me a model of wholeness, although I did not know this at the time. I happened to love music. I was steeped in hearing because I was made that way. I observed the manner in which others listened to music. I was especially drawn to my father in the presence of music. We all knew that father was very musical and that his parents and his sisters were musical too. I studied him closely. He became my teacher, my teacher 'of the ear'. If my father had been permitted to genuflect, he might have genuflected before sonata form. It occurred to me, even when I was quite young, that in the presence of this worshipful work of art, the sonata, my father seemed, in some way, covered and unavailable. As he approached his *sanctum sanctorum*, he assumed the singular, a man alone. His entire being changed, and it was both a fascination for this change as much as a fear for his unearthly knowledge that kept me a close observer of all his actions. I used to wonder what he heard through the gramophone that he should be so altered, and in what manner he heard. What was happening in him? I saw the rapt expression on his face. I felt his absence. What conflict arose in his mind because of hearing? And there was conflict in him because from young manhood my father suffered from an inexorable loss of hearing, a tendency that had also visited other musical members of the family. And as a result of his increasing deafness, my father sought a close alliance with the struggles of Beethoven. He embraced him with both arms. My father said that Beethoven, above all, was the greatest composer. He was the composer as hero, conquering darkness. He admired him and talked about him. And when he listened to Beethoven in that holy and reverent way, I knew that I must keep my distance.

As an interesting musical metaphor, I am thinking of the device that composers call 'an enharmonic change'. Sir Hubert Parry, the great English composer, says an enharmonic change occurs when advantage is taken of the fact that the same note can be called by a different name, this difference leading into an unexpected key. The enharmonic, a deliberate selecting of another dynamic within the harmonic, permits a subtle relocating of key in relationship to the original. The key now assumes a new modulation and is heard differently within the ear. This musical device, as metaphor and as a tool of transformation, offers me a model in changing the form of painful hearing within myself. Enharmonically speaking, what I now call pain may be renamed. To begin with, and before the arrival of any other name, I would like to call it 'non-pain'. The sympathetic energy of the crystal, working through my psyche, creates the change. I move into an unexpected key, delighted by the new perspective, the smooth continuum of things. Even in the absence of bliss, which is considered the most desirable transformation of all, non-pain now becomes the *locus* of further transformations, further possibilities; a place in which to experience the beauty of enharmonic hearing.

Darkness was the theology of my father's religious years. I do not believe that dark and destructive memory should be made to disappear, banished from existence. Where can it go? What energy destroys destruction? In my understanding of the behaviour of matter, the act of burning a book, for instance, does not make it disappear completely, except in its material form. The book passes immediately into smoke, an acrid, gritty mist, a visible suspension of carbon atoms. This is a transformation that may satisfy an inquisition in its need to burn thought. But a book belongs to language and to communication, not least a gift of trees, arising from earth. Can thinking be killed? Whatever is brought into consciousness, is simply there. It takes shape. As thoughts are things subject to countless mutations, the contents of books have proved difficult to burn. What is destroyed in one form will emerge elsewhere, at precisely the right time, in a new form. Extermination is a dangerous process to adopt as a way of dealing with perceived forces of evil. The very engine of evil in one shape or another was a fundamental part of my childhood. My father pointed to it. Evil had to be destroyed, completely and utterly. It was to be cut out at the root, thrown on the fire, or dashed to the ground and smashed into a thousand bits. So today, I am looking to a softer transformation, a movement within the psyche that some call healing. I know this to be a more wholesome way of approaching the pains of the past in a desire for inner growth. And in order to offer healing to another, the would-be practitioner should first effect a transformation within herself, observing the power of enharmonic change. And so I begin here, in a personal burning; burning myself into the fine violet ash of the mineral spodumene, acting as an auspex of earth mysteries, a modern woman in an ancient art, observing the flight of birds.

Some thoughts on healing now occur. The word healer unnerves me. As a healer of others, I do not know who I am. The healer is not yet realised in me. As I have already said, this is but a beginning. This is my journey towards significant change. Anyway, I know that the intellect alone cannot heal. It might think it can, but this is an error. My aversion to the word healer belongs to deep-seated religious prejudices arising from a childhood sensitised to ideas of heresy. Am I a heretic? My father asks the question, pointing his finger. He demands an answer. I am confused. I haven't the faintest idea what he means. Diagnosis is at work. Even though he was a doctor, I do not think I ever heard my father refer to healing in a spiritual context, except when he talked about the miracle healing of Christ. Jesus being the miracle healer *ne plus ultra*, anything was possible, even the restoration of the dead. Medically speaking, my father might refer to the healing of a wound, the disease of the flesh. He often talked about his patients and their physical and mental problems. The power invested in him as a surgeon led him directly into the operations of both the body and the soul, so he believed, and as a religious man, his licence to cure ills invoked a voice of judgement. He gave himself this authority. But heresy remained a deeply troubling preoccupation of my father for which there seemed to be no cure other than a ritual killing. At one in spirit with the Protestant reformer John Huss, he exclaimed, '*O sancta simplicitas!*' as an aged peasant threw a bundle of twigs upon his pyre. My father loved to burn. A true creature of Prometheus, fire was his element. Foxe's *Book of Martyrs* glowed mauve upon the shelf, like a sultry ember of the mineral spodumene. Burning the heretic, as much as being burnt, was a theological idea that appealed to him. I am not sure whether he ever resolved the problem in himself, although I like to believe that by the time he came to leave this world, the terror of heresy had relinquished its claim upon him. But throughout life, my father pursued the unorthodox choice that is heresy and resorted to music as his 'enharmonic change'. But for reasons I have yet to understand, he transferred the idea of heresy right into the *locus* in which no heresy can exist. He judged music so that music suffered its own martyrdom. The world of art that he worshipped so much was full of saints and sinners. He condemned and praised, all in the same breath. My father was a hard man. He was fierce, exacting, demanding. To be in his presence as a child was to be terrified. On the other hand, his patients accepted his authority in diagnosis and treatment. I observed their gratitude before him. They gave him gifts. Their indebtedness to him for his life-giving skills increased my own respectful fear of a man who had such powers. And from his constant pronouncements of certainties and absolutes, there was the darker side: shocking lapses into coarse jokes and obscenities, especially when he drank. In his own inebriated pilgrimage to filth, he used to recite pages of Chaucer's *The Miller's Tale* at the table while we, his children, sat strictly to attention. This memory of his cracked, laughing voice, rambling through the rhyming couplets, leering at the lewd, reinstates the hazy ways of alcohol; the awful disarray of my father with gravy and drink dribbling from the corner of his mouth. My mother was there, but she sat in silence. These lapses into his dark art were just as terrifying to me as were his punishments of wrongdoing. Yet deep within him, I knew that he wavered. He too had his terrors and his doubts.

I am bound to say that my father's darkest enharmonic change was indeed his alcoholism. My poor father, I say, and I do not know why, except that I feel such pity for him. This tendency to drink came upon him suddenly as a young man after he had shed the stern guardianship of his parents. When he reached his majority and qualified as a doctor, he drank. His parents had determined from birth that he would be a surgeon. He obeyed. At the same time, he grew up with the mind of a patriarch, surrounded by the structures of patriarchy, in a Calvinistic theology that summarised meaning from origins to eternity. His father, of whom I have only the faintest memory, was a Presbyterian minister. My father, Merton, was the son of the manse. Young Merton wore, for as long as he was able, the mantle of filial piety. I am quite sure he never saw himself as a rebel, but even if he was not aware of it, revolt was in him. His drinking 'just happened', my mother used to say, as it 'just happened' to most medical students. At home he learnt obedience to authority. He was subject to restrictions and moral mouldings of one sort or another that in more enlightened times would be deemed severe deprivations. Physical punishment was the preferred method of correction, all good instruction being inextricably beholden to the pains of the flesh.

Raised in rural Victoria, my father led an isolated life, denied friends for the sake of purity of person. The softest connections he had were a companionable attachment to cats. The household pets became his out of school friends, as there was no one of his age that he was permitted to see. He put his hand lovingly upon his animal companions. He looked after them. For his chores, he cut and stacked wood for the kitchen stove, he cleaned his room, prepared meat scraps for the cats, and otherwise jumped-to for any task that was demanded of him. Above all, he was studious. He read the intellectual books that his parents selected for him. He studied the Bible, instructed by his father. Every week he was given a text to learn for the edification of his moral being, to be recited before Sunday lunch, following a similar recitation by his older sisters. He was a clever young boy with the ability to absorb information quickly; eminently teachable, receptive to everything, except when it came to learning the piano. Music, in this strictly gendered household, was the preoccupation of females. And although his mother wanted to give him lessons, because he was so musical, she refrained from using force. She sensed his aloofness. She saw him resisting tuition, standing beside her as she played, refusing instruction. His mother thought that insistence might be contrary to a gift. And anyhow, it was enough that three women occupied the Bechstein in the front parlour, practising every day. So young Merton listened to the word of his parents in their authority just as he listened to music in its own. Music had a strong location in his psyche, a more mysterious vibration, in so many ways nearer to him than the ambiguities of language. Nevertheless, as he lived under the rule of word and its theology, music too began to assume the pre-eminence of *logos*: the word that asserts. Later on, medical indoctrination instilled a belief in the cutting and cauterising cure, while creation awaited final salvation through the science of the rational mind. Progress for humankind, or for *mankind* as my father used to say, was surely a matter of fact. He aspired to ideals of purity, but the controlling of his compulsive tendencies, his feeling world, so turbulent, so unexpected, was completely beyond him. I watched him closely. I thought I saw the silenced child in him, but I think this is an observation of the crystal moment. My father was seldom silent, except when alcohol made him morose, or when he was wrapped in hearing.

When I was a young girl, subject to the authority of parents, I was mostly afraid. Fear, though not a friend, was a familiar, so to speak. I learnt to respect it. My father instilled fear in his offspring as a matter of course. He used it as a tool in much the same way that it was used in his childhood. The teaching that issued from the mouth of my father reiterated the teaching of his parents. 'Normal' and 'abnormal' were words that had a certain ominous ring. There was such stress on the ab, 'away from'. I could never be sure to which category I belonged. I always feared the worst. As I grew older and my passive observation became a way of living, I could be overcome by a great sorrow for him, particularly in his deafness, when the high notes of his heroic Beethoven were struck from his hearing. I watched his faculties decline, his once clear complexion changing into the ruddy glow of the alcoholic. I felt his depression, afflicted for him. Only now do I know that the anguish I experienced then was, in truth, my very own.

All this seems to be about calling or not calling myself a healer. I have in mind, a better word, 'therapy'. The crystal in my hand vibrates towards a different linguistic root. According to the Greek lexicon, as a therapist, I may also do service to the gods; I may keep a day holy; I may care for the sick; I may cultivate and I may love the land. Each one of these occupations is purely creative. I wish to embrace them all, one by one, here on the page, in the *locus* that first caught my fall. I will follow my inclinations, leaning into the native place, relating from the heart, creating a worded form to occupy both space and time. Although my work can never be as beautiful as music's vibrations, nevertheless, I may aspire to sonata form, the vibrating beauty that has its root in *sonus*, sound. I bow poetically before the inspiration, honouring the crystalline earth from which sonata emerges. Now I must examine the transformations of my own psyche, paying attention to sharper seeing and deeper hearing. Crystals are my flight of birds, a promising augury. And so I look to the skies in order to descry the heavens on a bright autumn afternoon in England. Blue lace agate fades to pale rose quartz at the end of my first day: my day of feeling recall, under the auspices of crystals.

A problem of continuity has arisen; an uncomfortable pause. The cool green of my initial encounter has completely disappeared. I do not know where I am, or how to proceed. I sit in the midst of a mass of contrary feelings. I am in turmoil, for that is the only word I can use. I am in the turn and moil of things, the boiling sea of the psyche. I observe my inner state in having come thus far into darkness, daring to speak about my father. My heart pounds in my chest. The vast space of the white page reels. It is difficult to select just one element from the seething thing within me, one element to satisfy my desire for pattern. I toy with italics, leaning into the word, pattern. I like all writing in italics. I remember when I first saw italics on the printed page of a school poetry book. My eyes seized upon the textual difference, the forward slope in a structure of uprights. How interesting, I thought, relishing the arrival of a new, subtle energy. I studied two Latin words, *lapis lazuli*, meaning azure stone in Robert Browning's poem, *The Bishop Orders His Tomb at St Praxed's Church*. By this time I was in my matriculation year at The Friend's School, Hobart, struggling to understand, dreading a written examination. I was far from happy.

As I had been sent to a number of different schools to satisfy the whims of my father, uncertainty had eroded my confidence. But the first subject to attract me was poetry, for which I felt something, a bodily something. And the attraction to poetic form arrived with the pleasing feeling that arose from the page. My eye followed the ordered lines. Although I liked what I saw, the literal mind within poetry was much more difficult to acquire. I had no knowledge of classical mythology. Every reference needed explanation. Where was this ancient world of the gods? Our origins were so far away, somewhere beyond the tropic of Capricorn, north of the known. All I knew then was the change that came over me in the presence of the poetic, especially the poetry of the English Romantics. I learnt the opening stanzas of John Keats' *Endymion*: 'A thing of beauty is a joy for ever.' Oh, I knew what that meant. Our class listened to a line-by-line analysis of *The Bishop Orders His Tomb* by our teacher, Miss Ellis. In a Quaker clearing, she talked about the opulence, the corruption of the Catholic Church. My mind wandered off into an italic dream, stimulated by the Latin, lapis lazuli. How beautiful; a thing of beauty; a stone of celestial blue. What would it be like to rest eternally in a tomb of celestial blue? Lapis lazuli leapt from the page and kept me in the hope of seeing. One day, I vowed, I would find my mysterious lapis. In myself, I searched for the colour. It was not the first time that I had done this, because a few years before, I had been despatched to a Roman Catholic convent to be educated by nuns. I had seen icons and holy statues. I had gazed at pictures of the Blessed Virgin Mary. She was always blue. In those difficult years, I had lived under a canopy of lapis, and I hardly knew it. The transformation was in Latin, in the forward inclination of 'z' in lazuli; two little parallels connected by a diagonal, inviting a glimpse of the Pythagorian mystery. Patterns within patterns. Even now, I like names of crystals to be written that way, leaning into meaning, thrilling with a shimmer of antiquity. I ask, what is the pattern of lapis in my imagination? And this morning, as I write, there is such a jostling at the door, such a constant flowing in and out, that I am unable to catch anything of substance. What shall I do? I arrive at the enharmonic change; a voice reaching into unexpected keys; calling, not that, not that, but *this*. I seek sonata form born from the very depths of turmoil.

I admit a crystal. From all the crystal gifts that have come to me, tumbled stones, points, spheres, polished slabs and rough minerals from the earth, today's insistent crystal is rose quartz. I have no hesitation in approaching it; a familiarity is there. About ten years ago, rose quartz called me. I happened upon it somewhere in England. Its simplicity caught my attention. I felt an arousal, not unlike my response to *Endymion*. How feminine, I thought; a thing of beauty, a joy for ever. Something entered; I admitted its energy, full of hidden pink rainbows. I do so today, waiting for the next insight in my journal of feeling experience. The pink polished sphere is in my hand. I observe. Rose quartz walks in beauty, but not the beauty of the night. It feels to be an aurora of the far north, where I am now. In its own soft dawn it longs to bring me a harvest from the past; yesterday's dawn of the Southern Hemisphere. I agree to travel with it wherever it wishes to take me, simply because it is so beautiful. I trust its healing intentions. Under its cosmic canopy, what can go wrong?

In my crystal awakening, once upon a time, I was more delighted by obsidian than anything else. That was long ago, after my initiation into the mystery of the italic lapis lazuli and Robert Browning's poetry. Obsidian and I could not be parted, all because of the name. I saw my whole life then, in its turmoil, through dark, volcanic glass. And if the origins of the word turmoil can be unearthed, then the turn and moil of it belong to obsidian in the primitive, before it was flung as sizzling liquid to the surface in a seismic eruption. That this smooth, beautiful thing should have been born in such hot, geological confusion, to sit within the hand as cool as spring water is quite beyond the power of words to describe.

Obsidian vibrations incline to art, especially the great vibrating art, music. Obsidian with its sulphurous sibilant, a shape upon the page more pagan than Christian, has an interesting etymological history. It arrived in English in mutated form, a mistake having occurred in translation. *Lapis obsidianus* is a copyist's error for *lapis obsianus*, 'stone of Obsius'. The Roman historian, Pliny the Elder, recorded that a man called Obsius had discovered the stone in Ethiopia. Early in its long evolution to the catalogues of crystallographers and healers, the stone of Obsius became 'obsidian'. It was of great interest to Pliny in compiling his vast encyclopaedia, the *Historia naturalis*. Did he know that it was not a stone at all, but volcanic glass? In AD 79, while he was in command of the Roman fleet, Vesuvius erupted. The sight of an active volcano in full flow fascinated him. Seizing the opportunity to observe an eruption from the foothills, he dropped anchor and went ashore. Vesuvius exerted her magnetism; she opened her sulphurous crater. Pliny began his ascent. While climbing the smoking slopes, the volcano took him by surprise. Enthralled by nature, negotiating treacherous extrusions, he inhaled the poisonous fumes and began to choke, suffocating in the very *locus* of the mysterious stone. Where obsidian was born, Pliny died. But the credit remains with unknown Obsius for discovering it. I imagine that every stone arouses a sense of mystery and excitement in the discoverer, a delight in the hitherto unseen. Even the copyist's mistake in the story of obsidian brings another quality to the subtle appreciation of its operations. Although something was misheard and misapplied, fate would have it that obsidian should emerge this way, that we should hear it and see it in a linguistic mutation.

Obsidian is often called the reflector of the psyche. It holds within it the power of insight as well as other subtleties of psychic descrying. According to Pliny, when sheets of obsidian are laid in chamber walls as mirrors, rather than the image itself, volcanic glass reflects the shadow of the image. More than just a shiny surface, in an instant it becomes a rolling enfilade of softening visions, a parting of old forsaken curtains, the rediscovery of long forgotten sights and sounds, the velvet penumbra of memory. I love my dark, greening obsidian piece; a deep heap of solidified interior; a primal mound. It sits in the palm of my hand like an inverted limpet. It is not crystalline, but takes its organic shape from the sudden, disturbing operations of the earth. It cools too quickly to form crystals. I read it like a mirrored book; a book with an annotated text; footnotes and appendices of further refinement; a leaning into a glassy meaning of meaning. Obsidian becomes my mystical *enchiridion*; something small held in the hand. I see it as vision; I hear it as vibration.

It is while holding my obsidian sphere with its viridian sheen that the music of Beethoven occurs. Obsidian takes me to a vision of my father listening to the heroic composer. At the same time, it takes me to my own hearing; the experience of hearing Beethoven differently, from the operations of the form, sonata. The *sonus* of obsidian holds me by the ear. I have my own hearing, I tell myself. I am at last free to claim it. This discovery, that I too hear, takes me by surprise. It seems that only now have I come into true possession of this complex faculty with all its refinements. I approach the hearing of hearing, under the auspices of obsidian. The distinction, my own hearing and not my father's, is a great gift to me, something startling. Throughout my entire life, I have given to him. Even from the remoteness of this *Ultima Thule*, long after his death, I have given to him. He demanded the attention of his offspring, particularly his daughters. Observing him in all his moods, his fearful unpredictability, his condemnations and his drinking, I held on to the great fear that he had given me. Through conditioning, I came to need it, for I knew nothing else. My father shaped my psyche. And his power was always reinforced by the unquestioning support of my mother, particularly with respect to daughters. There may be a right son or a wrong son, but to my father, daughters posed a problem that he was never able to resolve.

The image of hearing comes in a rush, like a volcanic eruption. My father hears. Holding obsidian I see him once more. I hold the crystal that speaks to the heart of the world, as Beethoven spoke through his music, the oracle of the cosmos. Oh, how I see my father! He is listening intently to a recording of Wilhelm Backhaus playing Beethoven's sonata, *Appassionata*; a turbulence pervading the air from the woody interior of the gramophone, making the room resonate. The piano crashes forth. It is summer in Hobart, Tasmania. My father paces the floor of the sunny drawing room with its bay windows and its beautiful view. For an instant he holds up a hand to me as I stand on the threshold, a signal that says, do not enter. He is hearing nothing but his music; hearing and inhaling; exhaling tobacco; breath and Beethoven infused with the incense of nicotine. I watch him. He moves through the passionate sounds of the piano. Once more, the transfigured look is upon his face. He impresses me, yet Beethoven is even more impressive. There must be something unique within music that my father, who knows everything, should be compelled to enter the great resonating chamber alone. I stare at him. I wonder, but posing a question makes little sense. I simply wonder. My father, in his own deafness, listening to the deaf Beethoven. It is only now, with obsidian nestling in the palm of my hand that I can ask, to the very depths of volcanic glass, what was so powerful in music that affected my father? What exactly did he hear?

Before I continue with my narrative of hearing and seeing, I would like to relate a striking story in the life and death of Joseph Stalin. As this story has a certain insistence in my hearing, arising now as I lean into my newly discovered inner location, I must relate it, just as it comes to me.

The story concerns Stalin's connection with Mozart's Piano Concerto No. 23. Quite by chance, Stalin heard a performance of the concerto in a radio broadcast not long before he died. The concerto affected him profoundly. Stalin, whose fear of formalism in Soviet music kept him ever alert to his perceived enemy, found himself moved, not by the work of a Russian genius, but by a work of eighteenth century classical purity, with its indebtedness to sonata form, composed by none other than Mozart, an Austrian. Although the story that arose from Stalin's hearing of Mozart came some time later and is imbued with an apocryphal flavour, it is nevertheless a haunting tale that presents itself as fundamentally true. I trust it implicitly.

Mozart's A Major Piano Concerto with its second movement in the remoter key of F sharp minor, a movement of great delicacy and refinement, was played on the occasion of Stalin's encounter by Maria Yudina, a Soviet pianist who taught at the Leningrad Conservatoire. Yudina was a woman of exceptional musical gift. Her honesty and outspokenness were eventually to be the cause of her dismissal from the Conservatoire. She was, as was her contemporary, Dmitri Shostakovich, one of the great artists of the Soviet Union. After years of tirades against her for her anti-party opinions, she was finally accused of uttering the word God before her students and condemned for promoting religious propaganda in an officially atheist state. Admired still for her great integrity, her reputation remains to this day 'untarnished gold' among those who admire Russian art and artists. Dmitri Shostakovich tells the famous account of Yudina and Stalin in his posthumously published *Testimony*, and although this book has since been discredited for reasons that have no bearing upon what I am about to say, I remain under the spell of the event that Shostakovich himself found truly remarkable.

Whatever Maria Yudina played, said Shostakovich, she played 'unlike anyone else'. In her exceptional knowledge of the language of music, she had a profound effect upon how he heard the great keyboard works of Bach and Beethoven. As a Russian, he was indebted to her for deepening his understanding of German music, the pillar of twentieth century art. When Yudina played a four-voice fugue, Shostakovich said, each of the four voices could be distinguished by its own timbre. Her playing ravished the ear. He was struck by its interior nature. So subtle was her hearing that through her interpretation, she encouraged Shostakovich's own musical development, his own inner hearing. They often played the piano together. But when he asked her how she arrived at a particular dynamic, her reply was simply, 'because I feel it that way'. It was always a matter of feeling, her feeling. Apart from this, she had nothing else to say. Shostakovich found her response frustrating. What did she mean? He asked for her thinking, her method, how she reasoned as a musician. But Maria Yudina made no contribution to music and the mind. With her rare intelligence, she interpreted art through the heart. Her hearing of music came from the very spaces of its architecture and from a deep respect for subtle structures.

Yudina defended Shostakovich publicly when he was under attack. She spoke openly of the innerness of his music, as if there was no other way in which it could be received. His Forty-Eight Preludes and Fugues, she said, were keyboard masterpieces full of originality and pathos, and that hearing his music gave rise to wondrous possibilities akin to 'the identification of a bird by its flight'. Shostakovich had already been accused of sinning against surrounding reality and failing to reflect a contemporary image. Soviet music critics were deaf to the voice of Shostakovich, but not so deaf that they did not condemn him. Everyone knows the suffering of Shostakovich, the great *yurodivy*; the 'fool-for-God' who had the gift to see and hear what others knew nothing about.

As soon as Stalin heard the broadcast of Mozart's Piano Concerto, he demanded a recording, played by Yudina. He spoke directly to the Radio Committee. Had the Radio Committee that very record? Of course they had! In fright, they lied. There was no recording because the performance had been live. No one dared say no to the dictator, for the consequences could be fatal. Saying yes was an involuntary response to any demand. What on earth were they to do?

Stalin demanded that Yudina's recording of Mozart be sent to his dacha. The Committee panicked. They had to produce something that very night. Yudina and an orchestra were summoned immediately. All the musicians, with the exception of Maria Yudina, Shostakovich relates, trembled with fear. Yudina was uniquely calm, playing precisely what she felt within her, faithful to the work. Everyone else shook. She did not. She remained steadfast throughout the whole fright-filled exercise, immersed in the ocean of Mozart. Shostakovich said that for her the ocean was only ever knee-deep. Or perhaps it was that Yudina was never afraid of depth. In her art as in Mozart, she knew no such thing as fear.

The conductor was so nervous that he had to be sent home. Another conductor was called to take over, but he too succumbed to anxiety and transferred confusion to the orchestra. He apologised, but he was unable to complete the second movement. It took a third conductor to finish the task and to pull the work together. By the early hours of the morning, the panic had subsided and the record was ready. Only one copy of the work was made. As instructed, it was sent straight to Stalin's dacha. Then followed a tense silence, the awful interim before a reaction.

Some days afterwards, Maria Yudina received an envelope containing a payment of twenty thousand roubles. It came to her personally, on Stalin's orders. In reply, she wrote him a letter. Shostakovich said that it was the most suicidal letter that anyone ever dared write a dictator, and if that was so, then she wrote from the remote key of F sharp minor, deep in the ocean of Mozart. The letter said:

> *I thank you, Josef Vissarionovich, for your assistance. I pray for you day and night and ask the Lord to forgive your great sins before the people and the country. The Lord is merciful and he will forgive you. I have given the money you sent me to the church that I attend.*

Yudina posted the letter to Stalin. Opening it slowly, he read it without uttering a word. He showed no response whatsoever, not even a twitch of the eyebrow. His aides standing around him observed him nervously. When he had finished reading, he laid the letter aside on his desk. In complete silence, he stared at it. As a matter of course, at the nod of a head, the order to arrest Yudina was prepared. The slightest grimace, the merest indication of a mood change would have been enough to erase her from the face of the earth. But Stalin said nothing, nothing at all. He maintained an icy silence. In the light of Yudina's audacity, her amazing self-possession, Stalin's unprecedented response is also remarkable. Of Maria Yudina, instead of making a public example, he made a rare exception.

Nothing happened to Yudina. It was reported that her recording of the Mozart Concerto with its tragic middle movement in the remote key of F sharp minor was there upon his record player when the leader and teacher was found dead in his dacha. The music of Mozart, played by Maria Yudina, was the last vibration to die within his hearing. Music had silenced him. Right into the terror of his own death, Yudina's ocean of calm had silenced him, the audible still clinging to the inaudible.

What did he hear? I cannot help but ask this question. Over and over again, I ask the question, for it brings me into the realms of memory and my own father; it brings me directly into his locality and into his hearing experience. I repeat, it was my father who taught me how to hear music. And I ask again, how does hearing differ from person to person? Why did my father hear in that particular way? I watch him pacing the room, listening to Beethoven. And it was his unique hearing that was very soon to shock me. His exceptional, judgmental hearing of Tchaikovsky resulted in my lifelong attachment to his music, especially his Symphony No. 5, a work that to this day makes me feel altered. But as I write these words, my father remains in the grip of Beethoven.

Of all Beethoven's compositions, the pianoforte sonata, *Appassionata*, is consistent from beginning to end in its sense of tragedy. It is a work of feeling, communicating feeling. Composed in the distant key of F minor, it opens with both hands an octave apart playing a downward sonority, a descent into depths. There is fatality in what we hear. Descent and ascent oscillate within the ear. Into this motif comes the disturbing four-note knocking, *pianissimo*, and then increasingly *fortissimo*; four notes that are the voice of insistent enquiry. These repetitions admit the hearer to turmoil. There is darkness in the descent and great uncertainty. Everything is opaque. As the sonata unfolds, lurching through its mortal life, a kind of terror arrives. Percussive sounds alternate with the lightest finger upon the note. A spectre of the Scottish air, *On the Banks of Allan Water*, weaves through the turmoil, recalling a perfect place. But it is a paradise that retreats. There is little respite. Upon the spring banks of Allan Water, 'chilling blew the blast'. Throughout the work the underworld us augmented. Nevertheless, there is no wanton self-destruction, no such thing as total loss. The sonata is an ordered work. It is intrinsically formed, a creation, by its own means, existing outside the confines of time. The sonata, defined as 'something sounded on a vibrating instrument', has its own history, an evolutionary process that operates at the very depths of creativity. The sonata, as an enquiry into form, attracted only the most sensitive minds, expanding substantially with Haydn and Mozart. And however disturbed was Beethoven's inner world when he composed his sonata, *Appassionata*, form contains the chaos. Retrieved from seething depths, erupting hot and sulphurous upon the surface, chaos obeys the laws of nature. It moves from subterranean heat and disorganised matter to a beautifully integrated, cooling stability lying upon the surface of the earth. And by the end of the sonata, the hearer too has mastered a skill: the skill of ordered retrieval, a capacity for containment. In this way I describe the operations of darkly enchanting volcanic glass; obsidian in cooperation with the gifts of the composer, Beethoven; music as healing within the ear.

What evidence do I have that Beethoven healed my father? I have none. I cannot know my father as he experienced himself. I can only imagine through feeling. I remember what happened to me. And had Beethoven not been there, the past, with all its secrets, may not be willing to disclose its fragile vitality. As I have said before, it was the unforgettable picture of intent etched upon the face of my father as he listened to Beethoven that struck me as the highest example of how hearing should be. Music entered him. And even in these forward moving pages, I am compelled to return to my father pacing the room, listening, listening. Observing him from my own silence, my tuneless, amorphous state, I still wonder what magic carried him into the heart of another world. Where was this seemingly inaccessible place that had consumed his entire person? Could I go there too? I recognised a fear in my disturbance, an alluring fear. I began to sense turmoil in myself; turmoil that one day would have its containment and its resolution in my own hearing of music. The insights of experience were far from me then.

My father, at the time that I stood upon the threshold watching him, was fast advancing into hearing disturbances that were to result in deafness. I say now, in the grip of obsidian, that his inner hearing was so often distorted by morbid intrusions and strange thoughts that he was compelled to wreck everything that was there, even for a moment's respite. Alcohol was both his temporary ease and his final disease. In mid-life, he came to renounce even the palliative operations of music, hearing nothing but his own chaos, the distortions of the inner ear. But he was never able to renounce alcohol. For him, alcohol was always more reliable. He knew its ups and its downs, a moodiness that came and went so easily. He preferred the oscillations of inebriation to the question that the mind alone could not answer. Just like Stalin, my father rose to condemn art for its psychological subversions, its 'muddle instead of music'. He preached one composer as opposed to another. Where one was right, the other was wrong. In doing so, he ushered in a frightening eschatology invoked entirely by feeling. He burnt. In music, my father heard the worst, casting around for justifications in order to support his condemnations. He protected Beethoven from judgement because of his revered struggle with deafness, but upon later composers in the full flower of romanticism, he would have much to say. When music became pure feeling to his hearing, he loathed it. There was a time at home when the romantic was silenced, except for the labours of daily piano practice and my mother's sad drift in and out of Scottish songs. After the great exhortation, music next to Jehovah, at a single stroke, there was nothing to be heard any more. The new god of reason held us by the throat, forcing thought and assertion when once there was feeling. All that remained was the keyboard and my nervous uncertainty. Under prohibition, confusion reigned. I did not know what to do. I had reached an important feeling obstacle, an opaque, impenetrable state. Later on in England when I read about Stalin's acts of terror against art and artists, I returned to the acts of my father and his absolute ban upon the works of Tchaikovsky. I remembered how he had reserved the worst denunciations for his Fifth Symphony, raging against its turmoil in much the same way as Stalin did against Shostakovich and his tragic-satirical opera, *Lady Macbeth of Mtsensk*, the 'muddle' instead of music. I was shocked into a reflection upon the very nature of hearing, how sound and meaning fell upon the ear. What were hearing and feeling to each other that they should bring about such violence?

The vision of my father listening to Beethoven's sonata, *Appassionata*, had started a hearing identification in me, a hearing revolution. Throughout my life, the music of Beethoven would always be there to nourish my search. Though music unearthed and disturbed, it also offered shape and containment through the creativity of form. Composing music was as natural to Beethoven as his given senses, particularly his senses of hearing and seeing. Beethoven's affliction, which seems so tragic in a musician, contributes powerfully to his perceived fate, his suffering as absolute necessity. In the annals of conquering artists, Beethoven holds a unique place. It cannot be said that his deafness is anything other than a gift to us, feeding his spiritual life, emerging in the most triumphant way, in the actions of obsidian; erupting from an unfathomable hiddenness to an open fluidity within the ear, to a vitreous clarity. It is Beethoven that I thank for the gift of his inner ear, for the impairment that gave rise to so much more than mere hearing, reaching a spiritual heaven, where all form is transcended.

It is impossible to know just how we are moulded and changed by what we hear. Vibrations and the patterns they make are unique to each person and cannot be separated from the destiny of the individual. Both Beethoven and Tchaikovsky spoke of the operations of fate in their creative lives; fate and transcendence. All music is vibration. Vibration is the substance that comprises form. As living creatures, we are in a constant flow of energy, from earth to the vast unimaginable emptiness of outer space. But how we hear individually is held deep within our own uncovered depths. Sometimes I had a vague sense of what my father heard in music. I sensed fear in his hearing, a fear of wrong hearing, of letting in the bad. But it was not until I came to the operations of obsidian that I was able to see the shadows of hearing that so unnerved my father. I moved through passages of sound, dark mirrors of the inner ear, under the auspices of obsidian, the soft mound of glassy ground that brought the unfortunate death of Pliny the Elder, suffocating him in a sulphurous surround.

I need to say how the energy of obsidian left me. It left me suddenly, with the shock of a shattered mirror. As obsidian was the first palm-sized crystal that I bought, in my enthusiasm I passed it around generously, and as it turned out, indiscriminately. And then one day, having pressed it into the hand of a friend, saying, 'Feel this, feel this!' the obsidian slipped glassily from our fingers, hitting the leg of a chair. I felt an obsidian wound in me, a terrible shock. But as it was just an accident, I made light of it, picked it up quickly and put it away. Afterwards, when I came to examine it privately, I saw its fractured edge, the chip in obsidian beauty. Although I loved it still, I felt such regret for its imperfection, such guilt for its accident, that I decided to hide it. I took it to the garden and buried it beneath the holly tree. I gave it to the protection of my native *ilex aquifolium*, in England. And as I dug its small grave of transformation, my feelings changed. I thought about my father and Beethoven. I believed that the great obsidian work was, for the time being, over.

Before I move from obsidian to another crystal energy, I am bound to relate something else about my father's dark capacity to hear what others did not hear. My father's judgements upon music led him to a more sinister and far-reaching discrimination that I will attempt to explain. I say attempt because as I draw near to the past, the memory of what happened in the family seems to become less available to my verbal powers, as if I am forbidden to utter one word. In which case, my writing these crystal memories is an act of defiance that I hope will break the spell of centuries. Centuries? Perhaps the prohibition is much longer than I think. I believe it is. And it is certainly true that I speak from an enforced silence. My father's act of discrimination fell heavily upon my older sister, Fenella. She was to suffer terribly under his denunciations. It was she who became the receptacle of his very worst fears, especially his fears about women. He expressed a loathing of her person. Where once he praised her gifts, suddenly, and without warning, he changed. He looked at her and he hated what he saw. And what did he see? Whatever it was that disturbed him, in typical manner, he took charge of her life and directed the whole of her adolescent years from the nexus of his masculine authority. Every member of the family, my older and younger brother, and my mother, listened to him. Through his pronouncements upon his daughter Fenella, he educated the family in a very specific way. He demanded that we hear and see things as he did. So effective was his command that it was quite impossible to refuse.

But as I write, it is to earth's elements that I return as much as I return to music and vibration. Only now, in late middle age, am I able to include the living memory of fear in the child. I write from the safe location of natural beauty. I write with Maria Yudina, from the remote key of F sharp minor, deep in an ocean of Mozart. It is crystal power that I feel now, crystal power that assists my return to the opening cave of childhood. And this diversion into the operations of a dictator and how he heard music, and the similar way in which my father heard, begins my searching enquiry into the subtleties of the ear. I must ask the question, what did I hear? For above all, this essay-sonata, this work of art, is primarily about my own manner of hearing and seeing; a retrieval of the past in the language of the present. Its gestation period cannot be measured. How long has art been acting within me? Art is as old as Pliny's volcanic glass, and much older than that. Longing for my own art is ancient. I struggle with an emerging form. Upon this page, I negotiate my way through a compositional development; the dominant striving to return to the theme in the tonic, to the statement that began my crystal sonata. But a new attunement emerges. I must pay heed to its need for expression. Obsidian and my father now buried for a while beneath the holly tree, rose quartz and my mother appear within me. I pick up a polished crystal. Its vibration settles happily at the location of the heart. After the depths of obsidian, rose quartz is sky-high in a haze of drifting pinks. How I love it. With great relief I embrace the fresh, floral energy that flows through me. I feel the difference. This is not amorphous glass. Deep in the mineral mass, my gemmy rose quartz presents its trigonal prisms.

I thought I would be able to move smoothly into another development of my theme, the story of my mother and rose quartz, but once more I must pay attention to something else. I am pressing the opaque, waiting for a creative opening. Having glimpsed the aurora of the north, rose quartz is falling towards a deep pink, sinking to the earth, taking me with it. It is much stronger than the floral energy I first described. I am surprised by the exertions of such an innocuous colour. I had so wanted every day to be a gracious illumination, the pain of the past held together beautifully. This was to be an easy healing, every revelation a powerful strengthening of spirit. Something happened last night to change all that. I regret to say that I am still at the mercy of events, and that the present contains the destructive power of the past.

Reverberations of shock took me completely by surprise. Last night I found myself watching television in an idle sort of way, waiting to be distracted, allowing my eyes to follow the flickering images before me, disconnected from the story. I began to dose off, slipping gently into a dreamy world. In this floating state, partially alert to seeing and hearing, quite without warning, I was interrupted by an act of violence. I heard a gunshot, the sound of violent death, in the room. I leapt from the chair in fright, clutching my head, flinging my arms about my body. I tried to run away, but I was fixed to the spot. Panic rose in me; panic at being trapped. It was as if I had suffered the shooting myself. Shattered, I collapsed into the chair. I could not believe what I had seen and heard. And yet I knew what had taken place was just an act in a story. The shock lingers still. In my sudden descent from trivial viewing to disintegration, I am overcome by a sense of hopelessness. I see no point in anything. I wonder why I have allowed myself to be so injured by a passing image in a fiction that does not really interest me. In that act of destruction was a whole cosmos of cruelty, the feelings of annihilation I experienced as a child. These feelings being so difficult to express, today I comply with anything other than the truth. Evasion is comfortable. I cannot bring myself to describe in any detail what I saw on television, or what I heard. I do not want to spoil these pages with violence. Making pale words appear is a reassuring process for someone new to writing. Be mild, I tell myself, mild under the auspices of crystals. Crystals are so very beautiful. And anyway, why bother with describing something so very distasteful? I have heard enough. Old patterns return. Instead of continuing, now I want to burn my work. I see myself doing it. Everything I have written here is dangling precariously under the hand, ready for destruction. Oh, how familiar is destruction! The urge says, take it to the garden, all this written stuff, and put a match to it. Watch it burn! As soon as the words drop onto the page for the eyes to see, I resist. I fall under the spell of language. Writing breaks the mould. Surely, it breaks the mould. At the very beginning, I promised myself that I would absorb all the inner and outer signs that came to me, that I would descry the skies and see as deeply above as below. I must receive this immediate loss as a vital ingredient in my act of creativity. I must ignore, as far as I am able, feelings of utter futility.

It was in augury, before the awful event occurred, that I did see something wonderful. Yesterday, gazing at the skies, I saw a skein of white geese flying in typical formation, heading west. When I happened upon this aerial vision, my heart leapt. The geese were calling to each other, calling into the falling night. The sight of flying geese, on the way home, filled me with both joy and sadness. The contradiction was affecting. I envied them; I grieved for them. Why should I either envy or grieve for geese? I envied their creaturely existence, the winged movements of nature, the joy of natural flight. I grieved for their unknown fate.

Perhaps the abandonment and the death of a bird is terrible. And how could I know the sorrows of a creature? I felt that I did. I too know fate, in a human way. A bird, in its own being, could surely show me a simpler existence, moving more gently within life's natural currents. At the time of the arrival of geese, I happened to be tidying the summerhouse after an afternoon's writing. I was hastening to return to the cottage, gathering the fluttering leaves of my manuscript into a neat pile. Leaning into a different feeling, touched by rose quartz and thoughts of my mother, something stirred in me, but I did not know what it was. I am aware that the season is changing. I am adjusting to receding light, a damp wind beating at the shutters. But the day for me had been unusually bright. I delighted in a blue sky with its puffs of white cloud, the sight and energy of ancient chalcedony. I was just about to close the shutters when outside, above me, I heard the rush and flutter of wings, the fanning sound of flight. It was so strong and gusty, so full of power, I immediately dashed out onto the veranda to see. And there they were, the geese, flying low, passing overhead. The sight was another kind of shock, but a beautiful one, nothing like the disintegration that I was soon to experience. They were calling to each other from throbbing throats, encouraging each other in their homeward flight, these buglers upon the wing. I listened to the distant diminuendo. My mood changed. I am bound to admit that the image and the shock were really a memory, something I had forgotten. The comforting presence of my sister, Fenella, came to me. I saw her. I heard her voice calling to the glossy black ravens of Tasmania, 'My brother! My sister!' She danced. Her arms reached to the sky in an ecstatic greeting. We were together, at home, somewhere in the spicy aromas of the southern bush.

A sudden inhalation strengthened me. I felt hot, elated. Everything to do with location and experience returned in that split second of a bird's call, a summoning of the past, seeing Fenella. I know now that the flight of northern geese was the augury, a vision of my sister. The flight of geese tells me that I am to see yet more under the auspices of crystals. On the way home, I may not be spared any revelation, any awful truth. The creation of a work of art demands an acceptance of everything, no matter how dark. Even the separation that exists between my sister and myself must be integrated. I must bridge the gap of ten thousand miles and bring her here, to these pages. I must conquer death. An afternoon of unexpected augury brought our separation into a palpable, living loss. I saw her again. I saw her as Fenella, oh, rare Fenella! She was gazing at the skies, waving and gazing, counting the circling ravens, in a state of excitement. I looked at her. I observed her immersed in something I could not then experience myself. Seeing changed her, just as hearing music changed my father. And it was then that intimations of future violence entered me. Five feathered specks disappeared into the pale pink of a gathering sunset. As their cries died, the image of my sister died too. It was then that the operations of rose quartz came to me once more, the desire and a need to recreate a feeling for my mother.

Across the television screen, coloured images flickered. The picture of a cat appeared before me, a family pet, taken with a telephoto lens. The cat was on a night prowl, walking its suburban territory, happy in a nocturnal world. Nothing that was happening in the story interested me. A man pursued a cat. In the unfolding drama, I sensed something sinister. Murder was in the air. I wanted to rise from my chair and turn off the television, but I allowed myself to drift towards sleep. A question played upon my wavering mind. What is going to happen to the animal? I might have been a child, asking the same question of a parent. I could not imagine its fate, even then, after all my years of knowing about the fate of animals. I felt uneasy, but still did nothing. And then it happened. Caught in the gun sights, the face of the cat stared at the lens. Beautiful creature, I thought, vaguely. In the glare of lights boring straight into his eyes, his whiskers twitched. There was a long pause as the sights were levelled at the target. Only then did I become alert to the next event. A trigger was pulled. The sound of the bullet flung me from the chair. The little cat shot into the air, splitting to bits as it fell to the ground. The eye of the lens followed the deed. I screamed. I began to cry, to beat my breast repeatedly. I clutched my head. There could be no comfort in witnessing violence to an animal. What is the suffering of a cat to a callous human being? Enter, hopelessness. You are always welcome. Enter, meaninglessness. You have a place in this world.

It was not until today, after a fretful night, that I remembered the ways of obsidian. I consider the actions of a volcano, the power of aftershocks, the energy that continues the seismic shift to its very last tremors. My distress continued into the morning. The image of the shattered cat now fixed in my imagination, every burst of crying intensified the feeling of hopelessness. Misery might kill me. As shock worked through me, another reality made a tentative entry. There seemed to be a spectre in my weeping, a feminine figure with a vitreous gleam. I gazed into the obsidian mirror. Two women wept. The shadow of a woman imitated me. Or could it be that I imitated her? It was my mother. She was the vitreous shadow that wept and wept, beating her breast. She wore dingy pink. Grief was her reason, but it was not grief for a shattered cat. Her grief belonged elsewhere, to an intimacy with my father that was not revealed to me. As my mother beat her breast over and over again, her hand made a hollow sound, as if her bones were empty. Her head was bowed, her voice muffled. Her words came in a wave-like flow, breaking in her throat as sea upon the seashore. I could not hear what she was saying, speaking as she did through the streaked viridian, the volcanic sheen. But whatever she said, the feeling that accompanied her words carried the greater weight. It would not have mattered what she was saying. Feeling was everything. And I remember as a child, receiving nothing but feeling when she spoke about herself and her grief. For what can a child know of a mother? How could her language equate with my own? Now it seems that I can only meet my mother through the actions of obsidian after all. Be that as it may, if I remain faithful to the task before me, working with the natural elements and not with my own mind, I will arrive at my mother in the very heart of rose quartz. I thought that by burying the mound of chipped obsidian that it had gone and that strictly speaking its operations belonged to memories of my father. Such is the power of elements from which I write. Grief for the shattered cat led me, through the aftershocks of obsidian, to my mother's grief. Observing myself in the obsidian mirror, I also observe her. And having summoned my mother, I am able to speak about her.

I am trying to recall the first feeling memory of my mother, the small child looking up to see the face of the one person whose nurturing means survival. The depth of obsidian yields to rose quartz. I enter a manganese pink, a colour that is a little misty, swimming, dipping easily in and out of the earth. It is both airy and watery. The feeling of rose quartz is essentially feminine, but this does not mean that it is always gentle. The palest colour contains a power to shift mountains. From my experience of crystals, mineral strength increases with use. Its strength surprises. Sleep with rose quartz, carry it about with you, see and hear everything through manganese; observe, observe. Pay attention to every inner movement, every flutter. Deep within my own observations, I brace myself.

Crystallographers say that the colour of rose quartz can fade. Crystal healers say that this is not a sign of depletion or overuse, for in the natural world, the life that is innate can never be erased. Primary energy is eternal. Though the colour may fade, the power of the crystal does not. In fact, the operations of rose quartz can only intensify the more it is used, the more that it is respected. There is no such state as crystal exhaustion, not unless the healer herself, for other reasons, is exhausted. And I need to emphasise for my own benefit that working with crystals is the yoga of self-knowledge. Self-knowledge, by any chosen path, has its pains as much as it has its joys. In putting myself there, in a manganese childhood, in the very heart of dependence and trust, I invoke the power of place. I am going home, but from the safety of a location I know, from my other home here in England, the birthplace of the Romantic poets.

Perhaps it is no coincidence that I write in the Devon town of Ottery St Mary, where Samuel Taylor Coleridge was born. Feeling acts intimately with location. It does here, thinking of the poet and his mystical writing, *Christabel*, a work that was conceived in these regions and contemplated in agony for over thirty years. The story of Christabel, his 'child of nature', through whom he hopes to restore a fall from innocence, has no conclusion. It awaits a third part. Though the poet still breathes into the pause, his words stop suddenly. Though his hand hovers, his unique marks upon paper cease. I stare into the space. Somehow, his uncertainties consecrate my own. Through him, I tell myself, I may learn to accept literary difficulties. Coleridge gives the searching artist permission to leave a work unfinished, permission to tell, or not to tell. There is no presumption in a longing to complete the ballad of the lovely lady, Christabel, to know for myself what happened to her. It is only a simple desire rising naturally from the place of his birth. And the story of Christabel speaks too of my sister. She too was 'a child of nature'. On numerous occasions, Coleridge tried to finish the poem, encouraged by friends who had fallen under the spell. Unfortunately, the way was blocked. He could go no further. Feeling for the troubled poet, I might rush to assist him. I might offer him a crystal. But in truth, it is he who comes to assist me. He will guide me through these pages. I would not dare to interfere with his muse, for she is active still. Though his writing is over, his spirit is available to those who wish to be healed by the beauty of language. I use poetry as it occurs to me, for my own purposes, calling upon the subtle vibrations of his friendly voice.

The return journey to my mother and my place of birth is misty, a manganese memory. Holding a polished rock of rose quartz, turbulence is subdued. I see a land. Tasmania, from which I was to be separated for most of my life, gives rise to quite another kind of poetry, the poetry of location, a far more primitive language, *ab origine*, but one that could never be judged as inferior to the poet's imagination. Coleridge drew his visions from the caverns of his psyche. Tasmania, once a shaman's land, vibrates in my imagination with the power of rose quartz, the energy of universal love that is the great luminosity and the ground of all healing. Only now, after so much has passed, may I attempt to retrieve my own lost Aboriginality in that land of universal love, reclaiming a sense of security that resides like a god, deep within nature. I yoke myself to the divine. And I yoke myself to the living heart of rose quartz. There might be too much to assimilate if I did not first ask to be held. I turn to the poetry of earth.

There was a time when I had no security whatsoever, certainly not any that came on command. The security of location comes now. Some places feel safer than others, some are more or less inspiring, some are to be avoided at all times. When I was small, I was unable to take a conscious account of the ground upon which I stood. Everything was the same. I had no insight, no powers of discrimination. I awoke to life in the Southern Hemisphere. The mystery of my birthplace was veiled to me. The land, as birthplace of my parents, was also veiled to them. They looked away from the natural world, away from Aboriginality. Not only was Aboriginality absent, it was first and foremost, alien. Native Tasmanians, being dead, were too distant, too insignificant in their primitive history, their unreachable rituals. Superseded by the intellect and the enlightenment of science, they were gone for ever, a casualty of colonial conquest. As far as I knew, there was no trace of them, except for their reconstructed ghosts, the still, mute *tableaux vivants* of the city museum, seen through the eyes of the anthropologist. Fenella and I stared into their silence. We inhaled preservative. Naphtha acted upon the nostrils. A group of dark-skinned people stood by the seashore in Van Diemen's Land, the Eden of the Antipodes. Behind glass, a fire glowed. I did not know Aboriginal fire, the eternal burning in the heart of the earth, the manganese light, but Fenella did. I knew she did. I seemed to have little awareness of what was in my life, except for one awesome thing, the punishment of bone-pointing, killing through the power of the psyche. Bone-pointing was the weapon of Aboriginality that I did know about. There was always the vast unknown before me, and in that unknown the fear that one day I might be *thought* to death, killed by an idea. Old Tasmania was more dreadful than it was secure. I turned to Fenella for guidance. With her love of the bush and its birds, she was far ahead of me. I remained passive until I began to realise that I was a person in my own right, when my power to evaluate and discriminate began to emerge.

There are locations that assist memory, something special about a place that calls up a delicate pulse, a faint aroma. That this recollection might be a falsification, a need to reconstruct the past in a specific way, does not bother me. I draw upon all the strengths of the imagination, all the devices of the poet in my feeling journey. I seek memory as an art form, the past that will yield its primary truth, a knowledge that will heal. I wish to revitalise an infant awareness in a selected place, to call up a very particular sensitivity that will bring me close, so very close to my mother. It is only now that I know how an invocation to her sensitivity opens the door to her grief. As I become vulnerable before her, standing there as a child looking up, I see a woman, my mother, in disarray.

In many ways, and without the aid of crystals, I have tried to revitalise the child's experience of the mother, the singular recognition of a daughter. So many times I have set out from Ottery St Mary to the city of Exeter with the intention of finding my mother there, in a place where she never lived. In my striking out upon the well-worn way, I held on to the idea that I would happen upon her casually, as if she might be found walking the streets any day of the week. I searched as much for her physical form as I did for knowledge of her, a kind of *gnosis*. What was she doing there? She could be found, I believed, shopping in Exeter. As I walked, I was confident that I would meet her just around the next corner and that she would be carrying a basket of fresh vegetables. And she would be happy, skittering about, like a new bride with her first shopping list. This was how I was bound to see her.

Each journey I re-enacted is in truth a journey modelled on a passing event in my young womanhood, not long before I left Tasmania for England. I was wandering the streets of Hobart, savouring the last connections, looking for souvenirs to take with me, when quite unexpectedly, I happened upon my mother. She was in a hurry, buying groceries for lunch. Seeing her away from her domestic setting startled me. I think she was just as surprised to see me, her daughter. We stopped sharply in front of one another. I remember nothing but the awkwardness of our meeting, and then seeing her basket of fresh vegetables with its dangling carrot tops. She was buying food for my father. It occurred to me that I had never met her in the streets of Hobart before, even though we lived in the same city. We had never, as mother and daughter, shopped together. I had spent little time with her, except that I had lived only in her time, as a passive listener, receiving whatever she said. For a brief moment, I thought she might invite me to an Italian coffee bar, that we might, over cappuccino, make a final farewell. An Italian coffee bar? Just as soon as this most unlikely idea arose, it died. My mother looked the other way. She fluttered. It was a gesture, and so slight that it is probably more in my imagination than in reality. And I do not know in what way she fluttered. It is just that whenever I think of her in the streets of Hobart, shopping for my father's lunch, she is looking away, clutching a basket, fluttering. And it is this poignant memory that brings her essential self to me, the child longing for the mother, the memory that I have now made into my pilgrimage to the city of Exeter.

I need to explain that I had left my country of birth under a cloud, in a marriage that had been condemned by my father, with feelings in the family at their very worst. My sister and I did not see one another. We seemed to have forgotten the common language of our childhood, intent as we were upon our own individual lives. We never wrote letters, nor did we speak over the telephone. She was far away in the bush, she too in a marriage that had been condemned. When I recall the mood of those troubled years, my sister might have been living the life of a deranged thing, a native, tearing the flesh of wild creatures with her teeth, flailing about in madness. Fenella had, for some years, become dark to my parents. But her name being so very white in Gaelic, it was impossible for me to believe that *Fionnuala*, the girl of the fair shoulder, was in fact the dark daughter of the Grey family. Nevertheless, she was by now quite beyond my reach. I thought of nothing but my own survival. At the very first opportunity, I married, forcing myself to assume a role for which I was scarcely prepared. It began as a fearful fantasy that I struggled to resist, and then very soon it became a loveless marriage, from the outset an opportunity to escape. And escape I did. I knew that when I left for England with my husband, I would be leaving Tasmania for ever. I remember the stricken face of my father when we said goodbye. My father wept. My mother, whose tears are today my strongest memory, looked only to my father. Of this parting, there was nothing soft. I have no memory of her fluttering.

It was such a fleeting meeting, the tiniest entry into a vast imaginative space that in the isolation of this northern location has become a place of feeling interest to me, my mother, found in Exeter. And I know that my walking the streets in the hope and the belief of seeing her is an attempt to return to the past, to finish a story once so full of promise, to complete the mystery of the meeting. What might have happened? But my hope of finding her, of being with her in a coffee bar, in the babble of the morning, the Gaggia machine hissing merrily behind us, has all the potency of a dream. Just like the poet Coleridge and his creation, Christabel, who prays in her sleep, thirty years of pilgrimage have done nothing for the meeting but to bring me to these pages, to complete it here. Perhaps I am retrieving an aspiration so fragile, so unstable, a mere quantum of the psyche that over years of incubation has grown into something else altogether, a product of my own private laboratory. I do everything in secret. Living with crystals, secrecy will always exist, for crystals bring to the crystal companion a depth of feeling that also resists translation, except that I am attempting to overcome resistance, cooperating with everything that happens. Crystals exist for the speaking of feeling. The speaking of feeling brings me to my mother, to her voice, to the rose quartz of her expressions, the words that I heard so clearly as a child, sitting on the edge of my parent's bed, listening, listening to everything she said. Finding the key is the key, and in the integration of experience, rose quartz becomes an aliquot of amethyst. What ever arises will need to be received into the energy of amethyst, a violet vibration that seals the *gnosis* of all experience.

My wanderings in Exeter may not yet be over. I am loath to let them go, even if I do manage to see her flutter beautifully as she once did. There is still the journey, because it is always a joy to undertake, and then there is the search for something to represent my longing: a perfume, a pink face lotion, an emollient for the body. My mother had a fascinating collection of cosmetic bottles, sitting in a mess upon her dressing table. As I contemplate her crystal containers with their silver lids askew, I draw near the sacramentals of religion. I see a medieval pyx; the mother in essence, spiritually. I look for the symbol of a jewelled reliquary.

I had thought as a child, forbidden as I was to regard Catholicism as anything other than a heresy, that somehow Our Lady of Perpetual Succour would assist me secretly, simply because she had a name which meant help. She had been known to help others. An awareness of the mystery of her name came as a result of my being sent to the Convent of the Sacred Heart in my early teens. A convent education was my father's attempt to rescue me from the corrupting influence of my sister. Although I feared the heresy he referred to, I knew nothing of how it worked, except that my father made so much of it. How could an image, a mere painting, be a heresy? And what indeed was 'heresy'? Our Lady of Perpetual Succour was all mystery to me, unaccustomed as I was to seeing the mother of Christ as 'divine'. I looked up to her picture on the classroom wall. There was a little bowl of flowers placed on a wooden ledge beneath, with two low candles burning either side. The area around the icon was a sacred space. I noted the manner in which Catholic girls walked past it, in a kind of arc, giving Our Lady of Perpetual Succour the necessary air, the breath of sanctity.

By the time I entered a Catholic school as a Protestant, Fenella was far away. Our fleeting fascination with Aboriginality was over. Fenella was at home, but she might have been across the seven seas, she was so remote to me. I had transferred my gaze to the icon, to the passive mother of no recognisable human dimension. I was fixed upon Catholic representation. The mother of God was merely flat art, touched by deep purple and gold. She was immersed in the sufferings of her only son, already a little man. As a tame bird, he perched upon her arm, nestling into her neck. She knew that his great sacrifice and her own pietà were yet to come. Her gaze was oblique, penetrating the child, penetrating space. My desire for the Virgin troubled me as much as it decorated my imagination, a weight in my feelings, to which more weight was soon to be added. I had been sent to the convent for reasons of perfectibility, to imitate the nuns in their vocation to remain pure. Under no circumstances was I to believe anything theologically Catholic, certainly not words uttered by religious women, no matter how exemplary their behaviour.

I know now that my father had his own mysterious bonding to Catholicism. He too felt a kind of perverse comfort in pursuing theological faults. But my father maintained an open admiration for the nursing sisters of Calvary Hospital who served him so dutifully when he visited patients. The nuns respected his authority. It was at Calvary Hospital that notions of priesthood at the heart of his profession began to affect him. In the presence of women clothed in white habits, living under obedience, he sensed the power of his own vocation. He felt priestly before them. The nuns treated him with the utmost courtesy, following in his train, attentive to his every need, fluttering around him. They spoke in lowered tones, as if he were indeed a priest. In a way, my father envied the structures of Rome that permitted such deference to the consecrated male, even though he might dismiss ideas of consecration as so much Jesuitical distortion. But as a man with an eye, he felt awakened by the presence of Catholic colour and religious ritual. Somehow, it made him feel alive. Difficult as it might be to admit such an attachment, he approved of hierarchy, because he himself was of an hieratic disposition. As a man, authority came naturally to him.

All this brings me once more to my father speaking theology. For the moment, I cannot hear my mother's voice, because I must first approach him. He holds the key; he is the gatekeeper who opens the way to the female. My father speaks. I hear his didactic manner, the stress on certain words, the orator's technique acquired in a childhood listening to his father's sermons. I hear the intensity of pitch, his masculine emphasis. My father speaks of God, mankind and morality. 'In such an hour that ye think not, the Son of Man cometh'. He quotes St Matthew, the poet of the last trump, reciting the parable of the foolish virgins upon whom the door to the marriage feast was shut. It is a warning. Everything, he says in his preaching tone has a predestination, an eschatology, a logic that arises from a clear mind. This clarity is reason, the very hallmark of Protestant authority, the assertion that is *logos*. It is as reasonable, as it is inevitable, that we are judged. And in Calvinism, it is important that 'emotion', the disobedient thing, the irrational animal, should be kept under strict control. The animal must be contained, because she is dangerous. I heard him utter the word 'dangerous'. The meaning impresses me. I know I am in trouble. I am guilty of 'emotion'.

When I recall my years of convent education, I wonder how I managed to keep myself together, subsumed under such opposing forms of patriarchy. At home my father had already set up a scheme that was to all intents and purposes an apartheid in sisterhood, a regime that would keep both of us tied to male authority. He separated us, severely. My father was determined to eradicate all influence that might come to us in a fallen world. Though he looked askance at the robing of the mother of God, dismissing the icon of Our Lady of Perpetual Succour, he gave far more than tacit consent to the ideal of chastity. I was to have nothing to do with the blasphemy of praying to the Virgin as intercessor, the reckless *hyperdulia* of Rome. It was ridiculous. And more than ridiculous, it was wrong. So whenever the Angelus was recited, he instructed the nuns to usher me from the classroom. With certain strategies in place, the error of Mariology would be avoided. It was a matter for the reasoning mind, the supremacy of Protestantism. Greater than the Mary heresy, which he saw as a sign of weakness in women, was the worse sin of 'immorality'. He believed that fleshly corruption came all too easily to girls. It was a part of the female nature. And especially did it come as easily as it came 'naturally' to Fenella. After Fenella was pronounced a dangerous adolescent, he insisted that we live apart in the same house. We were each given separate bedrooms. In this respect, we did have something in common, alienation from each other. But in alienation, we were powerless. We were unable to do anything about it. And as much as I would like to think that we clung to a knowing of our innocence, I think we did not. We believed the authority of the father. How could we be absolutely sure that we were not at heart, bad?

At the Convent of the Sacred Heart, there was an entirely different world presented to me. Certainly, it appeared to be a different religion altogether because there was so much to delight the eye; so much illustrated by statues and icons, by religious clothing and by manners. Every saintly example cried, 'This, and only this, is the way to piety'. But where the eye delighted, the shadow appeared. What lay beneath the rituals I recognised as much the same. The Catholic Church was riven with obligations written in the absolute. Looking back upon my years enclosed by the convent, I can feel only the ritual atmosphere that was so very different from the box-pew theology of Protestantism. It felt freer, though it was not. Now I see gleaming wooden floors and walls decorated with pictures of saints. There are freshly cut flowers in crystal vases. The scent of petals and pollen hangs in the air mingling with the more domestic smell of polish and burning beeswax. A dazzling brightness strikes my imagination when I visualise the convent classrooms, a brightness that has more to do with the romantic adjustments of memory than the austere articles of religion under which everyone lived. It was a strict school run by the Sisters of St Joseph, a teaching order from Ireland. The nuns wore black serge habits and starched white gremials choking their throats, crackling with every turn of the head. I scrutinised their voluminous dress, the layered black body finished with the face, as the naked essential, framed by radiant white. From my desk in the front row, I observed all their Catholic attitudes, signing the cross swiftly in an airy kind of way, genuflecting deeply at the name, Jesus. Among the heavy woollen folds of their skirts, long wooden rosaries rattled as they moved. All academic activities were linked by a reference to the hours of monastic prayer. *Aves* and *pater nosters* interrupted lessons in mathematics. But it was a school where the arts flourished, where the sound of the piano was never far away. The piano seemed to be the only instrument in the whole world. No one studied anything else, not an oboe, a trumpet or a violin. It was always the piano and the classical repertoire. The sound of scales and arpeggios in every key and inversion were flung unceasing into the perfumed spaces of the convent practice rooms.

Music and the reciting of poetry were favourites of the nuns. But artistic display was always limited to a room no bigger than a chamber. The convent never presented major drama, or encouraged any form of theatrical flamboyance. In the classroom, the plays of Shakespeare were read more for the beauty of language than for their narratives. The moral teaching in literature was secondary to the moral teaching of the Church. Music examinations, poetry festivals and choral competitions were integral parts of an otherwise fundamental academic curriculum that offered only general science of the domestic kind. As 'the call' was the greatest spiritual honour to be bestowed upon a woman, the nuns scanned young faces for any signs of piety that might lead to early vocations. Several of my contemporaries were plucked from the classroom to be trained as teaching nuns, disappearing into religion. Their gifts were contained by convent walls solely for the edification of pupils, for the development of those better human inclinations, and for the promotion of religious life. Though the focus was subtle, it was nevertheless unrelenting. I thought much about vocations and how a Catholic vocation differed from a Protestant one. In the Presbyterian religion, God did not speak so directly to women. Protestant women were hidden behind their preaching men. They might be called, or they might not be called. It was not easy for a Presbyterian girl to respond to the voice of God. She had no convent, no religious clothing, and no hourly rituals.

But much that happened in the convent was familiar to me. Order and discipline being such important ideals, disobedience was punished in front of the class as an example to others. And disobedience was more than a messy exercise book or forgetting to wear gloves in the street, though these too were punishable offences. Slovenliness and what the nuns referred to as 'sluttish behaviour' were high on the list of female vices. And what was 'sluttish behaviour' to the nuns? I simply cannot remember. I cannot remember why a girl called Bernadette was always singled out for being a slut. And she from such a good family with a brother in the priesthood! How could she disgrace her parents so! Six swishes across outstretched fingers with a bright yellow cane was the standard practice for breaking rules, or for the unfortunate Bernadette, long, hard strikes across the back of the legs. Any nun might carry out this demeaning act, though one or two in particular were feared for their mannish use of physical punishment. Although it was dreaded, its place in our education was never questioned. It was always there. Fortunately I was never caned. I watched and was frightened. It was difficult to look at the poor victim, wincing under the whip. In the breathless hush my heart pounded. Even the image of the Little Flower of Jesus clutching a crucifix and pink roses could not soften the blows. Nothing connected. In the deep beneath, the reason for physical punishment had absolutely no meaning to me. As I could not understand anything at all, turmoil was the only real experience. I was confused. At home, I kept quiet about my fear and dread of punishment. To my father's way of thinking, notwithstanding the hocus-pocus of Catholic theology, the muddle instead of method, the nuns were exemplary women who offered the best opportunity for the moulding of my character. At the convent, there reigned the great trinity of ideals. There was order, discipline and obedience.

I was particularly bothered and guilty about one oppressive Catholic secret. Catholic girls were permitted something that I would never be allowed. Catholic girls had their own rosaries, delightful prayer beads with little silver crucifixes dangling at the end, swinging and glinting beneath fingers. I eyed them enviously. They kept their rosaries in neat leather purses with press-studs, deep in their desks among books and pencils. They were fetched in and out on all kinds of occasions. For articles of theological fault, of heresy, these simple prayer beads seemed to me more beautiful than sinister. How could they be 'bad'? It was the mere sight of them and their perceived beauty that exercised a power over me. I thought they were so girlish, so utterly desirable. As my father indicated, rosaries belonged to the feminine and to the irregular adoration of Our Lady of Perpetual Succour, the mother who offered her spurious help. To me her enviable help was always very distant, in antiquity, available only to Catholics. I saw myself outside the walls of Rome. Succour must be the most ancient form of assistance to ever come to light; sustenance in Latin made available through prayer beads. How desirable was a rosary! Sometimes made of pink glass or precious amethyst, the little chaplet slid easily into the palm of the hand, a trickle of crystals on a silver chain. I watched Catholic girls playing happily with their rosaries, swapping them in the playground, slipping them around their necks, twirling the crucifix. I wanted a rosary of my very own.

But whatever I desired at the convent in the way of rosaries and relics, my longings remained a guilty secret. Sooner or later my father would come to know the fantasies I was harbouring, for my devious thoughts were surely the enemy of his intentions. Whatever my fears were at school, there were other more pressing matters at home, other litanies to hear. As my father was preoccupied with his medical practice for most of the day, and often into the early evening, in his absence, my mother was central to my life. She exerted her own influence, but not one that was wholly independent of my father. My mother had no autonomy. Reared too in rural patriarchy, deference to the male was natural to her. She had her story, the story of her dreams, the bewitching ballad of great romantic love. Although she was unable to enter the world of her daughters, to hear what they had to say, for indeed, we had nothing to say, she required a receptive presence when she gave way to her personal narrative. The constant telling of her story became the model of all longing in my life. And the favourite place for the recitation of chivalry was always my parents' bedroom, from which we were never forbidden.

There was much traffic in and out of the bedroom. Of course there were areas that were invisibly cordoned. It went without saying that we touched nothing to do with father's cedar tallboy where he kept his clothes. High on the top were his shoehorns and boxes of shirt studs for formal dress. In the floor of one of the upper drawers was a secret compartment. It had a particularly cool, woody odour. Although it snapped open obediently on the release of a spring, it was too high up, too difficult to reach. Once or twice, we dared to open it, standing precariously on a stool, in freer days before everything went so badly wrong. Its aroma was wonderful. In it we found bundled letters from the war years and envelopes of army photos. We knew it was our parents' former life, the life of love that my mother talked about. But with the excitement of getting at the secret mechanism, there came a warning. And it was enough to hear the story as our mother told it. To my mother, my father was an Adonis, a man who made her feel proud, her handsome husband of superior education. And indeed, I recall my father's dark good looks with a certain frisson, a fascination that all too soon became a fatal attraction.

It was true what my mother said. My father was unusually handsome and would have remained so were it not for the distress of drink. But she never saw his decline, although she often railed against alcohol. Unlike my mother, although my father took pride in his appearance, I could never describe him as a gentleman, for he had such variable manners towards people and was so very unpredictable in his ways. He often looked exceptionally smart in his tailored worsted suits. He walked with masculine authority, the immaculate man, with a thrust that cut the air. Society liked him. Sometimes, in the early evening when my parents were to dine out, I would be summoned to help my father dress. He said my fingers were better able to press in the collar studs at the nape of his neck. At such times of obedience, I sensed the intimacy of skin. Nearness to him aroused strange feelings. I felt uncomfortable. His whole body, his clothes and everything around his tallboy was surrounded by an odour of bay rum and ether. I came quickly to his bidding, but I was repelled by his smell. And the smell of whisky never fails to summon up identical memories of my father, memories of fear and dreadful love, a desire to attend to his every need. These odours are, to me, powerful evocations of male power.

But it was to my mother's dressing table that I was always drawn, without any restraint. It was there that I found the mysteries of the feminine, to which, in my imagination, the rosary also belonged. Here was the mother. As a mother, she too must have the virtue of succour. For indeed, I saw my mother's dressing table as a kind of shrine, the place of the maternal image surrounded by a jumble of scent bottles and emollients. Central to the image was the glass itself that gave rise to gazing, a scrutiny that might even lead to a peek at the soul. And writing now from within the clearing mists of rose quartz, my mother's collection of cosmetics from the English house of Cyclax seem to cluster about her image as jewels cluster about an icon. I did not know then that gazing at was not necessarily gazing into. For my mother, her long cheval glass had not the dim, slippery reflection that is the gift of obsidian. Though the penumbra was in the narrative, there seemed to be none in the mirror. But the mirror did offer the trick of reversal, a fact that is seldom, if ever, realised, removed on the instant by the mind. What might be the truth of reversal? Only now, with rose quartz around me, does the subtlety of reversal occur. What does it say? It is difficult to reach the meaning of this optical trick, for I have not yet reached the end of my journey. After all, a plane mirror is to do with the translation of light to an image. A fraction is lost in the transaction. And what happens to the light that is lost? It is absence, as feeling, that is better descried in the mirror image. I am not yet able to weigh the heart in the balance against the weight of a feather. Pure reflection offered my mother a dream ideal, a space where she was able to breathe into the past, to reconstruct romance as it had been once when so new to the love of my father. Her gaze reinforced what she needed to see.

Much to her surprise, falling in love with my father, my mother became a minor celebrity to herself. Through marriage, she was able to enter society. Sitting at her dressing table, lifting fresh underwear from drawers, she dawdled through the painterly landscape of courtship and marriage, her eyes moist with emotion. Even her tears were of the age of chivalry to which her romantic heart belonged. She admired what she saw before her. And she loved the handsome mahogany dressing table, the altar of the feminine that was a wedding gift from her husband. Naturally, my sister and I gravitated to her daily mysteries, to the *levée* of the mother who gazed at herself. Sitting on the edge of the unmade bed, Fenella and I watched her powder her body and then hand over hand smooth her face with Milk of Roses, addressing the distant reflection of her daughters. She spoke of her husband, and of our brother, Edgar, who had been conceived on the first night of their honeymoon. His conception ranked above ours, cradled as it was in her first sexual encounter. She spoke of her delight in this child of her love, and just as Our Lady of Perpetual Succour gazed into her little manikin perched on her arm nestling into her neck, I saw my brother Edgar there, occupying his proper place, the son of the mother. My mother was indeed an icon of the young Madonna, and all too soon, an icon of the *pietà*. Fenella and I observed the transformations. We both listened.

In my mother, there was much to admire. I did not see her as beautiful in the same way as I saw the striking good looks of my father. My mother's physical attraction was to become inseparable from the story in which she wrapped herself, throwing pink silk around her throat, opening to her world of tender feeling, the vibration of rose quartz at one with the movement of the heart. What I hear is beautiful, and beautiful hearing may also be light reflected in a mirror, light with critical particles missing. Holding rose quartz, I can see the absence. This is the gift of the present. As children, my sister and I were drawn to the sound of mother's voice calling us to her dressing table, calling, calling to the telling of her story. We came in our night attire, early in the morning, after my father had left for work. On countless occasions, through so many of her emotional upheavals, we came to our mother. Rose quartz tints the image in the mirror. I pause for a moment to think about this. I do not believe that the crystal deceives. As I have said before, crystals exist for the speaking of feeling. 'It was like this,' she would say, touching her breast with her hand, squeezing it gently, responding to the reflection in the mirror. 'I was such an innocent thing.' Dreaming pink, her voice wavers. 'The day I married your father was the happiest day of my life. I was a mere girl.'

My parents met just before the declaration of war in Europe when she was nineteen, and my father mature and experienced. In her eyes, he was a man of importance. He had studied abroad. He was Merton Grey, a Fellow of the Royal College of Surgeons of England, handsome and talented, full of vitality. In Victoria, matrons who schemed for their daughters regarded him as an excellent catch. But flattery or the temptations of wealth never fooled my father. He would marry in his own good time. And he would choose a promising young woman. My mother, from a modest landed family in the Western District of Victoria, had taken a position as governess to a little girl, over a hundred miles from her home. She had longed for a proper education, to attend university and to graduate with a degree. But as her father was a hardworking farmer striving against drought on the land and falling wool prices, he could not single out any one of his four daughters for a special education. What he offered one he must offer another. My mother was the only daughter with an academic leaning. It was such a pity, my mother said, for she would have made a good student. She liked reading. A shadow passed across her face. 'Such a pity,' she repeated, with the emphasis of regret. So my mother made the best use of her situation by following her literary inclinations. After finishing matriculation by correspondence, she decided to strike out on her own, offering her services as a governess. She felt she had a flair for teaching and she thought she could pass on what she knew to an able child. With confidence and hope, she answered an advertisement in *The Age* for a governess. To her great satisfaction, and without any delay, she came to be employed by the Howlett family in a well-to-do region ten miles from Bendigo. Her six-year-old charge was a girl called Janine. My mother, Miss Margaret Montrose, took her by the hand and opened the doors of learning to her. And it was while she was living there with the Howlett family that she met my father.

His marriage proposal took her by surprise. Of course she had fallen in love with him. As soon as she was introduced to him, she loved him. He was so very attractive. He was the centre of attention wherever he went. But his proposal still took her by surprise, because being so shy, little had passed between them. She was not aware that she had been noticed. Well, not in that way. But Merton saw how conscientious she was with the child, how thoughtful and attentive. He observed her. So unobtrusive, so self-effacing, she seemed to fade in and out of rooms, noticed by no one but Merton. He began to follow her, leaving his hostess and her guests for intimacy with Margaret and Janine. The three of them walked around the garden together admiring the trees. In the cooling afternoon, they sat under the rose bower. Her interest in literature attracted him. He questioned her. What book was she reading? She was reading George Eliot. Merton thought it a good sign, though he had not read George Eliot himself. He liked her studious ways and her modesty. He especially valued her modesty and her demeanour. In fact, he had come to value the quieter manners of country girls over 'educated women'. To his way of thinking, university and the greater world ruined them. While Margaret was so clearly unspoilt, so promising, he decided to propose to her. And he did so, not under the rose bower with Janine, but he proposed marriage the next day, after lunch, when other guests were leaving the dining room. He needed to speak to her alone. He waited for a moment to establish the occasion. She found herself looking at Merton, her heart pounding. 'Don't go, Margaret,' he said. 'I have something to ask you.' And reaching across the dining table with its crumpled table napkins and scattered utensils, he grasped her hands and said without the slightest hesitation, 'Will you be my wife?' Taken completely by surprise, she thought she might never breathe again. Her answer came quickly.

'Oh yes,' she said. Still holding her hands, he drew her away from the table and kissed her.

It was a simple wedding. On the day, just six weeks after they first met, my mother wore street clothes to please her husband. She had so wanted to be a bride dressed in white, to wear a veil, oh particularly a floating veil with a scalloped edge. She had thought about pearls and white satin slippers, but Merton would have none of it. He was adamant. No, he had seen enough of society weddings and white brides to know the truth of the matter. It was so much hypocrisy. He knew what really went on. To his marrying colleagues, he had been best man no less than eleven times. No, his wedding was to be entirely different. It would be circumspect, in keeping with the Protestant faith they both professed. So he chose a tailored dress for her in pale blue woollen crêpe, a variety of grey. She liked it. Struck by his forceful voice, my mother's fancies faded to nothing but a little regret. She was to be married to a doctor, a surgeon, no less, educated in London. She was happy to wear whatever he wanted. Her first regret, small as it was, in time developed its own insistence. Whenever she told her story, regret became more urgent. She sighed. She wished he had not been so strict. There would never have been hypocrisy in their courtship. She would have worn white truthfully. They loved each other. They would wait. And on the day of her marriage, among a small gathering of friends and family, she felt nothing but happiness, overwhelming, all-consuming happiness. She was still a bride. Instead of the trailing veil of her dreams, she wore a smart straw hat with a drifting brim. Upon her left shoulder she pinned a corsage of pale pink sunny-south roses and asparagus ferns. This was her day of transformation, a day she would remember for ever.

They were married in St Andrew's Presbyterian Church in her hometown, Willaura. Of course she was sorry that Merton refused to hire a professional photographer. She asked her friend Anne, who happened to be a Roman Catholic, to take a few snapshots, if she wouldn't mind. She apologised to Anne, but she was not able to invite her to the wedding, because in those days, there was no mixing of religions. So Anne stood outside and waited for the bridal party to emerge. Although it was an autumn of intermittent showers, the day managed to yield the gift of one perfect moment. Anne took her photograph just as the sun burst upon the threshold of the church. The bride and groom, emerging from the dark interior, paused briefly, holding hands, inclining towards each other, Merton very tall, Margaret very small. She tilted her head upwards, very slightly, under the drifting brim, so that her full face caught the camera. Someone threw a handful of confetti. It was a lovely photograph. She was so grateful to Anne. And as it should be, the bride and groom were central to the picture. Family members standing behind them seemed shadowy, indistinct. With the passing of time, she forgot who they were. Did it matter? My mother treasured the one and only snapshot of her wedding. And when Merton went away to the war, all too soon, leaving her with a newborn baby, she used to gaze at it, hardly able to take in the sudden and unexpected events that had brought her to this; an absence, a terrible sadness. It was more than his being away, more than their separation just as they were getting to know each other, more than giving birth alone. She didn't know. She just couldn't say. But it was deeper, so much deeper. There was this, you know, *this*.

I hear my mother's voice trembling with emotion, her words in subtle patterns, setting the mosaic of intricate feeling. From the bottle with the purple top, she tipped a thin stream of Milk of

Roses into the palm of her hand. Smoothing her throat, as she so characteristically did, hand over hand, she cried gently, watching her reflection in the mirror all the while, tears mingling with lotion and the scent of distant England. As she thought about things, her hand often rested upon her breast. And when words and emotion overcame her, she began to beat her breast in a soft, percussive accompaniment. Although we could not know it then, listening to our mother's morning story, as young initiates, Fenella and I were refining our hearing, gathered unwittingly into the delicately expanding mystery of word and meaning.

It is not the same, the screw-top jar of cosmetic cream that I bought in Exeter, looking for my mother, yearning for her to appear as the original vision of my childhood. The image of my mother has long since left reality to become more like poetry, ascending to a ritual search for perfume. It has assumed all the potency of her literary longing, or a lost manuscript, the words uttered once that can never be uttered again. Now I am intent upon finding just the right bottle of lotion to bring her nearer to me, to smooth over face and throat with folding hands, just as she did. Milk of Roses, as a product of the cosmetic industry, is history. It is finished, gone for ever. The goddess Cyclax, in silver and purple, is just one of many fallen idols. Others have risen quickly in her stead, but they are far less appealing. They are slick creations. They have no memory. And so I sidle around cosmetic counters, looking for a substitute that appeals to me. Turning away from the names of glamorous women who make their lotions in laboratories, and with the minds of male scientists, I happen upon a herbal creation in a large shallow jar, a pale pink lotion of *bois de rose*. It speaks through the word 'pure' that is inscribed upon its aluminium lid. Oh, how it speaks! Pure, pure, pure! The heart of my mother is now pure *bois de rose*, the scented wood from which romantic love grows.

At home in Ottery, I cannot bring myself to squander this precious lotion by laying it upon myself. There is something to be done first. I must create a ritual. Very carefully and reverently, I remove the jar from its wrapping. Less sophisticated than any product from the former house of Cyclax, its fresh naivety appeals to me. It is a new maiden, just like my mother, better even than the original. In a way I prefer it, because it is entirely mine and appears only to me. I like the frosted glass, so soft upon the eye. And contemplating the heavy container with a lid that turns smoothly with one twist of the hand, I visualise the ritual to come and its connection with the operations of rose quartz. The precious unguent smells wonderful. It seems perfectly natural in my current inclinations, to take a pillar of polished rose quartz and sink it into the middle. I have, in my collection, a crystal that might have been especially prepared for this very act. It is just the right size for the jar. And how I love the pillar with its inner pink clouds. I take it now to the bathroom for cleansing. The crystal seems to sing with delight in the palm of my hand, changing colour, undulating in cold running water. Pink billows within it making my heart race with happiness. While it is still dripping, I sink the crystal into the viscous interior with my fingers, pressing it down, down, until the whole shaft sits upon the base of the glass jar. It is done now, finished. I replace the lid. This part of the ritual is over. And there is only a little cream on my fingers.

I sigh. It is not my mother's sigh. It is my own. I have something to cherish from my memories of the past. In my reliquary is a living relic. For the moment, I do not hear my mother speaking, taken as she is into the spirit of rose quartz, her coarctated heart embedded in a soothing emollient. I have in my possession a thing of beauty. I have joy for ever. Hearing myself, I become my own voice. Once more, I sigh. How long is for ever? I do not know. Surely poetic eternity may be translated into any romantic epoch. Now that I have something tangible, a creation of my very own, I must guard it carefully, protecting it from every kind of harm. I give it to five years, to a mystical period called a quinquennium. To that end, I carry the reliquary carefully to a chosen place of rest. It is here upon my windowsill that I keep a portrait known to both Fenella and myself, an image of Nijinsky in Fokine's ballet *Le Spectre de la Rose*. Nijinsky, with downcast eyes, is poised on tiptoe, in a position *croisé*. From his hourglass torso, clothed in exfoliating rose petals, arises a scented silence, the effortless illusion that is dance. Although his balance seems to be precarious, his high *port de bras* broken, he is upheld by the enduring power of beauty, a subtle strength living so evocatively in memory that it may be summoned on seeing. Because Nijinsky is the god of the dance and his beauty causes all things to be in harmony, I know that he can never fall. And because he can never fall, he is the perfect guardian of recollection and the rose quartz voice of my mother. In this ritual I feel happy. Something good has reached me.

Carnelian should be worn next to the skin, placed upon the body or taken as an elixir.

In the catalogues of crystal healers, there may be more strikingly beautiful stones than carnelian, but it is the gravity of carnelian, as much as its capacity to contain, that attracts me. It offers the comfort of internal substance, the invitation to return to the centre of the earth. Seduced by the sight of iron, the eye sweeps across it, and then on the instant returns to be held there, gazing, seeking its secret movements. Isobars of red-brown ferric oxide melt in waves through carnelian, planting the same molten feeling in the beholder. There is something wonderfully soothing about this stone, a downward movement that is by no means heavy or dry. Caught in its vibrations, the *locus* of carnelian becomes the inner beginnings of the body, the primal wetness the womb. It settles there, happily. In antiquity, it was highly prized by both the Greeks and the Romans. Not only did the ancients decorate themselves with polished carnelian, but in its long healing history it was also used to alleviate the pain of childbirth, staunching the flow of blood and calming terrors. Today, crystal healers speak of the energy of carnelian in much the same way, where physical symptoms may correspond with conditions of the spirit, the bleeding heart.

Thinking of marriage and childbirth, I am reminded that Plato, the father of European wisdom, says of the womb that it is arid and unproductive until irrigated by the waters of the male. Subjugation is natural to the female. Plato likens the womb to a restless animal longing to be tamed. The ancient Greeks praise male supremacy and believe that sexual intercourse is, for all young women, a necessity. Girls are in themselves, unhealthy. They are nothing until they become mothers of sons. To this end, the bridegroom grasps the virgin bride around the wrist on her wedding day, pulling her away like a captive, a reluctant child abducted from her mother's arms. In Greek art, wedlock is drawn from the depths of melancholy, a day of initiation entirely without joy. Hymen, the god of marriage and the marriage song, who had vanished on his own wedding day, is sought at every wedding. He reappears as a representation of Eros, a beautiful winged youth, but with a more serious expression, carrying in his hand the marriage torch and nuptial veil. In this veiling, with her head bowed, the maiden is taken to motherhood. The fate of Roman women is only a little better. The daughters of Rome are also required to serve the male and be fruitful. From twenty-first century augury, carnelian brings healing to erroneous understanding of the feminine. All such false thinking may be removed by acknowledging the deeper truths of intuition, and the healing that ensues. This can be felt by holding carnelian, the crystal that belongs to the ancient experience of women, the deeper knowing that they were so often denied. In the wide range of colours I have encountered, from dark red to racy orange, as well as a fluid intermingling of both, today I speak of the common iron-bearing stone that gives carnelian its characteristic colour, its liquid nature. Carnelian belongs with visceral movement, with the functions of internal organs deep within the watery cave of the sacrum.

    Etymologically, carnelian is flesh. As everything known or born may appear anywhere as an image, then carnelian manifests all the virtues, all the aspirations of the human spirit in its search for self-knowledge. The soul is conceived and suffers birth. The sacrum, as the bone sacred to animal sacrifice, traces psychic memory far back to antiquity, to a quivering fear, to an act that seeks the meaning of things through the scrutiny of innards splayed upon a sacred stone. The haruspex, a soothsayer from

Etruria, hovers over the operations of carnelian. Moaning ceremonially, the priest invokes the deity, his voice articulating both evils and omens. Haruspices, a priesthood adopted by the Romans, raised itself from daily acts of animal sacrifice to give a special utterance to innards, an oracle from the hidden depths of the body. It was the liver, gall, heart, lungs and caul of sacrificial victims that became the very image of divine will through minute observation of the way in which these internal organs fell upon stone. The question asked by the haruspex on behalf of the enquirer had to be so precise that the answer, arising from the seething midden of the flesh, could also be precise. The priest fingered innards. As he fingered, he spoke. Even the pitch of his voice mattered. Haruspices were revered men. Very occasionally, they were women. Augury and soothsaying were especially revered before the onset of war. Blood spilt upon the stone indicated the extent of human sacrifice upon the land. Just as in animal sacrifice, the stone is the *locus* of holiness, in war, the land assumes the same religious significance. It becomes the *locus* of human sacrifice. The oracle was nothing without a flow of blood, for blood was the symbolic heart of incarnation and giving. The prophet looked for signs of victory over enemies, seen and unseen, a way of conquering death. And when not interpreting the movement of animal flesh, weather in its extremities was observed. From thunder and lightning, the haruspex drew down power.

What can be discerned now from this knowledge? As I speak of carnelian, I speak of haruspicy. I become an haruspica. By evoking the higher part of an ancient ritual, carnelian brings healing. I say this because I have come to know this stone through experience. I place a large piece of polished carnelian upon my sacrum. The piece I have chosen has a running, circular feeling. Its energy is so appealing that I toy with the urge to place it my mouth. I would like to swallow it, to trace its symbolic journey to the womb. I wish to consume carnelian and to be consumed by it. And in my many conversations with crystal healers, whose utterances are certainly out of the ordinary, I listen to everything they tell me, observing the minutiae of body language as they describe what they know. I hear a slight tremolo in the voice, a subtle change of pitch. Women say that carnelian is strong, as strong as the uterine muscle, that it is both holding and propelling. Yes, it is succulent, fruity. And as a sacred fruit, it is entirely suitable for the healing injuries of the womb, at whatever level they may occur, whether physical, mental, emotional or spiritual. I cannot analyse with any logic my knowing that carnelian is a crystal manifestation of the feminine psyche. All I can say is that carnelian belongs to intuition and seems to run with the still, deep waters of knowing. I hasten to add that in my many conversations, no one has ever said anything of haruspicy. I have not mentioned the matter, simply because I wish to hear what others say. Considering my fearfulness, I am more than surprised that the image of animal sacrifice came to me through carnelian, the vision of a pagan priest cutting down the victim, the limp body lifted upon the sacrificial stone, the splaying of innards. I avert my gaze. I might collapse with fright were not my eyes fixed upon the priest, following his ritual gestures, alert to everything that he utters in his peculiar tones.

In childhood, there was a time when stones, as conscious energies, did not exist at all. My happening upon them was merely incidental in the larger scheme of things. Only a few exceptional objects caught my eye. I admired my mother's turquoise brooch set in Indian silver encircled by red coral, a present from my father during the war. I loved her sparkling diamond ring, my father's gift to her on their engagement day. But these were her private possessions and nothing to do with me. I looked at them from a distance. Sometimes, but very rarely, when my mother was busy in the kitchen, her hands in flour, I would lift her ring from the hook on the dresser and slip it on. The little golden band with its adamantine eye spun round and round my finger, winking as it turned. I remember gazing into its faceted face as I might into a crystal ball. I saw magic there. I believed I peered into my mother's secrets. The ring was made especially for her, a gift of tender feelings. She treasured it, as she treasured everything she received from my father. But she was particularly prickly about daughters touching her jewels. I think she felt that we might break the spell of golden memory. We might contaminate her joy. My mother said that this most prized possession, her engagement ring, would one day go to Edgar, her first-born. And when my mother died, it did. Well, I presume it passed to him, for it disappeared from all knowledge. I would not know, because Edgar too has long since passed from this existence. And although I sense that her diamond ring is far away, in these summoning words, and in the opening spaces of the heart, her diamond is very near, sparkling before me.

It must be the gently filling waters of carnelian that carry me now to the scene of my first emerging emotions. This is the link to my past that begs to be explored within these pages of words and images: water. I am compelled to do so from the very strength of feeling arising from my own haruspicy. The memory of a special place rushes back to me, and if I am correct, the first intimations of my present return journey began with the old willow tree I encountered on my walk the other day. I was struck by the ruddiness of the River Otter made turbulent by recent rain and the happy thought that the ragged willow beside it remained so firmly rooted, surviving season after season of violent change. There seemed to be a deep connection between them, the willow tree and the rivulet; an intimate exchange, a mutual acceptance. Such mutuality, such stability is all to do with healing. I felt the movement of carnelian within me. I placed my hand upon its rough trunk, attuning with the woody moment, gazing at the rushing water, and in doing so, another image came to me. It was the experience of the first living tree in my childhood. It too was a willow, but a long-leafed weeping kind overhanging a small, still pond in an ornamental garden; *salix babylonica*, the tree of the tears of exile.

After the war, my father decided that his family should be reared in Tasmania. In managing offspring, my father used the verb 'to rear' in much the same way, as in a land of graziers, it was used of sheep. My parents had spent their honeymoon touring the island state, and during their hallowed stay, they sowed the seeds of hope, that one day, when Europe had settled its disputes, they would return to Tasmania and make a home there. It was such a beautiful place, and though some distance from the rest of Australia, it nevertheless offered everything that a man of the world and a man of culture could desire. Both music and art were to be found there, flourishing in replicas of Englishness. And in the garden of our first home, Harringay House, I found such replicas, England in a walled garden, existing in the midst of native eucalypts. The willow tree leant over a weedy pond that reeked of rotting leaves. It was here that I experienced an English spring, bundles of blue grape hyacinths along the path to the pond, the scent of sap and stem. It was here that I met frogs and felt the soft bodies of tadpoles tickling the skin. I may say that the garden was English, but at the time, I knew nothing of the kind. I was young. Only now do I know that Harringay House in Davey Street, Hobart, was indeed a house in England, translated to Tasmania.

Our first family home, the foundation of my imagined England, belonged to Miss Hastings. My parents rented her Tasmanian property at a difficult time, the years after the war when there was such a shortage of accommodation. Miss Hastings had retreated to the Old Country, and in the meantime, while my father established his medical practice and searched for a permanent place, we, as children, enjoyed the remnants of Miss Hastings and her relocated England. Roaming the rooms and polished corridors of Harringay House, we were reminded constantly of the absent and ever important owner; we were not to touch this and not to touch that. And so, in my small mind, the image of Miss Hastings became attached to the warnings and prohibitions that were cast about by my parents. Miss Hastings was stern and English. She was both the person and the location, Hastings and Harringay, bound together as one. What a strange name she had, to do with hurrying; hurrying away from Harringay to the Old Country. I imagined that Miss Hastings did everything quickly. Haste was surely her nature. And as the owner of a substantial brick house with leaded windows, and a drawing room in which stood a glossy grand piano, Miss Hastings, in her absence, impressed me greatly. More than the weeping willow tree beside the pond was the sight of the huge musical instrument. This vast piece of furniture was actually hers. Did she play it? I imagined she did. I moved cautiously towards the instrument. Might I see inside? My father opened the lid. A strange, dry aroma arose from the keys. The ivories gleamed; the black and white octaves repeated themselves in patterns. Reaching up, I pressed a single note. Astonished by the response, I pulled my hand away. My father laughed. May I play the piano, I asked? My father said that I was too young, that I would have to wait. One day, when we had our own home, he said, we would also have our own piano. I resented the word 'wait', so I turned to other things.

One of the downstairs rooms, off a vestibule near the kitchen, was locked. Through the leaded windows outside, my sister and I saw furniture piled high, chair legs sticking up, cushions and standard lamps crammed to the ceiling. We observed Miss Hastings throwing all her possessions together in a hurry, locking the door and running away to England. Inside the house, Fenella turned the knob. Nothing happened, but we stood there, waiting for something amazing to intervene. The forbidden room seemed so alluring, the panelled door, fascinating. Fenella drew my attention to a large spider, a hairy huntsman clinging to the lintel above us. A peculiar light fell upon the lintel and the spider, a light that was different from anything that I had ever seen. For a brief moment, I enjoyed a delirious swaying sensation. It seemed to come from the gentle brush of the foliage outside the window, the call of the weeping willow. Without the slightest fear of spiders, Fenella pointed to it. I screamed. And to that frightening experience came a strong feeling of the colour yellow, the yellow of ochre. It was as if the spider, the willow and yellow came all at once to my consciousness. As I looked up, I saw a streak of yellow paint on the panelled door. And now my sister Fenella is standing beside me with a paintbrush in her hand and a palette of watercolours. She looks at the streak she has made upon Miss Hastings' polished wood, the brush dripping and glistening. She marks a warning on the door to the hidden and interior world of Miss Hastings; yellow paint and the hairy spider, the leafy light rippling; Miss Hastings, away in distant England. Would she ever return from her *Ultima Thule* at the very top of the globe? And how would she manage to survive so far away, a woman all alone in the wide world without a husband?

My father loved Tasmania. The scenery was so striking, the hinterland mountainous and deeply forested, its craggy coastlines merging into miles of white sandy beaches. South of Hobart, across the D'Entrecasteau Channel, was the pristine Eden of an elongated island, a bushy paradise that only a few ventured to visit. My father wished to escape into the wild, and whenever possible to leave city life and the responsibilities of medical practice. Now that he had discovered Bruny, my father decided to make this remote location his place of refuge. He spoke to my mother of buying a holiday cottage. There were simple dwellings for sale, weather board shacks used formerly by settlers clearing the bush for pasture. On Bruny Island was a small settlement with the Aboriginal name, Lunawanna. It was still an undeveloped area, difficult to reach, hidden away where the dusty gravel road disappeared into a rutted track. At the extreme tip of the island, ten miles along the stony Lighthouse Road from Lunawanna, where scarlet blandfordia bloomed on the edge of the button-grass plains, the sea surged upon the rocks of Cloudy Bay in the sonorous voice of the Roaring Forties. This was his Terra Australis Incognita. Since the days of my parents' honeymoon, it was to the sonorous remoteness that emerged from Antarctica, and to the gales that blow on the southern side of the sky that my father was drawn.

Of course my mother spoke constantly of their honeymoon. Although I have no recollection of her mirror image at Harringay House, her voice is there, drifting through the French windows, floating airily from beneath the weeping willow near the still, stagnant pond. Fenella and I are sitting in the drawing room looking at photos in an album. Apart from their wedding photo, there was another I liked just as much, a special image of my parents lifted from the stream of my mother's telling. At Port Arthur, among the scattered ruins of the convict settlement, in the midst of alienation, they stood under the central arch of the old magazine, their arms tightly entwined. My mother's face was turned towards her husband. My father pulled her narrow body to his chest, his fingers gripping her rib cage just under her breast. The southern wind blew her hair in a halo around her head. They were so in love, my mother said. Over and over again, she reiterated the bliss of their honeymoon; bliss in Port Arthur, their wonderful union, so very precious to her; the mysterious thing that happened in Tasmania. I hear the word 'union' but do not understand, delivered as it always was with a kind of thrust from my mother's mouth. She enunciated 'union' in a special way, her hand pressing her breast, her eyes misty. It was while they were at Port Arthur among the ruins, in their honeymoon union, my mother said, that my father first spoke of his intention to live in Tasmania, just as soon as he was free. And when would that be? There was a war looming. Everything was uncertain. As Australia was a part of the British Empire, her husband felt he had a duty to offer his services to his country. Besides, he was a fellow of one of England's great medical institutions, the Royal College of Surgeons. The time had its imperative. He must make the difficult journey north. He must follow his colleagues. She watched her husband pace the room smoking cigarette after cigarette, drinking whisky, speaking of the war and the call to arms. She could see now just how agitated he was. In the days of her naivety, when she was newly married, she hardly knew him. She just had to accept. And whenever that time and its awesome imperative were mentioned, the tone of my mother's voice would change yet again.

My mother was so lonely during the years that she called 'the war'. She was washed out, exhausted by not knowing what to do for the best. Every time her husband came home on leave, she would fall pregnant. It was always such a joy to see him, and she supposed they couldn't help it. They needed each other so much. What else could she do? Under his instructions, she used birth control. She tried to prevent herself from conceiving, she said, but nothing ever worked. It was her fault, she knew. And then the parting at the end of his leave was so terrible. It was the dreadful thought that she might never see him again. After he left, she wept for days. She wept and wept. And then she would discover that yet again, she was pregnant. So there she was, bearing her babies alone, traipsing from one rented house to another, managing everything in the absence of a husband. She had made her promise to obey him. She listened to him. And especially did she listen to him when it came to the children. He was a doctor. He knew best. He was worldly-wise, educated. But things cropped up unexpectedly. She had problems he just did not seem to grasp. She needed to talk to him. In her letters, she made little of her worries. After all, he was a surgeon behind the front line, saving lives. She always thought everything would fall into place when the war was over, when they had settled down properly with the children. But it just did not work out that way. She tried, oh, she tried to make him understand. He returned after an absence of five years to find himself the father of three growing children. It could have been a wonderful new beginning, wonderful, she repeated, but she was taken aback by her husband's attitude towards Edgar. He spoke to him so harshly, pulling him up, correcting him in army tones. She asked him not be so hard on the boy. She said Edgar was still a child and that his disobedience was nothing but childishness. He did not know what it was to have a father. She thought he would listen to her, that she could tell him all about the children and her pregnancies, the difficult births of the girls, but he seemed deaf, deaf to anything she said. She didn't know; she just did not know. She truly believed she had done her best. Now he criticised her. He made her feel so miserable. He said that she had not disciplined the children, that she had 'spoilt' the boy. She had 'ruined' him. How could he say such a thing? The criticism of Edgar was particularly hurtful to her because all through her husband's years of absence, the child had been her constant companion. They had shared so much together. And what had she done wrong? My mother pulled a hankie from her sleeve and pressed it to her eyes. She pressed it and kept it there. Injury made her voice tremble. It was all because of the method, the new method of child rearing. It was her fault. If only she had been stronger. If she had been brave enough to follow her natural instincts, none of this business with Edgar would have happened. But her husband believed in training children, right from birth. Ah, Truby King and his slogan, 'routine'! Practise discipline, her husband had told her, follow Truby King's instructions, *read the book*, and she could not go wrong.

And so she did. She followed Truby King's instructions to the letter of the law. She read his book from cover to cover, applying his rules so religiously, that she failed to notice her baby. She nearly starved him to death. Merton, agreeing with Truby King, said breastfeeding should also be a 'routine'. It must be ten minutes at each breast every four hours, ten minutes and no more. If he cried, he was not to be picked up. There was a pause while my mother stifled her distress, gripping her ribs with crossed arms, holding herself together as she spoke. It pained her to think of it now, but Edgar was a hungry baby, so hungry that he fell silent. He stopped crying. He all but gave up the ghost. Oh, how it hurt her to think about it! My mother covered her mouth with her hankie, appalled by what she had said. She had looked at the wraithlike thing lying in his bassinet, the child conceived on the first night of their honeymoon, and she knew, she just knew that something was terribly wrong. But she was torn between love for her husband and her own instincts. Could she not feel? Did she not know? She daren't go against the wishes of her husband. There was that book, and 'the spoilt cry'. Anyway, Edgar had no cry, no cry at all. There was nothing left of him left to spoil. It had all been done.

In an attack of terrible nerves, my mother took Edgar to her doctor. Dr Frankl uncovered the skinny creature wrapped in a bunny rug, the child that only five months ago he had delivered into the world, and looking straight at her, he said sternly, 'Mrs Grey, your baby is starving. What do you think you are doing? You have plenty of milk. Go and feed him. For heaven's sake, feed him!' And that was what she did. It was such enormous relief to be told. She hurried home to put the baby to her breast. She stroked his head as he sucked for his life. She encouraged him to take as much as he needed. She did exactly what she and her baby wanted. And she would pick him up when he cried. She would. She would tell her husband the method didn't work. She was not spoiling him. She was simply feeding him. She would tell him.

My mother wept, as she wept, she beat her breast over and over again. She wept in the manner of the tree, *salix babylonica*, in the supple way of the English willow, leaning over water. My sister and I watched her weeping in her pink flannel dressing gown, her body heaving beneath the folds of material. We watched her leaning and weeping, beating and fluttering, accusing herself in her distress. It was this, she said, '*this*.' She gave herself to the primal memory, the loss that lived just beneath her hand. Her loss dropped as leaves into water, carried into the stream.

There were many grievances to do with my father, not least his drinking. To my mother's chagrin, she had come to accept that most professional men, as she deferentially called doctors, needed to drink. She was now resigned to alcohol as a fact of life, even though it was alien to her experience. Her father never drank. Neither did her father-in-law, the Rev. Arthur Grey. Of course he never drank. Not a drop passed his lips. Even the Communion wine was grape juice. All alcohol was strictly forbidden. It had no place in their lives. And the absence of alcohol seemed to deny its very existence. Drink became a part of the darkness cast out by faith. Only sinners drank. A Christian could not admit such a thing. But my mother had difficulty in equating the simpler ways of her religious upbringing with the complex theological world that confronted her now. It went without saying her husband had authority. As for alcohol and religion, she floundered. She had no idea what to think. Her husband must lead. She must learn to understand him. She could never match the superiority of his mind, though she tried so very hard to please him. Somehow, it was not enough to be proud of her country education. He made her feel that she had failed when her own family looked on her modest academic success as a triumph. Merton and his sisters had opportunities not available to her. Her husband's family was ambitious. And her mother-in-law was a most capable woman. Not only was she an accomplished musician, playing the organ every Sunday at church, but she was also a wonderful cook. There was an unwavering purpose, a brilliance even, in everything she did. My mother studied the austere Mrs Grey, the domestic Mrs Grey. To here eyes, she was perfect. And when, in the brief weeks of her engagement, her future mother-in-law discovered that the shy governess could not cook, she took her aside and said both confidentially and firmly, 'Well, Maggie, let us go to the kitchen and begin with the rudiments.' My mother went willingly. She stood beside her, weighing ingredients, fetching utensils, while Mrs Grey gave her lessons, taking her step by step through a day's menu for the master of the house, finishing with a swift batch of scones, those indispensable teatime comforts, acceptable to all men.

My mother acknowledged that through marriage to my father, she had come of age. She knew how lucky she was. Educated men were in the vanguard of a new society. The British Empire, at great cost, had defended itself in all its territories. Just as in military conflict the burden was on the male, so it was in a time of nation building. After the call to arms came the call to strengthen the democratic structures of the Western World. That men should spend time together was perfectly understandable. Shared work and recreation were as much a part of being male as was a right to govern. Men liked to associate with one another. They gravitated to their clubs. Because so much was expected of them, my mother felt she must give way to her husband and his colleagues. Nevertheless, there was bitterness in her avowed subjugation to the male. She tried to rationalise her feelings. Life was ordered in an immovable way. There was the progress of the modern age. There was pressure. There was the war. Nothing was the same any more. Of course her husband would honour his religion. The war had not shaken his faith. He was a man of integrity. She knew this, right from the start. It was just that she did not know what to make of his drinking, except that all medical men drank. It was a fact. It was taken for granted. It was something she could not understand, essential to the male. She knew the dismay of his parents. She knew how shocked they were. She saw their pride in him hurt. But there was nothing she could do. She could only play her part by striving to please her husband. Her obligations were dual: to be a good wife and to control her emotions. Yes, control. She stressed the word uncomfortably. It was his word, not hers. And if this word ever felt comfortable, and occasionally, very occasionally, a state that she could manage, then it passed all too quickly. She knew what she was really telling herself. Was not the word, 'suppress'? And how was she supposed to suppress what was 'natural'? She was to use her mind. She was to think herself there. Once more, the irksome came with a flood of feelings, especially feelings for Edgar. She broke down in front of her husband. She wept. It was so shaming, her lack of control. Merton told her she was weak, that she must correct her feelings.

With respect to Edgar, she had tried, but could not use her mind, because she did not love him in that way. She loved with her feelings. She had nothing else with which to love. How could she discipline feelings? What was the method? He didn't say. My mother paused. She bit her lip. Who could understand what had happened to her? There was no one. Unaware of her difficulties, her own family spoke proudly of her new life. And because she had to uphold her husband come what may, she had no one. There was no one to hear her; not a living soul. To say anything to anyone, even another doctor's wife, would be unthinkable. She too had a position to uphold. Just as her husband was bound to confidentiality, then so was she. In this, she knew an isolation of her very own. She was alone. No, she must struggle on. She must try to be stronger. But it was always in this oft-repeated, overvalued 'trying to be stronger' that my mother floundered. Especially in Edgar's case, everything she held to, everything she tried to accomplish for the sake of her husband, seemed to fail. As she said before, if only he had not been so hard on the boy. If only she had been stronger.

There was the unforgettable occasion when Edgar, who was just six years old, took it upon himself to play with matches under the house. The area so described, under the house, was an unlit storage space exposing the foundations of the upper structure. It was tinder-dry and dark. As it contained many of Miss Hastings' boxed possessions, we were not supposed to go there. But Edgar was such an adventurous little chap, always exploring, running around the garden wielding his sticks of stripped willow, playing soldiers, conquering enemies. He was up to all kinds of tricks. It was so easy to push at the low door to this under the house cavity, just to see what was inside. He fancied, in his boyish imaginings, imitating his father, that he would light a fire to brighten the darkness; just a little one. If he lit a fire, he could explore. In the drawing room upstairs, he had seen his father crumple newspaper and split kindling across his knee, arranging a neat pyramid in the grate on top of the paper. When a match was struck on the side of the box and the tiny light poked into the paper cavities, there came a sudden burst of flames up the chimney. Kindling crackled. New fire spat sparks onto the hearth. He watched his father sweep them up. It was wonderful. Surely he could do that for himself? Edgar already had a box of matches in his hand. In the chink of light from the half-open door, he found strips of musty newspaper in the crate that contained Miss Hastings' china. The paper would do. He had his willow sticks. And searching around in the dimness, he found a few bits of dry wood lying on the dusty floor.

If my mother had not interrupted the fire under the house, the consequences might have been fatal.

At the time, she was working in the kitchen directly above the dark area below. She was not aware that Edgar was right beneath her feet striking match after match, lighting his fire. At first she did not hear the scuffling noise or the small voice calling for help. She happened to be at the sink, washing the lunch things, turning the taps on and off. The swish of running water hid all but the clink of dishes. And she was thinking, deeply. But then, through the open window, she smelt smoke. She sensed an absence. It was some time since she had seen Edgar running around the garden, slashing the air with his sticks. Where was he? Dropping the tea towel, she flung herself out the back door. She raced down the steps, calling as she descended, 'Edgar, Edgar! Where are you?' In the garden, she darted hither and thither. A thin stream of smoke drifted about her. Oh no! He was under the house. He was under the house and there was a fire!

Edgar shouted from inside, his muffled voice crying, 'Mummy! Mummy! Help me!' When she found him, he was blowing at the fire, trying with all his might to puff it away with his breath. Without a luffer or the guiding bricks of a chimney, the flames leapt and spread, leering at the tinder of Miss Hastings' things. He picked up a stick and smacked the burning bundle, catching his fingers in the heat. In her panic, she flung her son aside and began to dismantle the fire with her hands, trampling upon it, stamping the conflagration to a few smouldering embers. Smoke choked them both; their eyes smarted. Trembling all over, Edgar watched her. He coughed and shook with fright. He began to cry. Trembling with fright too, she went to him and knelt beside him. Squeezing him tightly, she pressed his sobbing body to her breast. It had always been thus. Their terrible ordeal in the dark was over.

When my father came home from work that evening, it was only natural that my mother should tell him what had happened. In her telling, she stressed that Edgar had learnt his lesson, and that nothing had been damaged. Miss Hastings' possessions were unharmed. They were intact. With wavering words, my mother tried to say that Edgar had been chastened by the shame of the little fire. And as he was so distressed, the poor child had gone straight to his room. She brought him milk and bread and butter. But he was too shocked to eat. She thought it best to tuck him up in bed, poor little chap. He was now fast asleep. Couldn't Merton speak to him in the morning?

But my father could not. At this point in my mother's narrative, my recollections take over. From hearing a story I move to seeing an event. An eruption equivalent to a seismic upheaval in the psyche of the family occurred. I cannot remember where Edgar's hiding took place, for it seemed to be in several locations and on several planes of existence. Dragged from his bed by my father, his body slithered along the polished corridor, his limbs pulled from his quivering torso, an animal forced from the comfort of the flock to be despatched from the land of the living. Was this a considered ritual, the hand of redemption at work, saving the son from the sin of disobedience? My father wanted to take him to the scene of the crime, to punish him in the very *locus* of his disobedience, but his anger was so aroused that he could not wait to lay his hand upon him. In my recollection, his hiding takes place all over the house, in each and every room. As this could not have been so, I attribute the distortion to the fear engendered by my father. Edgar was hauled through his punishment. It was so very shocking to see. Into the faint quiver of our existence, our short years of playing with dolls and frolicking in the garden, came the unimagined violence. Fenella and I saw the contortion of bodies, the large man towering over the small boy, a hand landing blow after blow upon the wetting, screaming child, the sound so sharp and percussive. It was a terrifying beating that seemed to go on for ever, a frenzy of limbs working like pistons in the machinery of parental discipline.

Partially blinded by fright, I cannot remember where my mother was, but in subsequent beatings, she was always nearby, weeping and wringing her hands.

The experience was a lesson to us all. It was no use thinking that as girls, we would escape such a fate. We knew there would be no exceptions. And if my mother had observed us, she would have seen the fright in our eyes. But in spite of my mother's identity with her first-born, she did not see the fears of her children, especially not the fears of daughters before the father. If she did see, and I know that the pains of her son touched her, she was so fixed in her own fragile security that she was unable to move. She was full of uncertainties; mesmerised by an authority over which she had no control.

It was shock that stopped time. The world froze as ice on a pond. My sister and I had been initiated into the rituals of a hiding. We had seen, and in that act of seeing, we had experienced something profound, standing before the cosmic event as *epoptes* in the fields of fear; a grotesque enactment not so remote from the ancient Mysteries of Eleusis, where death and all the cohorts of darkness were the infatuation.

After his punishment for the fire under the house, Edgar was sent back to his room, sobbing. Fenella and I retreated to the safe territory of our own room, to the canopy bed that we shared, a woven night enclosed by heavy linen drapes embroidered with exotic birds. We slept with Miss Hastings, in the deep folds of her distant England. Silence settled around us. Lying there, slipping into uneasy slumber, I heard footsteps along the corridor. For a brief moment I was roused to a hope that my mother might come to see us. Perhaps she would arrive in the night of our fears to put everything right, to cancel the terrible event. Only she could restore harmony. My mother approached Edgar's room. A door opened and closed. She was with her son.

I could not imagine what took place between them, but it felt to me then, as it does now in my recall, that between a mother and her first-born there exists a secret knowing, a knowledge that has its own ritual act, the *consolamentum*, an encouragement to banish fear. This was a sacrament not for me. Although I was unable to identify my turmoil, beneath the fear I most surely knew, confused with the longing for my mother, was the growing awareness that to be a son was to be special before the mother and despicable before the father. For my sister and me, there was no escape from a double fate. Without a defender, what might evolve for daughters before the father? Bound to both her husband and her son, my mother's gaze was elsewhere. There was no *consolamentum* for being female. My mother spoke to Edgar in a different way. And in the night of Edgar's hiding, we heard her murmuring voice, the muffled sounds that soothed. My mother was speaking softly, her words banishing all remembrance of injury. She touched her son with a healing hand. Everything would be all right, she said. Everything would be all right.

Carnelian should be worn next to the skin, placed upon the body or taken as an elixir.

Days shorten. In nature's augury, immigrant swifts swarm on high wires all along Yonder Street, waiting for the signal to begin their flight south. Soon they will be on the wing. Their impending absence brings a feeling of foreboding to our northern skies. The frantic breeding season is over; parents have thrown their offspring to the wind. I must look to other things. In the changing days, the long arm of the night draws me to itself. Future events cast their shadows. I approach an English winter, a hibernation that wraps the body tightly, taking us indoors. It is time to leave my summerhouse and close the shutters against the damp wind. I will not visit it again until the spring. In my small town cottage, curtains are drawn early. Outside, leaves fall from trees; the earth drifts towards sleep. Heat from the open fire nourishes feelings. I breathe, here in England, where poets breathed, where the hearth ministers to incorporeal thought, bringing living beings into my writer's mind. Imagination, as swift as a bird, has the freedom to fly anywhere in limitless migration, but as yet I am unable to rise from the south. How difficult it is to leave a sanctuary of so much creativity. I am reluctant to depart, for there is still something left to say, something gathering and fluttering, demanding attention. In the psychic plasticity of antiquity, I dance a mystery dance, perfecting a ritual purification of my life, with every movement fulfilling the responsibilities of the winged comprehensor. My learning is remembering.

It is clear to me now how colour first occurred at Harringay House, how ochre was drawn from Fenella's box of watercolours to be born upon the page. It was Fenella who knew how paint and water behaved. She knew in a way I could never know. Pigment was her *prima materia*, her lapis of transformation, a means of both imitation and expression. She approached painting with an unusual assurance, her purity of perception carrying inner knowledge forward. Dipping the brush in water, Fenella paused before selecting what she wanted. She held her breath momentarily, hovering over a row of colours, floating in the flow of anticipation. The saturated brush touched the parchment; yellow seeped in. Its uneven, watery distribution and the buckling page did not dismay her. She knew what to do, for she was already practised at her art, working with the power of insight. She looked at nature, and seeing the yellowing willow and the pond, she transferred the image to paper as if she had done so many times before. Stepping back, she observed her work, adding streaks and dabs here and there. I followed her eyes from nature to the page. The willow arched in the English garden. It swayed over the pond, moving at her command. She filled the picture with scribbled foliage and dripping leaves. The path wound round the garden. In the pale blue sky, the sun at the top of the tree appeared as a spangled stone in the midst of celestial activity. From billowing clouds, a bird of augury emerged. How could she know then, when she was so young, that her spangled sun would consume the dawn of her own creativity? The bird of augury flew from her inner world. Ochre swirled in the jam jar; the brush clinked against the glass. From wet blocks of paint and the glistening page, an earthy aroma arose.

My father too had his visions. Seeing mattered to him. He began to build up a store of visual experience, although it has to be said that in the cultivation of seeing, being so thoroughly trained, he found it difficult to relinquish his keen, diagnostic eye. But when the imperatives that drove his professional life were at rest, he inclined to works of art, relishing the change of mood that seeing induced. Art in all its forms was his *mysterium fascinans*. With a glass of whisky in his hand, he contemplated the delectable but disturbing possibilities of the senses, carried by the same stream of distant memory that had carried his mother in her love of music. Although he was not a musician, music was the first kiss that bloomed in his ear; it would always be his passion. But at the same time, now that he had proved himself as a surgeon, at home and overseas, he felt compelled to enter the other aspect of himself compatible with music, his love of visible order. There was something immensely satisfying in seeing a landscape set off by a handsome frame. It was the containment of the imagination as much as it was the work of art that kept him in thrall. The act of completion satisfied him. It was a job well done. It felt good. An awakening desire, to enhance his surroundings in a manner that was appropriate to a surgeon, occupied much of his fantasies. In this respect, a colleague, a distinguished physician who claimed to be a direct descendant of Donizetti, may have influenced him. Like a doge of the High Renaissance, Donizetti had cleverly constructed an elegant mansion in the Venetian style, not far away in upper Davey Street, all from the ruins of a convict building. Donizetti had invited my father to view his pride and joy. It was a beautiful house, but rather too like a museum for my father's taste. He had sent to Italy for craftsmen to carry out the work; he imported rare tapestries and antique furnishings. The garden was mannered and stylised with its patios, clipped trees and terracotta pots. But there was much more to Donizetti than the mere love of refinement. Everything in his elegant residence was touched by perfection, with a spaciousness that gave rise to feelings of strong, everlasting values. It was the timeless world of classical antiquity. Initially, my father wished to cultivate Donizetti's company, but found him remote, and with his faint foreign accent, somewhat phoney. Anyway, he was Catholic, and underneath his suave European veneer, there may have been a Jesuitic suspicion. To my father, this presented a social obstacle that it was impossible to ignore. He held himself ready, and then he hesitated. Donizetti was undoubtedly an attractive man. He had an aristocratic Italian wife who wore her black hair in a high chignon. She was the ornament in her husband's cultured world. When my father was first introduced to her, he almost kissed her proffered hand, but decided better of it. He was an Australian. And he was not a ladies' man.

In the end, my father turned to the familiar images of Englishness that surrounded him at Harringay House. There was a comfortable *déjà vu* about this substantial city residence, a harking back to the Old Country that was consistent with his own upbringing. England was always 'home'. My father awaited the day of his becoming, the day when he could gather his own chosen artefacts around him, an impresario setting the stage for a theatrical drama. He would like to begin with Persian rugs and fine art. He very much admired Persian rugs, and notwithstanding their oriental origins, he saw them as peculiarly English. For his fine art, he would cultivate indigenous talent, by which he meant local artists whose work was both romantic and emphatic. He need not look any further than Tasmania. Educating himself, my father had considered the paintings of Arthur Boyd and Sidney Nolan with their passionate love of native Australia. Though he craved freedom, he was always at his own extremities, fighting boundaries. He did not know how to manage blinding light and empty space, or the burning thirst of drought. Aboriginality unsettled him. In forgetting its own history, Tasmania seemed to modulate the harshness of the mainland. It was a varied wilderness, a land of ferny forests and watery gorges. Now that he had visited the Old Country, the archetypal island, for the family home he favoured a more utopian view of nature, something that might be realised in this nethermost location. He recalled the smooth, moist plane of an English lawn, the dressing of design. His dream of Albion was epitomised by the ha-ha, a grassy boundary below ground level that from a house created an undulating, uninterrupted view, as far-reaching and as misty as a sea vista. Thinking of this, his throat stimulated by spirits, he stood in Miss Hastings' drawing room contemplating the best of England. He listened to music; he looked at the pictures that hung upon her walls: pale family portraits amid chintz furnishings. In art, he knew he could do better for himself. He knew he could do much better.

His thoughts returned to London and the Royal College of Surgeons, to the temple of the elect that had admitted him to its halls of excellence. He remembered how strong he felt when, as an aspiring surgeon he approached on foot the location in which it stood, Lincoln's Inn Fields. By his own efforts, he had succeeded. It was in England that his education had really begun.

He found such freedom there; the discipline of intense study marked off by excursions into art and music. He heard Elgar at the Albert Hall; he delighted in Flanagan and Allen at the London Palladium. He enjoyed both the serious and the frivolous, a collaboration that he had never been permitted in his years at the University of Melbourne when he was still the son of the manse. The gaiety of the music hall was, in his opinion, no more corrupting than 'What the Butler Saw', a cheeky peepshow. He loved the stage, for it gave immediate relief from the exigencies of a religious existence. And in the same way that he extended his serious repertoire to include symphonic works, he took himself to the National Gallery as often as he could to extend his gift of seeing. He walked alone through its rarefied spaces, surprised at his elation, the lifting of his spirits at the sight of the great masters of the Renaissance. But his initial gratification at the stirring of his senses almost immediately gave way to doubts about what he was seeing. When it came to looking at works of art, he had no implicit knowledge, so deprived was his childhood of ritual seeing. He behaved as a man blind from birth that had just been granted his sight, confronting a visual world of which he had no experience. His vision blurred; nothing was clear. He wanted to believe that both science and art belonged to the mind, the god of pure reason, but he knew that his own response to what he saw had nothing to do with the rational. It galled him that he could not give an account of himself, that he could not be contained by the effort of his mental faculties. For it was in religious painting that he really became unstuck. The constant reading and reciting of the scriptures, always in the Authorised Version, so formalised his inner seeing in keeping with the discarnate loftiness of its language, that when his eyes alighted upon an artist's realisation of an original hearing, he suffered all the symptoms of aesthetic shock. So great was his deprivation, and so sudden the opening of his eyes, there seemed to be no neurological link between his seeing and his understanding. He had only an abstract knowledge of scriptural imagery, and in the absence of essential information, he did not know where or how to begin.

There he was, standing just a few feet from Caravaggio's great masterpiece, *Supper at Emmaus*, feeling the full force of his confusion. He was offended by what he saw lifted before him, an extravagantly laden table, as richly robed as an officiating priest; a flabby, beardless Christ in the midst, indistinguishable from the rest. Could the resurrected Jesus, on the brink of disappearing, really look like this? Could so much dark, oppressive opulence dissolve into the divine light from which it was created? Although alone in the gallery, a suffocating clustering sensation came over him. He felt crowded out by something deeply unpleasant, something that gave rise to a bad smell. He decided that this was Roman heresy at its very worst. It was inaccurate, untruthful. It was deprecatingly 'continental'. With such thoughts and such feelings, he reinforced a pride in the clean achievements of the Protestant Reformation. Religious works were not for him.

In affirming that Christ, in his one incarnation, was the sole and sufficient image of God, and that the Thirty-Nine Articles summarised truth, he believed that he need never bother himself with what reason had rejected. He would control his feelings. Protestant regeneration was his model. The Reformation had cleared out so much dross, once and for ever. Unable to see his own rebellion, he sanctified the teaching of his parents. He was now a father. His success as a surgeon supported and reinforced the supremacy of training. His momentary conflict with art was now in the past; a conflict that he was convinced he had won. In a battle with the primeval, he was the victor. He knew, from his now considerable experience, what was normal and what was abnormal. Most important of all, he knew what he wished to teach his offspring. It was this.

My mother was in a flurry the morning Mr Keller arrived to paint a portrait of Fenella. Although it was Saturday, the routine was the same. Her husband had calls to make, so having risen to cook his breakfast, and after seeing him off, she had taken her time with the dishes and had now fallen behind, for no other reason than fatigue. She would like to have gone back to bed for a while, but there were the children to see to, the housework to do. From what her husband had said, she thought the artist would come at about noon. She didn't expect him so soon. The children weren't even dressed. Anyway, as a portrait of Fenella was his idea, it would have been better for her husband to supervise the sitting. He had gone to such trouble to find Mr Keller. In fact, for the past week he had talked of nothing else. A demon of determination possessed him. She had listened to him all the while, but she did not understand. She could not grasp the urgency when there was so much that they needed. And he would have it that things should happen this way and not that. As discussion was out of the question, what else could she do?

My mother was hurt that her husband had turned away from Edgar, that he had nothing kind to say to him. She was hurt and upset. She dressed slowly, thinking unmanageable thoughts, dropping her nightwear onto the unmade bed. It was a lovely morning and she was so very tired. There was the tangled garden, the pond and the willow tree. She could see it all from the bedroom window. The girls were running through the shrubbery in bare feet. The garden needed attention. Her husband told her not to touch anything, that he would see to it. He had done nothing. He was busy with the practice, busy with colleagues. She liked Harringay House but it was not theirs. Miss Hastings would return and they would have to move. It would be yet another upheaval. My mother made a little gesture of despair, closing her eyes. Her husband was home, but somehow their relationship was marred. It was difficult. Having rejected Edgar, Merton had turned to Fenella. The daughter was in his eye. Nothing could have prepared her for this, his preferring girls. He might even be right about Edgar. Had she spoilt him? Perhaps it really was her fault. She thought it better to say nothing when he corrected him. She left the scene, the father admonishing the son, and retreated to the kitchen to wash the dishes. I heard my mother singing while she worked, her tremolo circling up the stairs. She sang of a land 'somewhere over the rainbow', where in eternal verses, she flew with bluebirds. But the feeling beneath the dream was pernicious and all too familiar. It was a wound that attached itself to an image, the impending picture. Merton's mind would not be altered. After the fire under the house, things were different. He picked on Edgar. And he had taken to art, talking about an exhibition at the Museum. Whatever she said made no difference. He was changing, changing before her eyes, intent upon Fenella. My mother was sitting on the edge of the bed, trying to do her hair with nervous fingers, dropping pins onto the floor. She didn't want to look at herself in the mirror, to see heartache and fatigue. Her husband's neglect hurt her feelings. It was a knife in flesh, and she hated it. Securing her hair, hope returned. She felt a rush of vitality. Hope returned. Somehow, she would manage. After all, she owed everything to Merton.

Indeed, my father saw Fenella in that watchful way because he could not help himself. She reminded him of someone he was at pains to recall but whose image eluded him; not his sisters, nor his mother; perhaps not his mother, perhaps not. Was it to do with music? He did not know. It was at first the spectre of a memory from a world of shadows and partial incarnations, and then it was a host of elemental beings that refused to address him directly. Something amorphous and distant had been laid down that he could not yet realise. Yet it was here, in him. To quell the disturbance, he entered his hiding place. He uncorked a bottle of whisky and poured himself a drink. It was to do with music, he decided. That was it. Fenella would learn the piano. His daughters would play the piano as his sisters did, and his mother. Oh, yes, his exemplary mother, the paragon of virtue. It was she. It was because consciousness and music had been awakened simultaneously. He had come to life listening to the beauty of her playing.

His feeling for Fenella was indeed a recognition, and much more than that. She was born to create. There was her art. Oh, always, there was her art. She painted effortlessly. He could see. He did not know that his attraction to her was a powerful, hidden resource. It pulled him. So hidden and so invisible was this *conjunctio*, having been pushed far down under the mountain of mind that rose above everything, that not for a moment, not for a split second did he suspect it or put any value on it. Anything that disturbed him for which he had no language, anything that could not be trained, he immediately denied. He masked his changing moods with alcohol. He was moving forward in his life, gathering the ornaments of culture, becoming a connoisseur, acquiring portraits of daughters. He was establishing himself as someone apart from his own father, a minister of the Church of Scotland. Reason permitted him to exercise his discriminatory judgement in this way. He was a man of the world. And he could go one better than his colleague, Donizetti. In spite of his illustrious name and his wealth, there were no portraits in his home, not one, and to his astonishment, no music. He had expected to see a beautiful piano, but in Donizetti's vain Venetian rooms there was not the faintest reverberation to be heard.

When my mother saw Mr Keller standing there before her in the front porch, she was deeply apologetic. She had opened the door to him wearing her apron. Placing his painting paraphernalia on the step, he removed his hat respectfully and extended a hand in greeting. Had he come to the right house? He had. My mother said that she had not expected him so soon. She was not ready for him. The children weren't dressed. But Mr Keller wasn't in the least bothered. He told my mother that it was the morning light that mattered to him. He would like to see Fenella and make some preliminary sketches. First impressions were important. He painted quickly so as not to tire the child. May he choose the room? My mother showed him in. She was embarrassed that we were still in our night attire, playing in the garden. But Mr Keller, who was used to painting children and had visited many homes, was quite at ease with the arrangements. He wished to begin immediately.

Fenella was called from the garden and hurried into the drawing room, just as she was, wearing her green flannelette nightie. As I was invited no further than the threshold, I stood there, watching the artist, observing the birth of an entirely new world. My sister was to have her portrait painted. What did this mean? Searching around for a suitable chair, Mr Keller selected one with a straight back and carried it to the French windows. He sat Fenella upon it, placing her hands upon her lap. Mr Keller looked at her. Yes, he liked her in her green nightie with its little bits of lace and its sprigged yoke, her wispy hair falling over her shoulders. He touched her gently, lifting a few dark strands towards her cheeks. As the chair was tall, her legs dangled and her toes peeped from the lower edge of the garment. He said she looked very pretty. It seemed a good idea, he said, respecting the gift of his surroundings, to invite the lovely garden into the room. He went to the French windows and pushed them open. Streams of green-scented air rushed into the merging spaces, spreading the freshness of the morning. The autumn day was so very beautiful and the light so soft. Mr Keller turned to Fenella. Was she comfortable? Could she hold herself very steady for a little while? He sat at his easel. He told her where to look, straight ahead if she didn't mind and slightly over his shoulder. Fenella remained perfectly still, fixing her gaze upon the glossy mass of the grand piano behind him.

The artist began his work of art. From a wooden box, he mixed colours upon a white china plate. He worked rapidly, dipping the brush in the pot of water, rushing paint onto the page, squeezing tubes of new colour until he achieved what he wanted. And so as not to tire Fenella, he took only a few pencil sketches at the side while he talked to her. Did she draw? Did she like painting? He could see the willow tree in the garden. It was so beautiful, just like the trees of England. Fenella told him about her picture, the frogs that hid in the pond, and the dark birds. She said she loved painting. One day she would go out into the world and paint everything she saw. She would have her own box of colours, and an easel, just like his. She would have all the colours of the rainbow, every tint that existed, and some of her very own that no one had ever seen before. She would paint the tall trees of Tasmania and lots of beautiful birds. Watching Mr Keller closely, his hand darting from palette to page, Fenella fell silent, enthralled by the magic of her imagination in the midst of living creativity. And when she said simply, innocently, 'I am an artist. I am just like you,' Mr Keller was pleased. He appreciated the simplicity of the child. He could see that she was observant. Her purity of heart appealed to him. And it was this fragile quality, her translucent purity, he wished to recreate. From his study of many children, he knew all too well that innocence was as fleeting as the bloom on the wings of a butterfly, destroyed by the lightest touch. Fenella saw the artist finish his creation, laying his brushes aside. She watched him rise from the chair. He examined his work, turning his head this way and that. Would he now show her what he had painted? Might she see herself as he saw her?

Mr Keller signed the portrait with his initial. As the brush was already drying when he came to the very last strokes, the letter K, circled in scarlet, showed hairs parting in the thinning colour. The diminishing circle of his signature was a curious sight. The disappearing pigment seemed ominous, the absence of a name even stranger. I examined the cipher closely. Was it really a secret? Perhaps it was. Though Fenella had been admitted to the mysterious world of art, I was still awaiting my turn. My father had chosen her; she was under his Seeing Eye. I looked at the portrait. Her face was before me, painted in watercolour, her dark hair tumbling over her shoulders. I was surprised and puzzled by what I saw. The artist's signature, in parting scarlet, was on the right hand side of the page just below the last dribble of thin green at the extremity of the picture. Little runnels of colour fell from Fenella's sprigged yoke, making the edge untidy. I looked closely at the unruly way in which paint behaved, colour that seemed to escape, running and running and then coming to a halt in a blob. To my child eye, this was a terrible mistake, something the artist had forgotten to do. He had forgotten to finish the painting. He had neglected something very important. I was so concerned about the dribbles that I pointed to them and began to cry. From then on, in my mind's eye, I saw myself correcting the artist's mistake, mopping up the liquid pigment, painting a strong green line underneath; a strong line that would contain everything above. I feared that if I did not do this she might be drained from the page. There might be nothing left for me to see. The more I imagined this, the more frantic I became. And just as I cried, the painting seemed to cry too, the liquid green falling not only from the yoke of my sister's nightie, but from her eyes. It was impossible for me to control the feelings that seeing suggested. It was so difficult then that it is only now, in present augury, that I am able to read the signs that are still there, as real to me in the summoning of memory as if I stood in the drawing room before the very portrait. And if my augury of innocence is true, then only now may I complete, in my terms, the portrait that the artist began all those years ago. Only now, after my sister's death, am I able to shape the work of art, painting a strong line in green, the colour that began my living enquiry, under the auspices of crystals.

My father was very pleased with the portrait of Fenella. It met with his full approval. When it was delivered to the house some days later, mounted and framed, he propped it up on the desk in the drawing room where he could see it. I thought he might be cross because of the artist's untidiness, but he said nothing. He stepped back to admire it. And as he was not at liberty to hang the portrait on Miss Hastings' walls, this impasse spurred him on to find a place of his own.

Our time at Harringay House was nearing an end. I know that moving yet again must have been a great trial for my mother, even though I have no memory of the event or her part in it. The last days at Harringay were dominated by the birth of my younger brother whose arrival in our life came without any warning. I remember nothing of my mother's pregnancy, or her changing shape. Suddenly, I see myself standing by a freshly dressed bassinet in one of the bedrooms upstairs. Light from leaded windows behind me makes diamond patterns on the floor. The bassinet is empty, but Nana, my mother's mother, is there too, smoothing the white coverlets with her wrinkled hand, speaking softly about my new baby brother. Very soon, my mother and he will return from the hospital. Nana said she expected me to be very good and very quiet. I look at the stark white bassinet, but I cannot imagine my new brother. Even though I have my dolls, I do not understand what a real baby is. The coming of this puzzling phenomenon is preceded by my father driving through the gateway of Harringay House in his black Plymouth, getting out, slamming the door and striding into the front hall telling us that our mother has given birth to a son. This image is particularly strong because his voice booms the news. The sight of him in the front hall wearing his houndstooth suit heralds the beginning of another era. It comes with a gush of masculine energy. And although the beginning of infant memory draws to a close, the time becomes attenuated and difficult. The birth of my brother is in itself a clean, sharp event, with certain brightness. My mother is very happy that she now has another boy. But soon distortion ruins the story. For only a short time does the shadow lift. The momentous event opens a new chapter of hope for her. She is determined, this time, to do things her way. She has done with the science of child rearing. Never again, she avows, will she ignore her instincts. She will not ruin her second son. I heard her say such things to my father. My parents argued, bitterly. My father dismissed her challenge to his rule.

The period between my birth and the birth of my brother had been extremely difficult for my mother. Hidden in those years was another event that she felt compelled to re-enact all the time. It was a personal tragedy that she had longed to share on his return. In fact, she had stored up all the details of her pain for that purpose. It was something she could not write about in her letters. In the year following my birth, she had lost a baby. She had lost a baby girl. The circumstances surrounding this event were very regrettable, my mother used to say, and might have been avoided if she had been stronger. Oh, she had a good doctor, she would say, and then she would pause, considering her words carefully because she really didn't like to criticise doctors. If only he had listened to her, was all she could say. In those days, everything depended on a doctor's skills. Dr Gilchrist reminded her that her babies came late. There was nothing to worry about, nothing at all. She had confused her dates. Dr Gilchrist held to his opinion. The fact that she was a fortnight overdue was neither here nor there. She should be patient and wait. The baby would come in its own good time.

But the baby did not come. Her sister Amy had come to help her during this difficult time. Amy was good to her. My mother said, in her increasing anxiety about the baby, she would leave the children with Amy and go for long walks. She would walk in the grassland behind their rented house in Ararat. She walked in the late afternoon with her hand on her womb, trying to feel movements. She walked further still, to the straggling pines on the outskirts of the town. Breathless, she stood with her back against a tree, listening to the soughing wind, praying. She knew that as her time approached and then passed, movements were becoming fainter. Now she believed they had stopped altogether. There was nothing. She pressed the distended flesh, hoping to feel a quiver. Sometimes she thought she did. But then she was not sure. Fear gripped her. She wandered back to the house, despairing one moment, hoping the next. Her sister Amy encouraged her to be strong. She told her she must go to the doctor. Of course she knew she must. But she did go, she went with a heavy heart.

Dr Gilchrist examined her. He listened for signs of life. He shook his head. He was very much afraid, he said, that the baby had died. Not a trace of life was to be found. He folded his stethoscope and turned away. It was her dread come true, the words so awful to hear. Lifting herself from the examination couch, she gripped the doctor's arm. What was she to do now? What would happen to the baby? Dr Gilchrist withdrew. He patted her hand. She must go home and wait. She must wait for labour to start and for the baby to come in its own good time. He was sorry, of course. He was very sorry. She would have what is called a stillbirth.

My mother went home and wept. Amy comforted her. Although she was not married, she felt for my mother. She had attended stillbirths of calves. And it broke her heart to deliver a dead animal. So Amy understood. Amy would stay, she said, to help her to recover and to look after the children.

This was the experience from which my mother never recovered. It was so much a part of her mythology, it moulded her as a woman in a way that no other event ever did, not even the events that affected Edgar. It was the one story that she repeated all her life to everyone but her husband. Her first attempt to tell him on his return from the war had failed. He did not want to know. Her pain had become so impacted that she found herself doing the unthinkable, talking about it to strangers. She said she wished to guard the intimacies of her life for fear of offending the reputation of her husband. There was such a thing as family pride, she would tell us, during our years of rebellion. But even her forays into fortitude were useless. She came to find comfort in the telling of her story, to us, her daughters, and to anyone; comfort in the sound of her voice repeating tragic things. She wanted to cry all over again. Years later, in middle age, she might find herself at the counter of James Beck the grocer, when next to her, glimpsing a baby in a pram, she would be awakened once more to the terrible memory. Bending over the child, she would hover a little and then she would say to the mother, 'And did you have an easy birth?' She was not interested in what the mother might have to say, but it allowed her to tell the awful story of stillbirth to someone near the experience. Carried away by her narrative, among coffee sacks and smoked rashers, she spoke softly, with all the potency of a new pain. She lent over the pram, her hand on heart. 'How lucky you are,' she would say, with a quiver, 'Your baby is alive.'

Into the eternal telling, there comes another element that brings deeper significance, a crystal understanding. Among the pieces of jewellery my father sent my mother during his years of absence was a moonstone pendant. She said she lost it, but then she would say wistfully, mysteriously, that it had simply 'disappeared'. It had disappeared at the same time she lost her baby. When she returned from hospital, she went to look for it. It was nowhere to be found. She longed for it, the Egyptian jewel from her husband. It distressed her that she could not find it. She pulled everything out of the drawers of her dressing table, shaking articles of clothing, getting down on her hands and knees, feeling beneath and behind, asking the unanswerable, 'Where is it, oh, where is it?' She sat on the bed and wept. Uncharacteristically, she spoke of a curse, a curse from the tombs of antiquity. And then there was the baby. That too was a curse. She had so much milk. The loss of the moonstone compounded her grief. If only she had been allowed to see the baby, it might have helped her, but after her fruitless labour, the doctor had handed her dead baby to the midwife. 'What is it?' she asked faintly. It was a girl. And the girl, the mere girl, was bundled up and whisked away never to be seen again. And when her husband returned, she had hoped that Merton would come with her to the cemetery in Ararat where the baby was buried. It was futile to even hope for such a thing. Merton declined, brushing the matter aside. It was over, he said. It was all in the past. Although the baby had been buried in its miniature coffin, and she and her sister Amy had seen to all the arrangements, she did not know whom or what she was burying. It was her first experience of death. Perhaps it was only a bad dream. She would wake up to find the baby in her arms, just as she would find the moonstone on the silver chain. Amy suggested that the baby be given a name. 'Isabel,' she said. 'I think her name is Isabel.'

During the hours that I have spent recalling the last days at Harringay House, summoned by my mother's voice, I have drawn near the mysterious energy of the crystal that is called moonstone. In the kingdom of gems moonstone is referred to an orthoclase because when it breaks, the fracture is always in a straight line, giving moonstone a shape that often suggests a square. It is a variety of feldspar whose inner structures bend light. Colours within it move from white to grey to peach. Held in a certain way, moonstone shimmers in creamy hues. Though it may appear to be dull and lifeless, the slightest tilt this way or that will produce an unexpected depth and fullness. Turning it in the hand brings a feeling of peace and joy. Wearing it assists intuition and dream interpretation. Even before I happened upon my crystal journey, I heard much about moonstone, not least because of my mother's story, and it did not surprise me to learn that everyone assumes its femininity, qualities that adhere to the insight of dreams. Moonstone is nevertheless different from the femininity that is carnelian. If carnelian is of the earth, then moonstone, as its name suggests, is lunar. Carnelian is of the day of augury as moonstone is of the night of insight. Crystal healers speak of it with respect to the phases of the moon, exposing their collections for healing purposes to the clear light of a moonlit night. Moonstone has the strongest affinity with the heart and with fertility. It is woman as goddess. It is moist. And in its moisture, it is the counterpart to the dry, masculine daylight energy of the sun.

The loss of my mother's moonstone pendant now takes on the significance that I first mentioned. It is significant because I need to know how it came about that my mother turned away from her daughters to see only her sons. I do not believe her turning away was conscious or deliberate. It was something that just happened in the complexities of her emotional life. Everything was as jumbled as the bottles that sat upon her dressing table. Fenella and I were to hear so much about poor dead Isabel, the baby that died in the womb, the mere girl. She remained always the stillborn thing, something regrettable, something denied. So powerful was this story, so strong was my mother at her weakest, that Fenella and I came to envy the unique position held by the dead Isabel in our mother's affections. She told us the story over and over again, but it frustrated her in the telling as it frustrated us in the hearing. It grew in significance with every repetition, swamping the fragile existence of the living sisters. How could we compete with dead Isabel? Having nothing but a partial, discarnate life, she was somehow secure. Just as the poet Coleridge, in thirty years of struggling, was unable to complete the story of Christabel, his child of nature, I am not able to create Isabel. She was born into the ghostly, into the mystery of the unfinished, the essential Christabel. She was never meant to live, except in these pages, shimmering through my mother's sad memories and my attachments, a dreamy moonstone pendant, under the auspices of crystals.

My mother argued with my father. She shrieked at him. She would do as she pleased with her new son. She would pick him up when he cried, she would 'ruin' him her way. She would 'spoil' him with her love. My parents argued into the night. I heard my mother weeping, speaking from swallowed grief. As for a name, my mother wanted to call him Benjamin, for just like Rachel, she felt she had died giving birth. But unlike Rachel, she had died giving birth to a girl. Benjamin was more than 'the son of her sorrow,' he was now the son of her better self. But my father put a stop to her ridiculous fancies. He would have none of it. And he would not consent to naming his son Benjamin. Never. It was a Jewish name. It was 'bad luck'. Didn't she know what Jewishness meant? It meant persecution. He would not tolerate it. The warning came from history. Under such a powerful argument, my mother acquiesced. She conceded to his wishes. And as her bitterness ebbed away in the presence of the living boy child that was such a gift to her, together they agreed upon a safer name with heroic Roman overtones. My parents called my baby brother Horace. Ignorant of the storm that raged around him, baby Horace slept upstairs in his newly fitted bassinet. I crept into the bedroom to watch him breathing.

Part II

The Reign of the Belvedere Apollo

The feast of Christ's nativity begins, announcing itself as *logos*, an act of creation first heard, then seen. 'When all things lay in the midst of silence, then there descended down into me from on high, from the royal throne, a secret word.' From indistinct origins, and from pages of Hebrew wisdom, the birth of Christ is called into the midst of our English winter, the mantra of its primal voice modulated by centuries of telling. Of greater antiquity, The Season of Good Cheer peers through theological structures into present reality, reminding us of even older rituals arising from the history of the season, adopted by the Church, celebrated in a particular location. Harking back is the activity, repetition the essence, listening crucial to the mystery. We are compelled to tell a story. We hear what others tell, observing the subtle differences in tone, colour, and rhythm. We submit unthinkingly; we reach our own meaning, we write our own bestiaries. The enclosure of northern darkness urges us to create both fire and light; fire for warmth in the freezing cold, for the purity of burning; light to see in the night and to enliven indoor life. We believe we have heard; we are sure we have seen; we are convinced that we understand what we are being told, but there is such a confusion of voices from the past, such a melisma of images, it is impossible to distinguish one from another. Where is the silence from which the mysterious *Ursprache* springs? Where is the one and only word? In the mishmash of the market place, we respond to everything indiscriminately, neglecting the deep significance of small things, the still crystal point and the trembling festinations of the mystic *this*.

In my daily walks, my earth connections, I am drawn to the ash tree, *fraxinus excelsior*. Naked to the winter day, the English ash is goblet-shaped. An elevated tree-chalice, its slim extremities terminate in fingers pointing upwards, indicating other insights and other times. Its tall spirit interprets the flight of birds in turbulent winter skies. As it lives, standing alone in the middle of a cold meadow, the ash, given to the Latin word *fraxinus*, expresses the power I desire for myself, impossible to extract, except by perceiving and apprehending. I feel its beauty. It appears to pierce the sky like a javelin. Seeing and hearing continue in the spirit of my initial descrying, my imagination speared by the sight of indicating nature. As the images change, feelings grow deeper and deeper. The words I write dissolve before my eyes, the page a palimpsest subject to sense mutations, rubbed to nothing by undulating sight and perpetually modulating sound. Under the influence of darkening enchantments swirling before me, structure and form disappear. At the same time, music's ever refining harmonic is never far away.

The Yule log is Teutonic. In mythology, it is a symbolic limb of Askr Yggdrasill, the World Tree, the treasured slow-burning wood of *fraxinus excelsior*, connecting the four elements, earth, fire, air and water. It is Fenella's tree. How appropriate to the cold, stormy season is the presence of the ash. I walk into the wet meadow to look for a limb felled by the wind, an offering to burn upon my hearth. I stand in the middle world, between the mystery of great extremities, feeling vital life flowing upwards and downwards along the axis of an imagined symmetry. My hand touches the trunk of the wet ash tree, the symbol of the north, freely suspended in the earth's magnetic field. I am reminded of the fiery mineral kunzite, rising in sheets of sheer pink, appearing in the midst of tree feeling as spodumene, the crystalline forms of lithium and aluminium. Spodumene, in Greek says, be burnt to ashes; become nothing but ash; be pale in the ways of love-in-obscurity. It comes as an instruction from antiquity. My Christmas celebration is to desire nothing but burning and the residue of burning. In the wet season, I am bound to the love of fire. After the fire dies upon my hearth, forbidden to scatter ash, I must gather and cherish everything that belongs to the Yule log, the World Tree. Ash contains minute crystals. I see before me the tiny word *quasi*, 'as if'. The healing of *fraxinus excelsior* is similar to the healing of spodumene. It is 'as if' the tree, through the gift of seeing, becomes the illuminating crystal spodumene. Art is the eternal burning, the life-giving transformations of matter to spirit, spirit to matter. Nothing is separate from anything else. And as the inextinguishable Yule fir burns, the crystal spodumene changes from sheer pink to pale, pale violet.

I travel to Exeter to look for gifts. With conscious solemnity, in tinselled shops, I search for objects that embody the essence of things seen and heard that point to what can never be understood. I walk as if an aspirant at Eleusis, a neophyte treading the way of the seer, gathering offerings. I am an *epoptes* preparing myself to witness the awful fright in the confusion of night, the ritual charged with emotion that precedes the *arrheton*, the hidden truth, about which nothing may be uttered. From the Teutonic World Tree, with spodumene, I descend to the Isles of the Blessed, to Demeter and Persephone, to rape and mourning in classical antiquity. I break into absolute secrecy. With the grieving mother, I call for the daughter, regretting her loss, angry at her violation. 'It is the sovereignty of nature,' the chorus of women say. 'It is life.' But cyclic fright is hardly a remembrance in Christianity in which sovereignty belongs to the intellect and where the dark underworld becomes a place of annihilation, an earth reasoned away by philosophy. At this juncture, I pause. Violation occurs everywhere. With one voice, the chorus speaks a universal truth. It speaks for all ages and for all women. I affirm my intention to find the daughter, my sister, banished from the family. I am thinking of Fenella all the time. I cannot get her out of my mind. The gifts I buy are now for her, aspects of myself that I wish to burn, spiritually speaking, in the winter season, so that I may be continually renewed, strong enough to face whatever I may find. Christ, in his secret beginnings, lives to bring dazzling openness, offering a heavenly reward through relationship of father to son. I cannot allow myself to believe that the message of universal salvation, engendered by man through woman, via the sacred *vesica piscis*, comes without a veil. Light and dark exist in unfathomable *conjunctio*. My father believed that Jesus gave his hidden power to elect males who in turn became priests of the sacrament and preachers of the word. He imitated the theological model. Right from the very beginning, the inner path has taken me into priestly prohibitions. I dare to break them, to say what terrible sights I saw at Eleusis, shattering the occlusion. I speak in enigmas. The maddening paradox of revelation and concealment, light inseparable from dark, is the force of opposites from which there can be no escape. Christmas belongs to the son; Eleusis belongs to the daughter. And in both rituals of light and dark, mothers are present. In searching, it is impossible not to rupture the delicate membrane that covers our darkest secrets, to observe undisturbed, an immaculate, pristine truth. Penetrating the chink, I see a vast world. Disruption being essential to the process, I am destined to appear as the *mystagogue*, the one who expresses the *arrheton* through the ancient mode of being, memory.

I do have a memory of Christmas, a memory above all Christmas memories, one that lifts itself from the turbulence without any effort whatsoever. I do not have to break open a door, or to go down steps, for it lives above me. I need only look up to the heavens from which the winged word descends. It is a memory I care to cultivate, colour as vibration, a visual experience that simultaneously gathers as it disperses, moving in and out of itself without ceasing. It comes with every Christmas I have enjoyed, and even the many I have not. The feast of Christ's nativity is the very receptacle of the colour blue, the treasure in the royal throne from which the message is sent.

Once more, someone is pointing. This time, it is not my sister who asks me to see. It is a nun at Calvary Hospital. She puts her arm around my shoulders, and as a small being, she pulls me towards her so strongly that I feel the texture of starched white linen, the curious crispness of consecrated virginity. Pressed into such a mass of material, she takes on the shape of a white column. Looking up, her indicating finger extends from a cuff at the end of a stiff sleeve. She points with an iconic insistence, the discriminating finger saying, 'Not that, not that, but this.' She asks me to look most particularly away from the huge Christmas tree and its glass baubles to the wonderful colour above, a blue ceiling studded with silver stars. We are standing in the hospital entrance, in the peculiar odours of medicine, in the heat of a southern Christmas, admiring the work of the nuns, who every year recreate the imagery of Christ's nativity with canonical correctness. Christmas is the heightened experience of seeing in a scent of pine needles and Madonna lilies; ultramarine the colour that I come to love so much during my years at the Convent of the Sacred Heart. It seems odd that my father should bring me to the hospital to see a Roman Catholic Christmas. I cannot believe that he thought I should receive a visual teaching. More likely, it was a distraction from boredom at home. Sometimes my father would take us on his hospital rounds. We waited for him in the car, waited impatiently for him to stride from the porch. On this occasion, I have no memory of Fenella. As it was Christmas and there was something special to see, instead of being left by myself, I was delivered into the care of nuns.

I have never forgotten the shock of the spectacle, the great impression that ultramarine made upon me. Once again colour mattered above everything else. Captured in the act of seeing, for the brief moment in which the eye is engaged, the colour blue uttered its eternal word, telling a story of blueness at one with *logos*, the primal cause from which all creativity flows as effect. Though I understood nothing then, blue pierced my seeing so sharply, just as Fenella had been pierced, that upon the instant, the story of blue began within myself. Blue is the very essence of the ritual act of annunciation. In this, the truth of blue becomes both a seeing and a hearing. And when many years later, I stood alone in the hallowed corridor of the Arena Chapel at Padua looking up to a star-studded vault, a cosmos impregnated with blue, I remembered Calvary Hospital and my southern Christmas. Beneath Giotto's painted firmament, I became the willing receptor of the message through the medium of crushed lapis lazuli from which the precious pigment is so painstakingly extracted. The ultramarine mantle fell upon my shoulders. From Calvary Hospital to the Arena Chapel at Padua, and to the moment in which I write these words, all shades of blue belong to the narrative of woman, moving in the depths of the divine as *sophia*. When I was a child, I thought that the *gnosis* of blue was Roman Catholic, and that it was a nun who, in her act of discriminating, revealed the beginnings of the mystery to me. Her finger had pointed to the painted canopy above, but most importantly, she pointed first to the area of the rejection of images, the *via negativa* of mystic teaching. She caught my attention. Giving a most particular instruction, the white nun told me, very strictly, where not to look. And it is this that has, since then, informed every act of enquiry, every occasion of seeing and hearing. I believe it was this first sighting of ultramarine that imbued my aura with blue. Or was the imbuing of blue more problematically connected with the priestly power of my father and his keeping of mysteries?

As I now lean into the words, lapis lazuli, the colourful stone, the poetry of Robert Browning returns. I find myself where I began, thinking of italic dispositions and Pythagorean mysteries. But before that meeting with European literature and my overhearing the voice of a bishop ordering an ultramarine tomb, and long before the annunciation at Padua, there is Christmas in another locality, a Christmas defined entirely by my father. I am now in our new home, Belvedere, bought so suddenly, so 'out of the blue', as is the expression, that it never occurred to my father to consult my mother. Well, I should say that his consultation was to declare that the house he had just inspected was to his liking and that he would bid for it at auction. Getting out of the car and striding into the front hall, my father made a last announcement in Harringay House, speaking with all the authority of a bishop, in pulpit tones. Something significant was happening, something bright and new. He declared that Belvedere was the right residence for himself and his family. And as the house was vacant, the transfer was to be swift. The owners, Professor and Mrs Rosenthal, had packed their bags and returned to the security of England. They had returned to their European roots, and to those of their chosen race who had survived the Holocaust. Apart from this, there was nothing else to be known of Professor and Mrs Rosenthal. Of course, in the very poetry of the name, they had left something to be explored. It was a feeling connecting near with far. Although the house was completely bare, in its musty spaces was a frisson of sudden departure, the ghosts of the Rosenthals fleeing from penal Tasmania. Why did they run away? There were not only signs of dereliction about Belvedere, but there was also evidence of wanton destruction. The damage seemed wilful. In the drawing room, which my father thought so handsome with its ceiling rose and its white pargeting, he was shocked to find holes in the wall where the mantelpiece had once stood. There was evidence of exertion in this act of destruction as plaster was scattered all over the floor. My father stood before the damaged fire surround, the blackened cavity and broken bricks, a hearth where logs of perfumed eucalypt had once sparked. He shook his head in dismay. 'Look,' he said, 'they've ripped the heart out of the place. They've ruined what was once a work of art.' He could not understand it. Casting his eyes about the room, he tried to envisage what might have been. What else had Professor and Mrs Rosenthal stolen and taken back to England? What was their game? After that, my father made a diagnostic inspection of the entire house, his footsteps echoing heavily through the empty spaces, the sound of doors opening and closing. Dust was the atmosphere. He stood in the midst of things making an assessment. With the orthodox eye of Athanasius, he said 'this' was right and 'that' was wrong. How would he fix the problem of the missing mantelpiece? He would remove the large cedar door to the inner vestibule, he would rip out a door that was no longer needed, and from its panels he would make a completely new structure. There was much to do. Yes, he could see it already, a polished surround, in gleaming cedar panels, with a curved and burnished copper smoke guard to set it off. On the smoke guard, he saw within a beaten circle, a raised *fleur-de-lys*, the heraldic flower that always points north. He toyed with the image, the pure lily. Yes, he would create something visually striking, a sign to himself and others of his European flair, his 'right judgement'. He would create a work of art of which he could be justly proud. He would bring beauty to the heart of Belvedere.

As for the garden, my father was convinced that the Rosenthals had planted weedy England everywhere. Inspired by my father's words, I carried their name through all the rooms, then down into the garden, where I saw Professor and Mrs Rosenthal broadcasting their English seeds in sweeping gestures. In my imagination, I created a floral professorship for the former owners and a whole expedition of planting, a migration from one hemisphere to another, just for this purpose. My father did not like the wilderness of Belvedere. He called the roses 'briar', meaning thorny and tangled. He pointed out that Professor and Mrs Rosenthal had destroyed the lower slopes of Belvedere by letting loose the English hedgerow. True to their name, they had created an anarchic flower dale of the south. I was puzzled. I saw them inspired by longing, calling upon the spirit of the north from which they had descended. And having planted a tangled paradise, recreating an English *locus sacer*, they too were called home, bearing the relic of an ornate mantelpiece, just as Miss Hastings had been called before them, called home to a land from which all antipodean life was but an imitation.

I liked the image of Professor and Mrs Rosenthal, much more than I did the image of Miss Hastings. I could move more freely into Rosenthal spaces, however damaged or neglected they appeared to be. And stepping into England was easy for my father. At last he had found a house that spoke to his understanding. Long before the Rosenthals had flung seeds and hips so indiscriminately, someone had thought about England; someone had remembered correctly. Although there was no ha-ha, there was a mass of trees. Stepping into Belvedere, I too remembered, though I knew not what. The rope of memory is the rope to Van Diemen's Land, a calculated policy. I remind myself that the settlement of the island began as a thought, a sudden blaze of reason, here in England, where I now live. Moving through the overgrown terraces of Belvedere, I visited history and its tyranny, spectres of the founding fathers of punishment. I lingered among Kentish fruit trees and the shadows of transportation. But in the dark garden of Van Diemen's Land, a jewel was hidden. At its very heart, nearer the lower edge of Belvedere, surrounded by a medley of apple, pear, peach and apricot trees, was a contorted mulberry tree that in ageing had extended itself so precariously above the ground that it was now propped up from beneath. Oh, how beautiful it was! In dappled shade, the venerable tree, from a mystic clutter, dropped its purple droops, the scent of moist leaf and wet fruit bleeding into the air, birds flitting and tweeting in its branches. Here was the original *locus sacer*, a golden place where everything in creation was sweet to taste, lovely to hear, beautiful to see. Nature offered healing. My father admired the mulberry tree. He was amazed to find it there. It reminded him of his ideal England.

For my father, it was his repeating pattern of fascination for age as much as his need to present himself as an Anglophile that attracted him to the old house and its sloping garden. He could alter all that was undesirable; he could change the shape, just as he wished. He could make it worthy of the mulberry tree. Indeed, he had found in Belvedere great possibilities for himself. I know my father liked it because although it had something of the character of Harringay, it was not a strict replica of England. It had its own poetry. In its curious, haphazard nature, Belvedere seemed to have lost its way. It wandered. It went wherever it inclined, speaking from an *ancien régime*. There was also an air of shame about it, exemplified by the wrecked fireplace and the obscurities that lay beneath. Even so, Belvedere had a certain character arising from the vagueness of its beginnings. Over one hundred years old, its longevity was exceptional. To its partly legendary history was attached much of its mystery. Belvedere, of beautiful seeing, grew out of the occluded narrative of southern earth; it rose from the primitive unseen called Aboriginality, the delicate thing so easily bruised. Complying with architectural ideas, it was required to adopt an upper civilisation that had forgotten primeval time, intent upon evoking the more shallow origins of Albion. But the intellectual ideal was not there. As an entity true to itself, imperfect, damaged, Belvedere had more allure. Named for its panoramic view, it sat on the side of a hill overlooking the city of Hobart.

In truth, the building served the confusing purposes of remembering and forgetting, weaving patterns of denial and affirmation that could never be separated. Constructed upon the pain of alienation and dislocation, Belvedere emerged from penal servitude, and from that necessity, the clearing of land and the obliteration of the indigenous people. And it was the obliteration of the native world in the midst of this that aroused spirits of discontent, a haunting by hungry ghosts. Belvedere appears to me now as uniquely Tasmanian, the upper house resting upon the foundation of an earlier three-roomed cottage with a riveted door and a barred window. The rough dwelling, to which the word 'convict' was given, was hewn from the raw hillside, completely hidden beneath the veranda that faced the main body of the house. The wooden trellis around the veranda was threaded with stems of white, honey-scented jasmine climbing in an untidy mass from the ground below. And so, concealed behind the scented curtain, the matted but nevertheless romantic English veil, was the disagreeable history in all its tyranny. Although the house had a placid presence, where its rendered skin fell away there were signs of affliction. Lower Belvedere was built from convict bricks, a cuneiform signature of servitude pressed hurriedly into every piece of fired clay. Inside, from the front rooms of the upper structure, through panes of hand-rolled glass with watery flaws, and especially from the bay windows of the tall extension, the River Derwent could be seen opening in ever-broadening ways until it reached the blue beyond. From the front veranda and the elevated new rooms looking south, there was nothing to fear. The vista was magnificent. What did this view mean to the first occupants? Were they filled with a desire to explore the nether regions, or did they stand amid the scented jasmine stroking the strings of longing, silently mouthing the myth of the eternal return?

    My father too stood upon the front veranda gazing into the direction of an imagined freedom. As his eyes swept over city residences and their gardens, the long horizontal thoroughfare of Davey Street shrank before him. He saw far across Harringay House to an unblemished brightness, far across its red roof and the scribbled willow in a walled garden. The river took my father in his visual explorations to the Tasman Peninsula and further south to Bruny Island, through ultramarine to the pristine unseen. Behind him, as behind the city, rose the mountain of eucalypt and fern, Mount Wellington, exposing towards her summit an ancient scarring, a curtain of basalt, the so-called 'organ pipes'. But as Belvedere was my father's choice and my mother had not inspected the house for herself, she could only take its virtues as described. She was to experience it quite differently. My father was so enthusiastic that my mother, for the moment, caught his mood and she too felt a rush of hope. They were going up in the world. They would own their own home. At last, at long last, she could embrace the vision that came to her when she was but 'a mere girl'.

But it was necessary for my mother to hide her disappointment. Reality was different from the dream. On first entering the house, with its rambling spaces and its poor state of repair, she felt nothing but dismay. In its heyday it must have been a remarkable place, she thought, with land stretching right down to the city rivulet. She could see that it had been a substantial property, distinct from the mass of surrounding weatherboard dwellings in West Hobart. Yes, once upon a time, it must have been very striking, sitting so prominently in the midst of things. Even as it had come to be, Belvedere was still a large property with a big garden. Its character was different from the Victorian farmsteads of her childhood, or the houses that she had rented during the war. Unfortunately, it was far less manageable than Harringay House. Its comfortable substance had degenerated into chaos. And Belvedere owned no tracts of land now except its own neglected garden. This was not the romantic Tasmania of her honeymoon. This was another Tasmania, with a strange history beneath. After the brief rush of hope came unease. She blamed the upheaval. It was the dread of moving again. As for the property, she knew only what her husband told her and the rumours that came with the purchase. Interested in history as she was, particularly the history of her Scottish forebears, with respect to Belvedere, nothing made any sense. All she knew was that its importance made it desirable to her husband. Besides, there was no time for regret. She must concentrate on the present. She must make the best of the situation.

Christmas was approaching. With four children to look after, my mother had dared to hope that her husband would make things a little easier for her. Merton's rush of enthusiasm could not be stopped, certainly not by anything she said. Anyway, she didn't want to doubt any more. She checked herself. He knew best. How could she not be pleased for him, and pleased for herself? It seemed so unreasonable for a wife to waver when her husband worked so hard for his family. She had waited patiently through all the war years for a settled life and a home of their own. Nevertheless, after her initial surprise at the sudden purchase, the underlying unease became real anxiety when she saw, with her own eyes, Belvedere's lack of modernity. To her dismay, once more the old question arose, how would she cope?

My mother stood in the dilapidated and dirty kitchen, a dark room at the back of the house that looked out through a smeared window onto a narrow strip of land. Strung along its length, with a tall fence behind, was a sagging clothesline still carrying a few broken pegs. In the kitchen itself, there was nothing but a rusty wood-burning range and a stained stone sink. The brown linoleum on the floor was buckled and torn; she could see that cupboards had been pulled away from the walls. And there was such a dreadful smell about the place. What ever could it be? My mother thought Professor and Mrs Rosenthal the oddest couple. She said as much. How could they leave the place in such a mess? Even though she was a country girl, and not averse to chopping wood and fetching water, she had hoped city life would be less arduous. Hadn't other doctors' wives nice stoves and new washing machines? She would like, no, she would love a bright white Creda instead of a wood burner, and a Simpson washing machine with an electric wringer, but she knew that her husband had bid every penny they possessed for the place. Belvedere had cost all of four thousand pounds. She would just have to wait. And again, surveying the inadequate arrangements, there was no door from the kitchen to the back of the house. There seemed to be nothing but a huge front garden. Did that mean she had to cart the washing out through the main entrance, up the side through a narrow gate and then to the scanty bit of rope that was the clothesline at the back? And where would she do the washing? The washhouse was a dingy weather board construction hidden away below the new extension in a jumble of plumbing. It was just a rickety room with a copper boiler in one corner, its roof and chimney covered in ivy. Inside, the ivy crept through gaps in the boards, even through the broken floor. And in the washhouse, there was the same awful smell. What ever was it? My mother sniffed. It was the smell of cats. That's what it was. She understood now. There was a cat door in the kitchen, a curious opening in the floor that led to an exit outside next to the gully trap.

The cat door, first discovered by Fenella, very soon became our delight. We loved it because of Alice in Wonderland and the tiny door in her world that opened upon a vast adventure. As we were too big to squeeze ourselves through the gap, perhaps Tommy the cat could do it for us? It was such a joy to see him disappear through the dark hole to emerge outside in daylight, his little eyes gleaming. After pushing him through, Fenella and I would then rush outside, down the wooden steps, to have the thrill of seeing him emerge. We would then pick him up and make him do it all over again.

But my mother could only remark on the peculiarities of the Rosenthals that they should have such odd arrangements and tolerate such slovenly ways. How could Mrs Rosenthal wash here, in a dank enclosure reeking of cat urine? How could she? This was a place of slavery, of backbreaking work. My mother turned the taps on and off and ran her fingers over the wooden wash troughs. The taps worked but the troughs were black with slime. It was here that she would have to boil the copper and scrub the clothes by hand. Then she would have to lug baskets of wet washing in a tortuous route up lots of steps to the clothesline. It would be such heavy going. My mother drifted into her familiar 'if only'. There was so much to be done to improve the place, if only they could afford it. The children's education had begun. There were school fees to pay and uniforms to buy. Merton had talked about bidding for a piano at auction, of lessons for the girls. In every direction, there was just too much to do, especially to the house. Where to begin? The roof, the outside, the interior, everything was in an appalling state of repair. She was disappointed in Belvedere, even ashamed of it, though she would never say so. How could she invite anyone here without feeling the deepest embarrassment? And then, there was the land. Who would take the garden in hand?

My mother resigned herself to her fate. Though it was not her habit to speak to us, her daughters, in an engaging way, we heard what she said and we observed her struggles, the long hours she worked in the kitchen preparing meals and the inordinate length of time she spent washing clothes. On wash day, the washhouse generated a steamy heat from within, while outside, smoke billowed from the chimney and sparks singed the ivy. Fenella rushed in to tell her that the washhouse was about to burst into flames. We could only be excited at everything we saw, getting to know the place, leaning from our bedroom window above the drawing room, delighting in the height that gave us such a splendid view. Belvedere was ours. We lived in a house that had a front veranda, an upstairs balcony at the back, numerous corridors, rooms leading from rooms, ceilings both high and low with small doors and tall doors, lots of inner steps, and best of all, a cottage below with a barred window. All this, as well as briar roses and fruit trees in a wild garden at the heart of which was a mulberry tree, 'over a hundred years old'.

While my mother was preoccupied arranging the place as best she could, and when we were not at school, there were adventures to be had, both in the house and in the garden, especially under and around the mulberry tree. For the first time Fenella and I enjoyed real happiness, relishing the sense of wonder with which all children are endowed. And in some of our adventures, because we needed the expertise of an older brother, Edgar played a part. We were particularly dependent upon his initiative in exploring the cottage below. How could we resist its charm? How could we not be fearful of its secrets? Edgar descended the wooden steps from the far end of the front veranda carrying a torch in one hand and a hammer in the other. Fenella and I followed. Considering the restrictions, it is with a feeling of freedom that I recount the story of the exploration of the convict cottage. This must have been a wonderful time for us, as remembering the event over fifty years later, I find myself rushing into the story without hesitating or searching for a word.

What was so intriguing was the fact that, although the cottage consisted of three rooms leading from one to another, the only entrance being to the first room with a very low ceiling, the third room was inaccessible. The way in had been boarded and nailed. In the middle room, which seemed to be sunk into the ground like a roofed cavern, there was a diminutive cast iron range covered in dirt and fallen plaster. Underneath the rubbish, in the thin light of the torch, we saw a small work of art wrought with iron flowers and leaves. A relic of another time, it was so easy to imagine smoke rising from its dark and beautiful hearth, its embers still burning. But the chimney was completely blocked. It had disappeared into the structure above, drawn up by the power of higher intentions in the building of Belvedere. What had happened to it? Once more, the cavern had no luffer and the fire no oxygen. And because of the veranda above and the overhanging jasmine, the smothering greenery, only a dim light filtered through the barred window. The first two rooms were empty. As this was Belvedere, we had hoped for more, far more. The emptiness, which at first disappointed me, came to fulfil a negative and necessary importance in the perfection of all things, the small flaw in paradise. Soon, it didn't matter. I turned to other attractions. Through what appeared to be a cupboard door in the back wall of the middle room, we peered at the hewn rock of the hill into which the cottage was so closely cut, making it such a useful foundation for the upper storey. The cottage supported the entire upper structure, with the exception of the bay-windowed extension at the far end. And it was here in the cottage that we discovered the best evidence of convict labour that had begun the story of Belvedere, the pale pink thumb-printed bricks.

I heard my parents discussing dim beginnings, speculating about what might have been. My mother said that Martin Cash, Tasmania's most notorious bushranger, had once occupied the cottage. A bushranger? How did she know such a thing? She was hovering between the kitchen and the breakfast room when she first uttered the word 'bushranger'. I remember the moment so well, because in the very ordinariness of the morning routine, serving porridge to my father, the fearful word seemed to cling to the air. I was frightened. And then, as an addendum to the slender legend, I heard her say that Martin Cash's mother had even lived there. His mother? Had the mother of this horrible man really lived and slept in the cottage? Had she cooked his dinner on the pretty little stove? Why had she come all the way from Ireland to live beneath our feet with her mad, dangerous offspring? My mother spoke of the 'terrible child', the baby ill-rocked in his cradle, sung to sleep like a changeling. From birth, he was doomed to become a criminal, an outcast.

As every Tasmanian had heard of convicts escaping Port Arthur to set up their ranges in the bush, making murderous raids upon settlers, these fragments bothered me very much. How did I know that there weren't such men now? I confused bushrangers and muskets with Aborigines and pointing bones, for both evoked the same paralysing terror. Both could kill, but in different ways. An intention could kill as surely as a bullet. There was no sensitive perception of Aboriginality then, no awareness of the delicate veil that covered everything long since lost in our cultural conquests, our necessary tributes to science and enlightenment. We had smothered our own intuition. We thought we understood when in fact we had obliterated a *knowing*. Aboriginality was judged to be dark, obscure and very heavy, quite without the superior power of reason, the great thought that had carried us so far into the future. If we had failed to recognise our own precious psychic flowering, how could we nurture the same fragile creature in another? The word Aboriginality, in early Latin, a back formation of the noun Aborigines, describes indigenous people as, at best 'primitive', and at worst, 'bestial', attaching to the image the innate impulses of animals which in persistent Medieval spirituality served as models of sin and degradation. Our bestiaries cast out instincts. To the child that I was, the effects of all ghostly narratives in Tasmania's recent and distant past were one and the same. Shock was responsible for much of my ignorance. And no one could reassure me that threats from unregenerate history did not exist. Was the cottage truly empty? Was there not a hungry Aboriginal hidden deep within the convict, *an animal*, making him behave like a madman, his insane, crazed face still peering through the bars?

Although the notorious Martin Cash might have been one fragment in the history of the cottage, the unlikely presence of his mother seemed to fling the fabulous net 'back home' to the unreachable north that was the Old Country. But my father pondered upon a more plausible story. A ticket-of-leave man could have lived there, he said; a convict released for good behaviour to work on the land. Yes, he continued, the cottage must have been a night lock-up for a criminal who had 'forgotten how to behave'; a pathetic failure transported to Van Diemen's Land in a commuted death sentence. This would explain the small rooms, the heavy door and the barred window. In the frail aptitudes of a fallen humanity, the cardinal sin of forgetting demanded a bodily reminder. With such hardened criminals, my father said, even earned merit was a doubtful virtue in Van Diemen's Land. At the beginning of his remission, the ticket-of-leave convict mixed clay for the bricks of his cell, marking each day's output with a thumbprint. Alone, he constructed his own enclosure. How he must have longed for England then.

Edgar had little difficulty in opening the way to the third room. Fenella held the torch while Edgar, using the claw end of the hammer, pulled manfully at the nail heads. As it was a narrow entrance, there were only a few panels to prize away. We squeezed ourselves through the opening, holding on to each other, stepping across the threshold into the sudden dark, the torch casting a single beam in front. Still holding on to Fenella's skirt, I followed her tentative steps into the terrifying hole. I could see nothing but black. Edgar swept the small torchlight over the walls and up to the ceiling. It too was very low. He could almost touch it. For a moment, he was excited. He began to kick about the floor, shining the torch, searching for the smallest discovery. But there was nothing to interest him. His excitement suddenly over, he wanted to go. Edgar flicked the light about the room once more just to make sure and then kicked against the cracked wall to see what would happen. A slab of plaster gave way. We examined the wall. What were these weird bricks with human marks? We took it in turns to see if our own thumbprints matched. Some were too big and some were too small. Was that all? There was nothing for Edgar. Might there be something for us? Fenella took the torch and shone it into a corner. In the small light, a white object began to take shape. It was a china ewer. It wasn't mysterious. It was a jug, a Victorian water pitcher, just like the water pitchers of

Harringay House. Those we were never allowed to touch. But this one was ours. We had discovered it.

Fenella took the water pitcher into the light underneath the veranda. Was there anything in it? Putting in her hand, she pulled out a grey rag. She flung in on the ground. It was dirty. Had it been clean, it might have been beautiful. Then looking at it more closely, we saw that it was a piece of bobbin lace, the sleeveless top of a garment covering the shoulders. It had a neat collar and a wavy edge. As we examined it, the lace began to fall apart, its patterned leaves and flowers unravelling rapidly. In an instant, it became a heap of tangled cotton, a bit of old rubbish. The dream of finding something had come to nothing. I had so wanted to wear it. It might have been so pretty. But while I was picking over the dirty lace, regretting its disappearance, Fenella plunged her hand into the water pitcher for the second time. She pulled out something even more desirable, instantly recognisable and completely intact. It was a necklace; a long necklace made of tiny pearly shells, each one ending in an iridescent point.

Although Fenella and I had heard only a few desultory facts about native Tasmanians, and many of them distorted by fear, we knew the significance of threaded shells through a heightened seeing. Our eyes did not deceive us. There were pictures of Aboriginals in pamphlets about Port Arthur. In Tasmania, what could be more compelling to the visitor than the war between bushrangers and natives? These slanted histories sometimes included early photographs of the remnants of the race, women wearing Victorian garb, arranged in depressing groups with dogs sniffing about their feet. One such female remnant we all knew. Her name was Truganini. As she was believed to have been the last full-blooded Aboriginal and in her final years celebrated as a living relic, her emergence from banished Aboriginality to sit for a photograph was regarded as a kind of triumph. For whom was this a triumph? *Oh, cover her face! Cover her face!* We cannot bear to see it! Truganini was remembered for nothing but the Christian virtue of resignation, and her simple shell necklace. In an advancing civilisation, what more was there to know? Although she had long since surrendered her native dress, the most famous photograph shows her with three strands of shells threaded around her throat. The shells rested upon folds of coarse material, a Christian mantle to hide origins. Fixed in sepia tints, Truganini's shells gleamed as jewels of Byzantium gleam around the image of a saint. Even so, being similar to digging sticks and dilly bags, shell necklaces adhered to primitive beginnings. They were trinkets, not treasures. They were valueless. My mother had proper jewellery. In her worldliness, she wore a first-water diamond. And as Western gems conferred status, shell decorations were regarded as pathetic dressings from the sea, passing childish amusements. What could they possibly mean beyond the naïve adornment of a native female?

But Fenella and I were seized by delight. 'Look what I have found,' she said, dangling the delicate strands above my head. 'I have found Truganini's shells!' Truganini's shells? Of course this could not have been so, but the threaded shells were now before us. We touched them. There was only one image to which our limited knowledge might have recourse, the photograph of Truganini. The picture came to us instantly. I grabbed the necklace. The shells were ours. They were still shiny, hidden as they had been for years under the protecting veil of greying lace. Though the English garment had disintegrated and was now a meaningless heap, the shells were perfect. They were pristine things from an Aboriginal Eden, pointing to the myths of a southern land, just as Honiton lace, made in Devon, had been a poetic illusion of idealised England. And, as luck would have it, Fenella had discovered the tiny sea creatures herself. She had put in her hand and pulled the pearly necklace out of the ancient water pitcher. Truganini's shells would do the precious work of remembering. They were hers by the right of finding, just as the pitcher was hers. I wished it might have been otherwise, that I had found them, but it didn't really matter. Fenella and I would share the bounty. We could take it in turns to wear the shells, just as Truganini had worn them. To us, they were just as desirable as any jewels in our mother's sandalwood box, if not a great deal more desirable, because they seemed to be within reach of our girlish dreams. We knew them, and better still, we had found them.

After that, we took the shells into our possession. We showed them to our mother, but in her preoccupation with unpacking and getting ready for Christmas, she was too busy to notice. She saw only a string of shells, unremarkable and common. She warned us not to go into the cottage again. It was dark, dirty and unsafe. We were certainly not to light a fire in the range. Nor were we to go anywhere near the old incinerator at the bottom of the garden. The weather was hot and dry. From distant bush fires beyond the suburbs, a grey eucalyptus haze drifted across the city. As for breaking into the third room, because Edgar had carried out the mission so successfully and no harm had been done, she let the matter pass. Oh well, we had found an old water jug, a bit of filthy lace and a shell necklace. Her disinterest seemed to us tacit permission to carry on playing with our treasure. Yes, we may keep the necklace. Heeding her warning, we would be reluctant to go under the house again. Now that we had conquered the third room and divested it of its secrets, though the cottage lost none of its potency, its gloom seeping through the ceiling to the living rooms above, its call was not so magnetic. My mother told us that the cottage was to be a storage place for things that did not concern us. My father's army paraphernalia, albums of photographs, and all their wartime letters, were lowered into his big tin trunk with layers of camphor and naphthalene to preserve them. In addition, there was a curious red fez that he had picked from the head of an Egyptian boy, and several bolts of Syrian damask. All such relics of the past were packed away from our prying eyes; the trunk pushed into the far corner of the first room. The door was closed. So having gained an unexpected freedom through an under-the-house conquest, and having escaped the humiliating punishment, a hiding, Fenella and I skipped through the house, in and out of rooms and up and down stairs waving our lovely shell necklace in the air.

It is clear to me now, in this thesis written under the influence of mystical things, that the Aboriginal shells, however they came to sleep in the depths of Belvedere, exerted a palpable influence over the family who were fated to inhabit its upper spaces. I now know that Fenella and I were affected, though I hasten to deny any such influence as a curse, a pagan power giving rise to 'bad luck', no matter what my childish fears were at the time. I know better than to bow to crude superstition. I would not be committed to these revelations today had I surrendered to the thrall of Hades, or succumbed to belief in a place called Heaven. The nun at Calvary Hospital had pointed insistently to the highest, to ultramarine, a pigment extracted from the depths of the earth. But it was art that elevated the colour to planes of spiritual meaning, its origins hidden in its destiny. Who cares that the most valuable lapis lazuli comes from Afghanistan, from a blue seam called the matrix? Who speaks of the colour and the motherly connection? It was only as a child that I believed everything I heard, indiscriminately, with the one exception that my sister was 'a bad girl'. For all hearing and seeing is mystery, and in these pages, I seek to enquire into the nature of the mystery that is my very own creation.

In those days, there seemed to be a primal power to which the demonic entities of unregenerate history had become attached. Indeed, these supernatural afflictions lived and moved in the timeless cavities beneath Belvedere, working at the depth of baneful consequences, whispering all the while, 'Hear me, believe me.' Shells awaken us to Aboriginal origins. They are 'the ears of the sea'. They share with crystals a psychic energy, an aspect of the soul. They are tools. And if they succeed in arousing our sensitivity to the presence of an ancient indigenous people, then they will also awaken us to a real awareness of our very own losses and to our own deliberate forgetting. Our losses are *ab origine*. In recalling the past, for whatever purpose, it is possible to know far more than mere facts. Where facts cannot be known, there remains the reading of the auspices. It is only after the auspex has uttered her words in an 'altered' voice that the real evaluation can begin, at that moment of insight when all fragmentary experiences, historical and mythical, have been collected. As facts generate their own poetry, history is a matter of the most scrupulous, delicate interpretation. Only then can we make a pronouncement upon the importance of events and the significance of the objects that played a unique part in the rituals of the past. First of all, there needs to be an enquiry into oneself. Truganini's shells speak of primordial misfortune, the clash of myth and history, of terrible loss. This tragedy touches all those who have ears to hear.

It is essential to say that shells are a universal image of female fecundity, central to many cultures and rituals. Shells participate in the sacred movements concentrated in the waters, in the moon and in woman. They are specifically, creatures of the sea. As emblems and ornaments of the matrix, a symbiosis of both sea and sky, their creative powers have always played a part in funerary rights, activating and sustaining a longing for the eternal return. The sacred power of the pearl, for instance, arises not only from its marine origins but also from a gynaecological symbolism. It is conceived in a uterus called 'mother-of-pearl'. Through this symbolism, the shell and her offspring are inextricably linked with birth and rebirth. On Roman tombs, the scallop expresses the hope of resurrection. Though we have forgotten the spiritual origin of the scallop, its psychic significance may still be reached. It need only be contemplated. And in the most famous Western image of the shell, Botticelli's *Birth of Venus*, the goddess of love and sexuality, as genetrix, emerges from her watery world to be carried towards the shore on the very symbol of her own generation. In the mannered realms of art, an act of conception and birth is depicted. All kinds of seashells, as well as the most highly prized jewel, the pearl, appear constantly in aquatic cosmology and in sexual representation. Pearls are, to this day, the quintessential decoration of the virgin bride. Even after the degradation of the symbolism is complete, when the loss of memory has destroyed all transcendent and all magical properties, the sea jewel is still capable of performing the one remaining cultural function, value. It is how we interpret that value, whether in money or in mystery, that determines the outcome of our journey to the past. However corrupt our use of its virtues, the shell will always retain its inherent power.

Once upon a time, as the telling of myth traditionally begins, a native woman on Bruny Island, in the midst of her *locus sacer*, taught her young daughter the secrets of the shell. In the last ash of the Aboriginal fire, the dull outer skin of the tiny shells was burned away to reveal the pearly sheen beneath, shells born into their ritual meaning. Here I draw back respectfully from what is not my own knowing. Silence descends. I stand on the veranda at Belvedere, gazing into the distant blue, just as my father did. Although I may not hear or see the shell ritual so cruelly interrupted by the violence of invasion, I can speak of what I now know has been interrupted in my own experience. Nor am I free to articulate the story of Truganini. I speak in my own language, *ab origine*. I speak of Fenella. The story of my sister, an infinitely small part of the vast canon of human experience called loss, is the medium through which I may enter the universal. For just as the story of Truganini is an historical fact, it is also, and more importantly, a myth from which the truth of any history, whether personal or universal, may be recalled as an act of regeneration. It is only regenerate memory, the recollection of truth that has the power to heal.

The joyous skipping continued. So magical was the power of the Aboriginal necklace, that Fenella and I spent what now seems to be a long period of time living in the delights of our bounty. But as we were young girls, and often fickle, our living enjoyment probably amounted to no more than a day or two. It may have been only an afternoon, one golden afternoon in a summer *ab origine*, in the Eden that was Belvedere. Fenella looped the shell necklace around her head. As I followed her into the garden, she became the caller and I the called, the shells a chaplet of transformation. In the freedom of restored experience, she laughed. She offered one end of the long necklace to me, and under an influence drawn from the deeper Eden of Bruny Island, linked together, we responded to the call of a timeless dance, recovering the myth of a native girl and her death. It didn't matter who she was, but for her deeds, whatever they may have been, neither good nor bad, she had to suffer. In order to fulfil her destiny, the hope of the future, she had to die. The law of life demanded to be enforced. The shells inspired a telling of our own story; they pulled us into an inner world. We wanted to penetrate and to experience all that lay beneath; we needed to know what was there, caught as we were in the fully flowing, glowing power. As we descended to the depths of the sea, we ascended to the heights above, re-enacting a rite of water and sky.

For a measureless period of time, living in an altered state, we fulfilled all the intentions of the shells until the mystery ran its course. We beat the boundaries of Belvedere, weaving our way through the tangled undergrowth, holding the necklace above our heads. We danced round and round the mulberry tree, binding ourselves beneath the bleeding fruit of our southern Askr Yggdrasill to the local goddess of the elements. Who was she? That she had no more exotic name than Shell mattered little. And then, happening upon Tommy sleeping under the mulberry tree, we wound the jewels about his neck, and carrying him ceremonially up the side steps to the kitchen, we lowered him gently through the cat door into the dark beneath. He gave us the pleasure of reappearing outside near the gully trap with the shell necklace still intact. We loved him even more. The moment he emerged, the shells gleamed as green as his eyes against the black gloss of his fur coat. This was his living apotheosis. He danced with us. And when Tommy grew tired of his ritual activity and ran away to a hiding place in the garden, we went inside to our parents' bedroom, ascending to another aspect in the telling of shells.

We sat close together looking into the long, clear mirror, our two heads encircled by the necklace. In the midst of our mother's precious things, in the odour of Milk of Roses, we spoke the language of 'the mere girl'; we uttered the *Ursprache* of our own Aboriginality. And as our desire for the necklace increased, and our self-regard became more intense, we invited the inevitable presence of decline and decay, a return to the matrix. As the mood changed, a far more demanding reality emerged, a time saturated with consequences. Very soon we fell to arguing as to who really deserved it. Fenella insisted that she did. She had pulled it out of the pitcher. She was older than I. She had black hair. Black hair? 'Truganini had black hair,' Fenella said, holding a few strands of her long hair against my head. I looked at her in the mirror. I looked at my own reflection. It was true. No one with fair hair could be Truganini. I tried to wrest the necklace from her, but Fenella acted quickly. 'You'll break it,' she said, running from the room. She ran along the corridor, out onto the front veranda, down the wooden steps and into the garden. She flew like a bird of augury, carried by the spirit of shells. In no time at all, she was climbing the mulberry tree, walking out along the propped branch. She pranced like a dancer, pointing her toes before her all along the length, the shell necklace dangling from her hand. She swung it above her head, skimming it through the air over and over again until it caught on a twig, tangling among green leaves and purple mulberries. 'Oh, look what's happened,' I said pointing to the necklace in the tree. 'They're stuck. Now the shells will have to stay there for ever.'

The dance was over. Fenella and I left the garden. Very soon, we forgot about the shell necklace hanging in the mulberry tree. Christmas was near. It was time to think about other things. Indoors, there were new events of darker magnetism. There was also the longing for presents, our small dreams of something exciting and very different, the hope of a pine tree decorated with tinsel. My mother was preparing for Christmas, baking cakes and puddings on the old wood range, the smell of eucalyptus fire and splintered cinnamon permeating every space. In the dingy back kitchen, with the window flung wide, my mother laboured late into the night, the cooler temperature making the heat from the wood stove more bearable. She waited for my father to return. She waited and waited for the long domestic day to end so that she could be with her husband. But there was a palpable hopelessness in her waiting as she pressed on with the cooking, stoking the fire, the red flames flaring. There was something desperate about those hot nights.

Later, when the sound of my father's distinctive footfall in the vestibule signalled his return, disturbances that we heard even from our bedroom upstairs very soon followed. Awakened by voices, Fenella and I would slip out of bed and tiptoe along the corridor. Hanging over the banisters, straining forward to catch a glimpse of movement from the kitchen to the drawing room across the vestibule, we peered and listened. What were they saying? I did not understand. Oh, I understood the words, but there was something in the mounting intensity, the sudden bursts of anger, and my mother's shriek that carried the meaning of 'heard words' to dreadful regions. There was a sobbing to drown everything, as if my mother only ever spoke with her hands over her mouth. The arena of misery was now familiar to me. I recognised it, because it was always accompanied by my thumping heart. And in the morning, I could see from the painful way in which my mother moved, just as I could tell from the uncomfortable silence and my father's irritable expression at the breakfast table, that something dark had happened. When my mother served breakfast in her pink dressing gown with the thin belt, her eyes red with crying, we knew that the night had exerted its powers. From a very early age, we had come to expect morning consequences from things that happened out of sight, behind closed doors. It was my father's drinking that caused the difficulties between them, his coming home late from the Club. It was drink, always drink, and as my mother constantly repeated, his refusal to discuss anything.

That first Christmas at Belvedere, in the summer heat, my father set about ripping the garden to bits. It was Christmas Eve, when at the end of a long afternoon at the Tasmanian Club, he began with a vengeance what he had wanted to do ever since he first set eyes on the briars and brambles of Belvedere. Early in the evening, and quite unexpectedly, my father returned home. A car drove up to the house. It was not my father's car, and my mother, who had come to the front door, alert to a development, was taken by surprise when she saw her husband walking unsteadily along the veranda, supported just as unsteadily by a colleague. My mother was embarrassed. It was so shameful to see her husband like this, on Christmas Eve. He reeked of whisky. She didn't know what to say. For a moment, she covered her eyes with her hands, hoping that the scene would go away. Then she looked at him. 'Oh, Merton,' she said, 'Oh, Merton.'

My father reached for the railing, his feet tangling in the greenery that fell across the veranda. Caught in its fronds, he stamped on the trailing flowers, cursing them. He said he hated English brambles. He called the jasmine blackberries, which they were not. And then he said they were 'bloody, bloody briars'. As he confused everything, he swore all the more. He was behaving in a way I feared the most. My father, so strict and correct, my father who looked so holy in church praying with a bowed head, was now reeling across the veranda slurring his words. He vowed to rid the place of all English weeds once and for all. He said he would act now. My mother protested. She thought he was going to do something dreadful to the jasmine. 'You can't destroy a plant, Merton,' she said, a shrill edge to her voice. 'It's not a weed. And it's in full bloom.' And at this sign of trouble, the development of matrimonial difficulties, my father's colleague left, making his stumbling exit down the stone steps to the wooden gate that was the main entrance to Belvedere.

There was no stopping my father. Brushing my mother aside, he made a precarious descent to the garden. Fetching a few implements from the convict cottage, he staggered through the shrubbery, making his way to the lower slope where the fruit trees clustered protectively around the mulberry. He began with the briar roses and the ground elder, the twining morning glory with its pretty trumpets and the soft grasses now beginning to dry in the heat. He cut and slashed at every plant that represented something repellent in his ideal England. He was clearing the way for the true vision of things, creating order out of chaos, correcting faults in nature. In the heat, perspiration ran from his brow. He threw off his jacket. As his determination increased, he began to work more steadily, wrenching stems and gouging the ground. A new madness controlled his actions, the terrible sanity of the sobering drunk, pushing the effects of alcohol through his body by strenuous exertion.

For a while, my mother watched him from the veranda, then she went inside. It was useless appealing to him while he was in this mood. He was deaf to her pleading. But once my father had tasted the gratification of effecting a visible change, of making things different, and to his mind better than anybody else's making, he could not stop, not even to draw breath. My father worked all round the fruit trees, piling up weeds in clumps. Eventually he came to the mulberry tree in which Fenella had left the shell necklace. My father did not see what was above him, glinting among the leaves in the waters of the firmament. He had no idea that origins covered his head as he worked around the tree, stripping the ground of its covering. He was clearing undergrowth. He told himself that he was getting rid of the worst of England. And having done all he could, working from one side of the garden to the other, he then lit the old incinerator and carted the clumps of tangled green to be burnt. The drying stems made the green easy to light. Summer heat assisted the conflagration. Very quickly, new flames leapt from the plant matter and smoke curled into the evening air, enveloping the mulberry tree and its hidden gift of the eternal return. My father poked the weeds with a stick, beating the side of the incinerator every now and then like a drum to encourage burning. This was his holocaust, destroying the remnants of the Rosenthals.

And just as the last briar roses were crackling low in the depths of the incinerator, the night beginning to fall, my father remembered the articles of his war years packed away in naphthalene flakes under the house. With determined and sobering steps he made his way there. He entered the low room. Moving confidently in the dark, he went to the trunk and pulled it towards the door. Opening it, he plunged in his hands to feel for the bundles tied up in ribbon, all the correspondence that my mother had gathered and matched letter by letter for the five long years that he had been away in the Middle East. While the fire was still burning in the incinerator, he would dispose of them. He would destroy every word he had committed to paper. It was dangerous to keep expressions of feeling. My father believed that the word, this word, exposed him to something menacing, something beneath reason over which he had no control. He feared what he had written. And so to the holocaust he committed memories, taking the camphor-scented bundles down to the incinerator. One by one, he thrust them into the hot ash. The flame flared more brightly now, inspired by flammable naphthalene, the crystals clinging to the paper leaves, the inked language of love crinkling and curling on its way to obliteration. He worked in the frenzy of pyromania, watching the scented smoke rise high into the night sky. Once more he beat the side of the incinerator with the stick. He beat the incinerator over and over again, investing more power in the ritual, seeing the whole wretched business through to the last dying ember.

My mother came to the veranda in the fast falling night to see what had kept her husband for so long. She stood peering into the dim descent of the garden, into the darker side of Eden. In the gloom, she could see the arching shapes of the fruit trees, the tall canopy of the old mulberry in the midst. Merton was there, at the incinerator, but he was not burning weeds. The leaping flames illuminated his face, shining a flickering torch upon his actions. She screwed up her eyes. What on earth was he doing? He was throwing bundles of paper into the incinerator, flinging things in one after another. She could not believe it. Could it be true? Was the light playing tricks on her? But she really could see. It was true. The bundles were her letters, her carefully collected letters, prized memories of separation and reunion, their first words of expressed love, and the last that they exchanged at the end of the war. Her husband was burning them. He was turning everything to ash. He was destroying her love, the love of 'the mere girl'. My mother collapsed onto the veranda rail. This was too much. There would be nothing left; nothing to remember. She could feel herself breaking apart. With her hand she struck the rail, beating the little white flowers in her repeating grief. The smell of burning naphthalene drifted from the incinerator up to the house, mingling with the scent of jasmine in the warm night air. She buried her face in perfume and wept. 'Merton, Merton,' she wailed. 'Why must you do this?'

There seems little left to say about our first Christmas at Belvedere. Christmas Eve, the unique day that was called a night, had its darkness. My mother had cried at the destruction of her love. My father, drunk, had frightened me. In horror, I shrank from the scene. But with the new dawn, and another summer day, something much better emerged. Fenella and I knew that we would be given presents. They had been promised. Although the receiving of gifts would depend on behaviour, whether in some way we might 'deserve' a reward, I believed that the great expectations of Christmas, central to which was giving, could never be denied, otherwise Christmas itself would not exist.

My parents avoided spoiling us. We would be given one present each, and that was all. My father quashed the existence of Father Christmas, deriding his pet name, Santa Claus, shaking him out of the whole idea of the Incarnation. We were forbidden to believe in him. Saint Nicholas emerged from a European Catholicism condemned by the Protestant Reformation. He belonged to the opaque, forbidden ritual, the 'Mass of Christ'. Stockings stuffed with presents and hung from the mantelpiece were images of England where it snowed and where, according to my father, all kinds of fantastic theological ideas raged. Compared with pictures on greeting cards, what happened in Tasmania seemed less true than Christmas in England; a southern fault that the tyranny of time and geography had fatally distorted. We could never recreate an authentic meaning in our alien location. It was just too far south of the Equator. In my small mind, the Northern Hemisphere and snow would always remain the very perfection of giving: a distant, glittering ideal.

On the subject of Christmas, my mother adopted a softer interpretation. She tolerated some talk about Father Christmas, because we knew that he had appeared in Myer's Department Store. Father Christmas was taking orders from little children. Into his ear, they whispered their wishing words. For the children who saw him in the store wearing his red and white robes then riding with reindeers through the night sky in the streaming green of the aurora australis, surely he must exist? As we were instructed not to believe in him, I found it impossible to penetrate the visual hint. Our parents, for the sake of 'this' and not 'that', had reformed the corrupt story of Christmas and the birth of Jesus, eliminating the saintly giver of gifts, the visions of Christmas Eve. If God had entered history as a tiny child, what was right and what was wrong? And what were the responsibilities of an incarnate god if not to love and to give to his creatures? For me, the mystery of the season was hidden somewhere in lapis lazuli, and in the colour called ultramarine, a name that told of origins 'beyond the sea.'

That Christmas, Fenella received what she wanted, more coloured pencils and a koala bear. She was so happy with her koala, she called her Belinda. I was entranced by the name, Belinda. How did Fenella know where to find such an elegant name? She had found it, all by herself. Belinda was a word from Fenella's magical world, from our shell dance round the mulberry tree. And Belinda Bear lived up to her given name. She was a buxom creature made from biscuit coloured fur. In creation's hierarchy from angels to ants, I suppose her fur had once belonged to another creature, and that a lesser being, probably a kangaroo, 'a nuisance to farmers', had been sacrificed to become the beautiful Belinda. Then, we thought nothing of Belinda's origins. Fenella tied a pink ribbon around her neck and held her above her head to admire her. I watched her as she danced. I envied Fenella her Belinda.

But to my delight, I was given a gift that I had wanted for so long. I had begged my mother to buy me a doll. I had been brave enough to stand in the kitchen and ask. My mother had acquiesced. On Christmas morning, as Fenella unwrapped Belinda, I unwrapped my doll. She was a baby doll, a pink plastic creature with a hole in her red lips to take the teat of a tiny feeding bottle. Another hole in her lower back allowed her to eliminate, but neatly, the nourishment that was given her. Turning her over, she cried 'mama, mama' and then stopped. Although she was a cold, inflexible thing, I loved her. I wanted her to be warm to the touch, as warm as our little cat Tommy, but it didn't matter. I swaddled her in a bunny rug. I wrapped her as tightly as I could and slipped her into my bed. I looked at her adoringly, her head resting on the pillow. Everything in my world was, for the moment, perfect. All my fears had vanished. I would never be parted from my doll. She had arrived with her name written on a tag tied around her neck. It wasn't anything like the beautiful Belinda, nor had she arrived on the shore of my life carried by a scallop shell, bearing the great name of love, Venus. Nevertheless, 'Patsy' seemed to belong to her smallness, her emerging infant person. She was a creature that needed looking after. Without the slightest hesitation, I made my vow. She was mine. And I would always, always love her.

In childhood, when desire for new objects is so very strong, forgetting is also easy. Just as one hope is realised and its usefulness exhausted, then another is soon born. So it was with the necklace. The shells had come to light; they had been celebrated. Once they were abandoned to the mulberry tree, they ceased to exist. We no longer thought about them. But their coming to consciousness had happened. From this event, which seemed so casual in the greater scheme of things, consequences began to emerge, taking shape little by little. The changes that were ushered in were of both kinds, benign and malevolent. At first they were very subtle. As I have already said, the shells were not in themselves to blame for either good fortune or misfortune. In fact, blame of any kind I am at pains to avoid. I wish to speak only of the events that followed the opening of the third room under the house and the discovery of its hidden jewels. For the shells 'happened'. When history ends, the making of the myth begins. And unlike history, myth exists outside time, moving within the eternal, subject to delicate transmutations of the imagination.

After Fenella danced the shells around the garden, there could be no going back. The great wheel of cause and effect had been turned, and although I am tempted to say that Fenella, as a child of nature, had unknowingly turned that wheel, I am not sure that she did. She just happened to be an actor in the unravelling amnion of consciousness; she was chosen to carry a part of the whole meaning of meaning that was already turning. How can I tell the story of Belvedere, making judgements and apportioning blame? That would be pointing the bone. All too easily, blame makes its entrance upon the stage accompanied by a retinue of fresh causes. No. Complexities demand that nothing less than an extraordinary reading will do. In the telling of the auspices, my attention has moved elsewhere. It is only a very subtle alteration, but nevertheless it is greatly significant. I need to pay attention to it and to observe, observe, without judgement. For it seems to me that I have at last arrived at a more stable location in my writing and that my faithful connections have brought me to a sure understanding of how to proceed. I now know that even though my narrative will end, in that I will suddenly stop writing, there is no goal, no *telos* as philosophers might say. There is only 'the way', a passage through darkness that will become whatever destiny dictates. As I feel the stream that carries me forward, I arrive at the celebration of the sea, the nacreous creatures that Fenella so creatively named 'Truganini's shells'.

Within two years of our moving to Belvedere, my father, in one of his characteristic rushes, began the changes that would transform both house and garden. Looking back, it seems that my father was the initiator, but strictly speaking, this is not true. It was my mother who caused things to happen. The real transformations came about because of my mother's extraordinary actions on a very ordinary day of the week. She altered something. She attempted to mend a hole in the dining room wall, but instead, created a situation. In frustration, she mixed plaster and water in a pudding bowl and then spooned this over the exposed laths, smoothing it with a carving knife. So furious was my father when he saw what she had done, what a mess she had made, that he was forced to call in the decorators to put it right. The moment the decorators arrived to repair the wall properly, he asked them to take on the entire house.

Although my mother was upset by my father's outburst, the harsh manner in which he spoke to her on the day she made a mess of the plaster, her relief at improvements to the house was reflected in the way in which she related to him. Once more, he entered the myth of man perfected. She listened to him and agreed with his decisions. She would retain a bitter memory of his angry words, but only as an aspect of her bedroom telling, when things were not going well and she needed to speak before the mirror. For the time being, she was interested in all my father's ideas. Now that her husband was releasing her from domestic slavery, she could see herself as a real wife of a professional man. She was happy for him to take charge of everything, including curtain fabrics, floor coverings and pictures for the walls. He had such a clear instinct and a fine understanding of things.

My father visualised a scheme for every room. Once he had decided that the time had come, he walked about the house with a glass of whisky in his hand considering what was to be done for the best. Yes, he could see curtains with a regency stripe in the drawing room, and floral curtains in our bedroom. He would select antique furniture that was distinctively English. As for the floors, by a happy coincidence, he had just met an Egyptian guest at the Tasmanian Club, a travelling salesman who had arrived with a fat roll of oriental rugs of every size and design. He would invite him to Belvedere so that he could choose suitable coverings for the drawing room and the vestibule *in situ*. And when the Egyptian gentleman arrived, wearing a red fez, just like my father's souvenir in the trunk under the house, the two men, sharing a predilection for spirits and cheroots, spent hours together swigging and smoking convivially. The sounds of hoarse laughter and backslapping interrupted the silence of an otherwise ordinary Saturday afternoon. And from this consultation with Egypt, in the pungent fumes of black tobacco, came the darkly beautiful Bokhara rug for the drawing room floor.

To my mother's delight, my father said he would buy an electric stove. Yes, they could now afford a refrigerator and a washing machine. It was to be a great improvement. He would add more cupboards in the kitchen, and new linoleum. As his visions took shape, there was nothing he liked better than to give voice to his ideas, talking and drinking, wandering about as my mother prepared lunch, describing colours and antique furniture and great changes. Vistas and visions seemed to extend far beyond the boundaries of Belvedere. He was bringing great distance near. To my mother then, my father was the exemplary provider, and as children, she was at pains to point it out. We were extremely lucky to have such a good man, a good doctor as a father; a man who was lavish in his gifts; a man who wanted nothing but the very best for his offspring. Did we deserve such a father? And hearing praise of the man who was my father, 'such a good man', I believed every word, for I saw him as she saw him. He was the miracle worker. He had nothing less than the power of a god to inspire such awe in those who beheld him, such fear and trembling.

So the decorators duly arrived, a team of men in overalls, bearing all the paraphernalia of their trade. For months we lived in disarray, but it was a joyful confusion of shifted furniture, the piling up of things that in due course, when relocated in their freshly painted spaces, set a stage that was a feast for the eyes. I loved the happy noise, the scraping and hammering, and the smell of wet paint slapped upon walls by workmen joyously restoring glory to the upper part of deserving Belvedere. It seemed such a contrast to the hidden and punitive foundations. Once more, my father declared his attraction to the realms of art, poetic worlds that were such a mystery to me. The dramatic stage was in the process of being arranged. He bought a Chesterfield for the drawing room, a curved rosewood settee for the space in front of the bay windows, and a cedar tallboy for their bedroom. He also bought a mahogany dining table that sat on four turned legs. It came with six matching chairs that my father referred to as 'spoon-backed'. Week by week, as rooms were completed, another piece of antique furniture appeared, the installation of which re-enacted a kind of reverse homecoming in the southern English kingdom that was Tasmania; an up-turning in the order of things that though very confusing, possessed its own immediate meaning. And then, when the drawing room was finished, and the central rosette of acanthus leaves painted so white that it sparkled, my father supervised the restoration of the great fireplace and the installation of his much awaited work of art, the cedar mantelpiece with its copper smoke guard. The winter would attest to its burning virtues. It looked so splendid, so very important with its burnished *fleur-de-lys* that Fenella and I stood beside it keeping watch over all that was happening in the room. My father was hanging pictures on the peach-coloured walls. To begin with, he chose the paintings of Max Angus, an artist whose visions of Tasmania's peaks and high places delighted him. He liked seeing Tasmania through the eyes of this man. And at a local exhibition, he found an etching by Lionel Lindsay that caught his attention: a crow with ragged wing sitting dejectedly on a burnt stump. In the artist's hand, it was titled, *Depression*. My father laughed at it, but he fancied this etching of depression enough to add it to his collection. And in a very special corner of the drawing room, directly above a small rosewood occasional table with a pretty splayed leg, my father hung the portrait of Fenella. I looked at her image suspended from the picture rail, giving it a slight forward tilt, a downward gaze. Although Fenella was older now, she was much the same. And I had come to accept paint dribbling from her sprigged nightie, the awful feeling of her portrait being unfinished. Fenella was there, overseeing the restoration of Belvedere, at the very heart of my father's golden renaissance.

But the work was not complete until the piano arrived. I will never forget the day. The new Bokhara rug had just been unrolled. And it was summer, because the sash windows were flung up, and the side door that gave access to the front veranda was propped open all afternoon awaiting its arrival, saving a tortuous and probably impossible route through internal corridors. At Burns Mart, my father had found the piano that met with his requirements, a German piano. Four strong men, sweating in the heat, heaved it up the side steps on a wheeled platform and then along the sloping veranda into the drawing room through the summer door.

The birth of the German piano in our life was momentous. It was such a solid piece of furniture, its handsome black lacquer finished with gold scrolling on the front panels. Hidden beneath the lid was the name of its makers, R. Lipp and Sons, Stuttgart, inlayed in brass. Gothic lettering made the piano even more alluring. To me, it represented the archetypal image of a pianoforte, the original instrument from which sonata form was born. It might have belonged to Beethoven. All that was required now was that it should be played, and played beautifully, meeting the harmony of it proportions and the intentions of its creator.

My father was especially proud of it because it was not unlike the piano of his own childhood. It was his mother's opinion that German pianos were of the highest standard, higher even than pianos manufactured in England. And it was R. Lipp and Sons of Stuttgart whose robust craftsmanship not only withstood the rigours of transportation but could also endure life in hot, dry climates. This was the piano on which we would learn to play. As soon as it was installed in the drawing room, in the place that had been reserved for it, my mother polished it with a soft cloth, bringing its dulled lacquer to a high shine. My father admired it, picking out a few chords up and down the keyboard, testing its resonant voice. He said 'the Lipp' needed tuning, but how did he know? I wondered what my father had heard so keenly that I could not hear. What were the tiny intervals between notes, the space in which the sounds vibrated? Ever since I had seen and touched the grand piano of Harringay House, I had dreamt of music. At last, our very own piano had come into its destiny, its southern inheritance, given to a freshly decorated room. Here music would arise and I would learn to listen, just as my father listened. Here too would my father play his records, giving his undivided attention to Beethoven sonatas and Mozart operas, venturing forth into the heart of great works that were soon to include a romantic symphony of Tchaikovsky. In such manner, the drawing room of Belvedere became the very birthplace of art.

Our education began in this manner, with music and literature. My father was so specialised in his patriarchal thinking that he believed science in its highest pursuit belonged to the male intellect, and that as long as we knew enough to get by, the rest was superfluous. His eyes were on Fenella. He watched her with growing unease, his gaze changing imperceptibly from her works to her. He could not see a daughter of his becoming an artist. Where might that lead, but to a Bohemian world and to moral degradation? No, the home was the safest place, the right place, and the stable place. Because his mother was skilled at tatting, my father admired all crafts of needle, hook and shuttle. It gave him pleasure to see me sewing clothes for my doll, Patsy from little scraps of material. I was aware of his scrutiny, and sitting in his company before dinner, I felt the difference that his judgement made to my stitching. But it never occurred to my father that women might not like domesticity. In the fortress of the Protestant family, women and their work were essential.

My father expected my mother to be orderly in the house and scrupulously clean in the kitchen, which she was not. Professionally, he expected nothing less than the highest standards in the operating theatre. For our own good, he told us of an occasion in which one of the theatre nurses at the Royal Hobart Hospital handed him an instrument that was not only unsuitable for the task but was one that he suspected of not being sterile. My father flung the instrument and its tray onto the floor. The nurse was dismissed from her duties and never assisted him again. After this, the sister in charge of theatre drew up a list of rules to follow when her staff assisted Mr Merton Grey. My father made it quite clear to us that, in his opinion, nurses possessed poor mental faculties and from necessity were merely servants of the medical profession. He disapproved of women doctors. But such was his authority, this man of the Royal College of Surgeons of England, that everyone, however inferior, tried to please him.

At the time 'the Lipp' arrived, as my father always called it, his passion was for our learning the piano. This was his time for the arts, for music, literature, painting and briefly, ballet. My father had arrived at his blue period, living under the auspices of ultramarine. We were coming to the end of our primary years as pupils of St Michael's Collegiate School and the mood was changing. Edgar and Horace attended a similar Anglican foundation for boys called Hutchins School. Both these educational establishments, at first highly praised, were now falling from favour.

My father's abhorrence of heresy and his suspicions about the Church of England required him, from time to time, to criticise Anglican theology and practice. I noticed stark differences when I attended St John's Presbyterian Church, the most noticeable being kneeling. In the school chapel, as soon as Sister Dorothea intoned the words 'Let us pray' in her faint, throaty voice, we all slipped as one body onto our individual prayer cushions with our hands clasped before us, fingers erect. She prayed to the Lord that he might 'open our lips'. According to my father, this abject attitude was a sign of 'theological weakness'. It was idolatrous and in need of reforming. I think kneeling at prayer began to bother him so much that he was forced to remove us from the school for fear of its corrupting influence. In a moment as swift as the utterance of a syllable, he sacrificed his belief in single sex education and decided that state education was the better system. It was better because it was free from the inculcation of heresy and its spiritual stumbling block, obstinacy. But my father was so often charged with the absolute in what was good for girls that we were subject to these seemingly immutable convictions right from the start. Everything he said assumed a truth and carried the weight of a commandment. By the time we moved to Belvedere, my father thought music should be the foundation of our education. He would direct our religious education, just as his parents had directed his, curbing the insidious tendencies of the world, the flesh and the devil. As it came from him that the arts had supreme value, I saw no difference between the veracity of literature and the everlasting truths of religion, except for the presence of poetry, the tiny vibration that altered everything seen and heard. I had no notion of a fall from grace for anything other than humankind, *en masse*. All art attained to the eternal and in some unverifiable way existed in passionless detachment. Imitating my father, creativity was therefore exempt from laws that governed ordinary mortality. As for domestic training, we needed no formal instruction save the practice we received at home, washing dishes, preparing vegetables, cleaning rooms, waiting at table.

With the arrival of a tall glass-fronted book cabinet came an array of books with titles and names to inspire poetic dreaming. My father subscribed to a renowned English book club called Readers Union. Every few months, a bulky package wrapped in brown paper and tied with string would arrive by special delivery, posted from a noble London address: 38 William IV Street in the City of Westminster. I watched my father unwrap the selected literature that came all the way from 'home', the land that he knew. He inspected the contents saying to himself, 'Good, good, excellent, good', affirming his own authority. He commented on the wisdom of his purchases, passing the books to my mother for her approval. He was, to a certain extent, dependent upon my mother for guidance. Listening to her awakened him. He became alert to something wholly unexpected that at first delighted his mind and then all too soon troubled him deeply. But I am for the moment observing his delight. One by one, my father's newly acquired works would be greeted and placed in the bookshelf, the titles recited to us as if the gods had inscribed the books themselves; *I Too Have Lived in Arcadia*; *The Wilder Shores of Love*; *Too Late the Phalarope*; *Random Harvest*. These were the first purchases of his literary life. Bound essays on John Calvin and the Protestant Reformation were to come later. My father believed that reading, by which he meant carefully selected reading, 'improved the mind'. None of the above-mentioned I read, for they were not for me. I proceeded no further than the poetry of titles to satisfy the desires of my childhood. Although I opened the pages and peered at the script, there was little written within the covers to equal the infinitude recessed in gold ink upon cloth spines, the outward for the inward. All books, whether read and unread, were indications of other realms hidden within my own reality; possibilities that were there before me in the space books occupied.

Following fast upon reading parcels came the 'high-fidelity' gramophone with long-playing records made of the unbreakable material, vinyl. To my father's gratification, he was now able hear a complete symphony without having to interrupt it half a dozen times. I remember my father entering the drawing room one afternoon carrying a large cardboard box of new records for the hi-fi. And there were pictures on their record sleeves, pictures and words about famous artists from the world of everything poetic and beautiful that was born 'overseas'. Out of the box came a recording of Tchaikovsky's Fifth Symphony with a portrait on the front; a portrait of Dimitri Mitropoulos, the stern-faced priest of music whose interpretation of fate was to influence my father so much. We could not know then that we were soon to live in the strict singularity that my father drew from the multiplicity of hearing in this great Romantic symphony. We were soon to hear as he did.

Although symphonies did not inspire my mother, she assumed quite another personality when the books arrived. In literature, she knew she was the stronger. And so my mother abandoned her mirror gazing pathos for vocal force and authoritative gestures. Reading changed her whole manner. She was altogether haughty in her demeanour. Whenever she was taken over by literature and knowing, I felt her to be even more remote. It was impossible to interrupt her or to ask her anything. She went on and on, quoting, but it was always her own myth that she quoted, the myth that kept her central to her husband's affections. She drew upon the nascent power of the jealous female that banished all rivals, and especially the rivalry of daughters. 'You girls have no idea how lucky you are,' she would complain. 'You ought to be grateful. You do not deserve the good things your father gives you.' What did she mean? She meant our newly painted bedroom with its floral curtains, the piano that had been bought especially for us. My mother recited these words of resentment and others like them so often in endless variations on the theme of undeserving that naturally we believed her. Why would daughters deserve anything before the superior birth of sons? But even my mother's idea of paternal reward was flawed. Horace had now superseded Edgar in her husband's affections. There was a biblical precedent for this in the law of ultimogeniture, where daughters ranked below all males. As she could do nothing about it, she came to accept it and by using it herself, eventually gave it her endorsement.

My mother loved to talk about the classics of English literature, and in happy times, when my father was in a good mood, she would describe particular passages that animated her. It was through listening to my mother's voice reading extracts from *Adam Bede* in the kitchen that he became familiar with narrative, feeling the great authority of language, extending his understanding of human nature. It was my mother who first raised the name Hetty Sorrel, the unfortunate girl who was condemned to death for the murder of her illegitimate child. Her death sentence was subsequently commuted to transportation 'for the term of her natural life'. Together, my parents discussed 'poor Hetty' in detail as if her story were the latest news from England.

They entered a desperate, shameful drama in which they experienced and expressed a similar pleasure. It was vanity that trapped Hetty, my mother said. She was a 'weak thing' who could not look after herself. As my father sipped his whisky, he said, 'True, true, oh, yes, true,' snapping his fingers when his understanding reached a crystalline clarity. It was like this: Hetty had succumbed to a terrible sin. My father heard my mother's words and accepted her interpretation. I wondered what was so true in literature that my parents, who argued so violently in life, should suddenly agree. If the story of Hetty Sorrel was true, was it her fate to end up here, in Van Diemen's Land? Was she, 'the weak thing,' confined to a single cell with a barred window? I now fancied that it was she, and not a ticket-of-leave convict who had suffered beneath us, the fallen girl with an animal hunger inside her that had to be locked up every night. Hearing my parents talk, I very soon developed a fear of the writings of George Eliot. Her books were dreadful history, terrible myth. But apart from the tragedy of Hetty Sorrel, which would continue to haunt me, there was always the poetry of the English Romantics and my mother reciting *The Isles of Greece* over and over again. After we had gone to bed, it was not unusual to hear my parents discussing literature late into the night. And literature was nothing if it was not at all times and in every respect 'true'.

Books worked their magic. Now that the practice was well established and the house refurbished accordingly, my father responded to my mother's requests for domestic help. In due course, Mrs Hussey, a rosy faced woman wearing a grey felt hat came for a few hours every week to help with the washing and the ironing. Mrs Hussey liked to work wearing her hat and apron, and whenever she happened to meet my father in the course of her duties, she gave him a little nod and then moved swiftly and respectfully out of his way. He was 'the doctor'. Under the liberating arrangements at Belvedere, it was Mrs Hussey who laboured instead of my mother, dividing her time between the hot copper in the washhouse and the whirring washing machine in the kitchen. It was Mrs Hussey who lugged wet clothes in creaking baskets to the back line. The inconvenience no longer mattered.

My mother instructed Mrs Hussey in every detail. She taught her the correct way to iron and to fold 'the doctor's handkerchiefs' and how to starch his shirt collars and cuffs, just as her future mother-in-law had instructed her before she married. I felt sure that the shy Mrs Hussey felt awkward pegging 'the doctor's' underpants and singlets on the back line, shaking out creases from the electric wringer. It embarrassed her to see him through the window sitting at the dining table having his lunch, she being entrusted to such private things. He was such an important man. But the assistance of the diligent Mrs Hussey meant that my mother could sometimes rest in the afternoon. There was nothing she liked better than to retire to her bedroom to read, forgetting the chores that she found so tedious and demeaning. And toppling upon cosmetic bottles on the dressing table or thrown upon the unmade bed were my mother's open books, their printed pages fanning languidly where she had hurriedly left them.

Besides books and Fenella's works of art, which I often copied, we were allowed to play the German Lipp, learning to hear by picking out tunes. We made ourselves familiar with the piano while we waited for a suitable teacher to be found. My father instructed me, suggesting the correct way to hold my fingers, diagnosing errors. It was winter now and the fire blazed. Thinking deeply, and for his own comfort, my father often stood with his back to the heat in front of the smoke guard with its burnished *fleur-de-lys*, drinking whisky, listening to my efforts, a proud man in the midst of his new surroundings. He said that I reminded him of his mother. But how could I reach his ideal? It was impossible. I knew that I would fail. And because I would fail, I could never stop him from drinking or from behaving as he did. I nurtured the secret that if someone in the family could play the piano as his mother did, then my father would attain to the perfected peace he so dearly desired. I knew too that my mother was quite unable to do this, in spite of her superior knowledge of literature. For in the hierarchy of the arts that my father taught, music was central to the seventh heaven. The language of music was the greatest language of all.

My mother, in her desperation, was driven to exploit the one tool available to her in order to gain her husband's attention. And looking back, it occurs to me now just how powerfully my father's expectations for daughters threatened my mother. Although my mother liked to play the piano, for she too had music to remember, her tunes were altogether different from the academic *Albumblätter* known to my father. She played Scottish folk songs and Sankey and Moody hymns that were dear to her childhood. Unhappily for my mother, although she was a good sight-reader, my father often dismissed her efforts. She longed for confirmation of her gifts, but my father could only compare her with his own mother. I remember how often she burst into the drawing room when I was at the piano teaching myself a song, and pushing me aside, she would begin *The Road to the Isles* very loudly with lifted hands and swaying body. I felt confused by my mother's manner at the keyboard, the way she pumped the pedal and hummed, filling the room with deafening discord. She received and performed music in an another kind of hearing. But in her dreamy hours at 'the Lipp', playing and singing songs of the Highlands and Lowlands, my mother was blissfully happy. Sitting at the keyboard, and sitting before the mirror, she lived her very own myth.

It was while we were waiting for a teacher that my father decided the time was right to introduce us to the ballet. The Borovansky Ballet, Australia's first professional company steeped in the great Russian tradition, happened to be touring the state capitals and had chosen to visit Hobart's Theatre Royal. Although my father had never seen the ballet, he appreciated the art of dance as a feminine ideal, and in his pursuit of beauty, he thought it would do us no harm to see a performance. He responded to the notion of stylised movement derived from French sensibilities. Indeed, he wished to see the ballet for himself, to confirm his discrimination. The visiting artists had trained 'overseas' and the list of their members included names ending in the foreign and wonderfully evocative 'ova'. The legendary Pavlova had visited Australia in the early twenties. Her ethereal grace, her Slav mystery, had so bewitched everyone who beheld her that very soon an exotic dessert made of whipped egg whites, sweetened cream and fresh passion fruit, peculiar to the perceptions of Australians, was created for her. Though unable to see her for myself, I consumed her as metaphor in the culinary perfection of a trembling delicacy. I ate her as dessert.

And it was to the Theatre Royal, Tasmania's golden baroque beauty and Australia's oldest theatre that my father took us to see the Russian trained Helene Kirsova in works of art that she had received directly from the famous choreographer, Mikhail Fokine. It was Fokine who had partnered the immortal Pavlova herself. So it was to living Russian refinement that we were taken, a land whose poetry, translated to the stage, seemed even more inaccessible than the gifts of England that came in the immediacy of reading. In Russia, with its indecipherable language derived from glyptic Greek, ancient words etched upon a precious gem, the *intaglio* art of dance had attained to the paragon. And it was the very potency of Russian remoteness that lent to the French perfection I saw that night in the Theatre Royal and in the classical dance called the *ballet blanc*.

There is no greater example of academic dance than Fokine's *Les Sylphides*. And if ballet is expressive of life, which it most surely is, then what aspect of life does the music of Chopin and this sylvan vision express? For Fenella and myself, there could be nothing further removed from our lives than an Elysian glade in which winged tree spirits flitted in and out of its blurred boundaries. The undulating white in moonlight, to the knowledge usually given to eyes, was entrancing; the plasticity of form, ecstatic. For the briefest moment, we glimpsed the Isles of the Blessed, where feminine perfection danced in circles, amassing a filmy radiance that the ancients referred to as the *augoeides*. Was I seeing the glorious vesture of the soul with my own eyes? I felt sure that I was. And who were these sad and seemingly disembodied creatures whose hems were always moist? On the stage was a scene of passionless serenity; a world in which feelings moved without the slightest disruption to emotional integrity; where even a finger's gesture retained meaning. Here were subtle maidens, their highly arched feet enclosed in pink satin slippers, criss-crossing ribbons tied about their ankles. The blocked ends enabled them to lift themselves upon the points of their toes, extending the airy language of dance to its zenith. And then, when extreme beauty had been achieved, the male dancer caught the ballerina in his arms, raising a dazzling display above all heads. Held so high, the ballerina soared through the scented night, her flimsy skirts ruffling. Oh, look how she holds her perfectly pointed feet, one behind the other in a little ankle knot! Look at the grace of her *port de bras*! In our delusions, Fenella and I believed the scene to be nearer than it was, and that after the curtain had fallen we could return to Belvedere of the beautiful view and recreate the high white arabesques of *Les Sylphides* in our own lives. We could recreate them somewhere in the garden around the mulberry tree. Had not Fenella danced along the branch? Had she not invoked the power of shells? She was always there, travelling beautifully in her world of transformations, in *mouvements perpetuels*, as swift as the wind, as turbulent as the sea.

After our night at the Theatre Royal, I fell upon pictures of the ballet. I studied every image I could find. In *Theatre Street*, one of my father's books bound in blue cloth with gold embossed lettering, Fenella pointed to a photograph of the Russian ballerina, Tamara Karsavina. The dancer posed for the camera wearing exactly the same white gauze dress with a pinked hem worn by Fokine's sylphides. She stood with her arms modestly crossed upon her breast, her eyes gazing heavenwards, her white body cast in an eternal *arabesque à terre*. Underneath the picture was the caption, *Myself in Giselle, Paris, 1910*. 'Myself in Giselle!' Oh, to be able to utter such words, to be such an artist! But who was the maiden Giselle that the Russian ballerina Karsavina should move into her being so completely that there should be no discernible difference between them? Who was she? I could not answer this question. I was unable to penetrate a world of such extreme antipodes. Fenella stood up and assumed the attitude of Giselle, adopting her earth-bound arabesque. I looked at her. She was both Giselle of the *ballet blanc* and Fenella of the portrait. In my eyes, she fulfilled the ideal. She had the classical black hair of the ballerina. And it was Fenella who read the story of Tamara Karsavina in her autobiography. Although the language of Tamara Karsavina was not too difficult for me to read, it was beyond my understanding. The faculty of seeing European myths required a different kind of knowing than hearing European music, for hearing was a language nearer to my inner expression. Nevertheless, the moment I saw the picture of Tamara Karsavina holding an *arabesque à terre*, her image continued to provide me with an ideal so powerful it was almost too painful for the eyes. Somewhere within me, I inhaled a forgotten fragrance. It seemed that an artist might experience more than one existence. Art permitted Karsavina to live all the roles that she danced: Giselle, the Firebird, the maiden in *Spectre de la Rose*. Fenella read the story of Giselle. She insisted on my hearing. She told me that Giselle, after being seduced and abandoned by a nobleman, 'went mad' and dropped dead. In her grief, she was unable to die properly and so became a hungry ghost, a white *wili* of Elysium who haunted the forests at night, charming men into a deathly dance, a frenzy of revenge. The *wilis* killed their former lovers. I believed her. Of course it was true, just as my parents believed the story of Hetty Sorrel to be true. And since my night at the theatre, I knew I had really seen the unhappy Giselle and her shimmering *augoeides* in *Les Sylphides*. For the time being, the moving vision was enough for my dreaming. I put the beautiful book back on the shelf. There was now another image to see, another voice to hear. My father made the long-awaited announcement. At last he had found a teacher of the pianoforte for us, a true musician, a person who was 'entirely suitable'. With emotion in his voice, he referred to this true musician as 'the soul of music'. He had invited her to visit us at Belvedere. Her name was Miss Colleen O'Hara.

From the moment Miss Colleen O'Hara appears my father becomes the principal actor in the creation of music's 'soul'. He causes the artist to enter. As I draw near the piano with a teacher at my side, it is her skill that begins to direct my hearing. I close the story of 'Myself in Giselle', the poetry of Tamara Karsavina. Even though I no longer look at the limbed beauties of the Russian stage, images of *Les Sylphides* still inspire me. Somewhere under the house, where history sinks into myth, all wronged maidens exist as ghostly modalities, their wordless epitaphs a derangement of veils. Intent upon the upper world of my life, Miss O'Hara sits next to me. In the spirit of the dance, she lifts my hands from my lap and places them gently over the keys, showing the relationship between fingers and notes. Her instruction in the art of music is completely different from my father's. But because my father has appointed her as an authority, very soon I accept her completely. Music is really like this; my ears have not deceived me. Art is its own achievement. It is nothing else but the practising of art. Miss O'Hara says that even Haydn 'borrows from himself and returns as himself retuned', but I do not know what she means. She speaks from her experience of hearing. And I love Miss O'Hara. She moves in music and in life with the assurance of a trained ballerina. She is small and dark, daintier even than a dancer, her physique, bird-like. She dresses in the latest New Look fashion: long swinging skirts, nipped in waist, high, peaked collars. About her neck is a single strand of graduated pearls. Somewhere upon her neat, discreet person, crystals of marcasite glint. My mother remarks upon her Irish colouring, her fine black hair, her white skin and her pale blue eyes. It is not surprising that in memory, I move from the image of the Russian ballerina to the image of the Irish musician. The insistent allusion of the *wili* now settles upon my piano teacher. And in my imaginings, the title '*Myself in Giselle, Paris, 1910*', might even be the secret life of Miss Colleen O'Hara herself. My father tells us, with that peculiar tone of honour in his voice, that Colleen O'Hara has studied 'overseas'. She received her musical training in Italy.

Having seen the ballet, I longed to dance. It was a dream that could never be fulfilled, except in a far distant crystal experience. Knowing nothing else then, for an intense period, I immersed myself in visions of moonlit Elysium. I stood before my mother's mirror with my arms above my head, yearning for the extraordinary flexibility of the body, the fluid movements that conveyed so much without uttering a syllable, imitating the girl with fragile wings fixed in the hollow of her shoulders. Following the example of my mother, I participated in the dream of Venus. The white was so exquisitely beautiful that very soon this inner structure begin to collapse, causing a hard crush inside. I could not bear to look. At the very heart of music and ballet, I saw feelings arrive as pristine art. In this new reflection, entering my mother, yearning and making gestures, though nothing happened, everything happened. What ballet revealed in its dance of veils and what my life was unable to realise became the poetic memory within me that neither time nor circumstances could ever obliterate.

For a short while, before the arrival of Miss Colleen O'Hara, my father too fell under the spell of dance and its power to enhance the senses. It was the very veiling of Romantic ballet that drew him nearer to a specific vision of women. Ballet enthused him as much as it confused him, his analysis tempered by the intrusive puritan with the pointing finger. The moment he first met Miss O'Hara, who came to him as a patient, he saw her with his theatre-eye; he the surgeon seer, she the gifted pianist. He had seen young women on stage dancing individually and as a corps; women moving in their very own art. His perceptions were sharpened by the refined musculature of these young women whose delicate steps were so sure, whose *pas de bourrée* so smooth. To the eyes of a physician, the extreme arching of the foot achieved by stretching the instep fascinated him. The extension of the leg in a *grande arabesque* he found quite remarkable. It was with a diagnostic eye that he examined the way in which the turned-out feet of the ballerina appeared to be boneless in some attitudes, or as flexible as the spine of a fish, and then as rigid as steel when supporting the body *en pointe*. The display of such physical health upon the stage after seeing the very opposite in medical practice only increased his initial attraction. In that dance was accompanied by music, he thought it secure, but because he was so overcome by what he saw, his security contained an inherent weakness. He was unable to abandon himself to the appreciation of feelings inspired by seeing, or to approve of them, so yet again, he was driven to suppress their full flowering by an act of will. He recognised the needling. It had happened in England. As he did not know what to do with this feeling, he gave it once more to the mortality of alcohol. From the beginning, music was his mother around whose image an abstract strength gathered. But the straightened mind of Calvinism was trained to resist the unnecessary decoration of dance. His mother's creativity, which he both feared and loved, was not clothed as the *ballet blanc*; her playing had never exposed his imagination to such naked seeing. In a way he found the allure of dance anathema to theology, the safeguard of faith. In a surge of visual energy, ballet as art inspired him. Then suddenly and just as unexpectedly, it threw him earthward. It was the lifting of the woman, he thought; it was her elevation that bothered him. Like a veiled disc, a peerless queen, she skimmed through the ether illuminating the night. And because a partner was essential to her heightening, he found fault in the eccentrically mannered presence of the male. Strength and mastery, yes, but ballet's gestures were surely incompatible with 'the man'. They were effeminate.

My father voiced the opinion, with some self-satisfaction, that ballet lacked intellectual rigour and moral strength, no matter how celebrated an art it happened to be. In spite of the virtuosity and grace of Helene Kirsova, who was cast in the mould of the celebrated Karsavina, he believed that the aesthetic was somehow false. It deceived. He demanded of ballet an ethic that it did not and could not have. Was it a 'lack of morality' in the manner in which ballet displayed itself? Perhaps it was. All he knew was that his analysis changed his opinion. As an art, ballet interfered with the settled course of how things ought to be. And so he judged it unsuitable for men, and yet he could not conceive of the art supported solely by women. Was it possible for a man to dance without such ambiguous gestures? To his way of seeing, the attitudes were so very unmanly. Its very expressiveness might even be the source of homosexuality. At the Tasmanian Club, he talked about the visiting Ballet Company in the most unflattering terms. In the ribaldry of drink, he ventured to call all male dancers 'jumping buggers'. Wasn't the mad Nijinsky, another Russian, one of them? His colleagues laughed. Ballet was 'peculiar'. It was dangerous to surrender maleness to such blatant femininity. And as he continued to drink, the effects of alcohol assisted the dismissal. He need not struggle with this art. He did not want his daughters to dance. Nor had he suggested that his sons should be exposed to it. My father returned to what he knew from long experience. He returned to music.

The presence of Miss O'Hara stirred up different feelings for my mother. She liked the ballet, she thought it attractive, but she was ruffled by her husband's reaction to it, the way he talked about a dancer's physique. She felt a vague unease when the limelight fell upon the ballerina making her pirouettes, turning and turning in such a physical display, keeping her white body in an eerie glow. Ballet was all very well, but what did it mean? Although my father did not read *Theatre Street*, he liked to see the book sitting on the shelf with its handsome binding. It was a part of his library. When he was sober, he spoke about the life of Tamara Karsavina as he spoke about the life of John Calvin, as if he *knew*. At such times, there was nothing to hurl against heaven.

And then one day, he came home for lunch saying that in morning surgery he had found the ideal teacher for his daughters. My mother did not know what to think, but once more she sensed a kind of inner turmoil. She sensed something in herself, a quiver of insecurity that she needed to protect. Miss O'Hara had come to him as a patient, in the confidentiality of the consulting room. She pictured the event, her being shown in by his secretary, this beautiful young woman, as her husband described her. She saw her taking a seat in front of his desk, her eyes downcast, her musician's hands clasped in her lap. She heard her husband say as he always did at the beginning of a consultation, 'And what is the nature of the trouble?' And never before in a consultation had he heard what he then did. He hadn't expected to be enchanted. My mother saw her husband's attentiveness to her physical needs, whatever they happened to be. She wondered. Had he examined her? Her husband did not say. It was not her place to ask what was wrong with Miss O'Hara, even though her curiosity was aroused. If he thought there was a moral to be learnt, my father was not averse to telling my mother, or telling us, what secrets he had heard in his consulting rooms. He told us about 'wayward girls' and the fearful consequences of 'kicking over the traces'. What did he mean by these expressions? He warned us sternly. But in this instance, it was not like that. His mood being so very different, my mother felt she could not ask. He would tell her what he wanted her to know. Her husband said that in the course of the consultation he learnt that his new patient was a teacher of pianoforte. My father often used the formal word, 'pianoforte', in memory of his mother. Miss O'Hara taught both pianoforte and singing.

A doctor of necessity being a kind of inquisitor, at the mention of music my father began to ask his patient one question after another. He wanted to know all about her. He wanted to know her family background, where she grew up, where she was educated, and how she had come to study overseas. Her experiences fascinated him. He was interested to learn that she was born in rural Huonville, and that because of the isolation, she and her brothers and sisters were sent away to be to educated at various convents and colleges. Her mother, widowed when the children were young, became postmistress at the local store that her late husband used to manage. She had made great sacrifices to educate her eight children. My father was very impressed. As a young child, she had shown promise in music. Listening to her speaking of her beginnings gave rise to impressions of another pianist, someone that everyone knew by reputation. Who was it? My father asked the question. Ah, yes. It was Eileen Joyce, he said, Tasmania's most famous pianist. Eileen Joyce had been born in rural isolation. She was born in Zeehan on the West Coast of Tasmania. Her early talent being recognised, she too studied overseas. Had she, as had the celebrated Eileen Joyce, studied with Artur Schnabel? Was it not at Leipzig? Miss O'Hara shook her head modestly. Oh no. She was flattered by the comparison, but she did not have that kind of talent, nor did she have that great ambition. Not at all. Nevertheless, she had been most fortunate. She had studied at the Milan Conservatory with excellent teachers. Although the experience had been most inspiring and had run its course, homesickness had forced her to return to Tasmania. Homesickness? My father looked at her quizzically. Oh yes. She wanted to be near her family. And she was soon to marry. It seemed sensible to establish herself here where she was known. She had already advertised for private pupils and had been engaged to teach at St Mary's Convent as well as the Convent of the Sacred Heart. She was very happy to be teaching at St Mary's where nuns had taught her.

With her subdued manner, her measured speech bereft of self, Miss O'Hara reminded my father of the sisters of Calvary. It was the deference of Catholic women that he admired so much, the interior silence, the subdued feminine. Although my father believed that the Roman Catholic Church had constructed a fictitious form of worship and that her dogmas were merely 'delirious fancies', he was nevertheless impressed by the monastic discipline that governed their educational establishments. Notwithstanding the superstitions surrounding relics and rosaries, he thought Miss O'Hara a shining example of Catholic training. He once referred to her as 'a living rule', a satisfying Catholic expression that surely sprung from his reading. The Church very properly nurtured praiseworthy and above all *safe* capacities in women. And he was impressed that she had given recitals for the Australian Broadcasting Commission. Miss O'Hara had not expected to meet such a doctor, a good physician who enquired after her career in pianoforte and singing. And when my father asked her whether she would be willing to teach his two daughters the pianoforte, his new patient said, 'Yes,' without a moment's hesitation. He then invited her to Belvedere. He would like her to meet his wife and daughters. And of course, he would be honoured if she would play for him. He told her that he had only recently bought a splendid German Lipp. He would be grateful if Miss O'Hara would test it and give him her opinion. Commending the arrangement to himself, he hoped that her judgement would confirm his own. Well, he felt sure that it would. He thought it appropriate to put it that way.

But before Miss O'Hara enters Belvedere accompanied by her husband-to-be, there are other observations to make. The coming of Miss Colleen O'Hara begins so many moods, I must be sure to establish all new causes so that the effects that issues from them may flow smoothly. After Colleen, music and practising the piano dominate my life, and to a lesser extent the life of my sister. Although I did not want to accept it, I knew that Fenella was moving away from me into her own world, and that she was occupied 'elsewhere'. We were now at separate schools. As she had a new friend, a girl called Coral who lived nearby in Goulburn Street, Fenella and I spent less time together. I knew that she was not as keen on learning the piano as I was. There was a deep resistance in her to my father's instruction that she should practise every day and that she should read every book he put before her. She resented the ordering tone in his voice, resented his unreasonableness when she did not obey. And I don't think she liked Miss O'Hara at all. Her resistance confounded my father. He thought he had never met such opposition. As we were not encouraged to entertain our friends at home, she took refuge from his unpredictable presence in contemplating her paintbox and in the rituals of the artist. She did not know why it should be so, but squeezing colour from a tube onto her palette somehow squeezed her, carrying her bodily to another feeling existence. It was so pleasurable to see how colours changed as she mixed them. It was inexplicably strange and inexplicably beautiful all at the same time.

And when she was not experimenting with paint, Fenella liked to dig in the garden, to nurture cuttings. Under the veranda, she kept a collection of terracotta pots in which she had set soil and seeds. When the time was right, she brought the tiny green shoots outside, arranging them in rows on the wooden steps so that they could absorb the rays of the sun. The garden was another place of freedom and experience, a natural environment where she was always happy. Looking back, it is not strange that it should have been so, for Fenella was always a girl of the elements, drawn to extracting and examining things. But my mother, sensing that her elder daughter had something that she did not have herself, a *gnosis* all of her own, that she participated naturally in mysterious, initiative rites, resented her. And under a compulsion to rupture the luminous web that connected her daughter with the *Creatrix Universalis*, she had no compunction in showing her resentment.

One afternoon in late spring, Fenella left her household chores for the garden. She went to her plants, to remove dead leaves and to loosen the soil around them. With a small gardening fork, she began to lift a cranesbill geranium, separating last summer's growth from a tangle of lady's mantle. The soil was dry and crumbly, the roots willing to be lifted. She thought it a good idea to give each plant a new space in the herbaceous border. My mother came to the front door looking for her. Where was she? She called from the veranda, 'Fenella! Fenella!' She was in the garden. What was she doing in the border near the old incinerator? She was digging. My mother was furious. At the sight of her daughter absorbed in her activity, something tore inside her. 'Fenella!' she shouted, 'What are you doing?' Her voice was agitated. Fenella heard. It was not the question that shocked her but the power with which it was delivered. The jagged edge caught her.

Fenella straightened herself immediately. She asked herself what she was doing. She was examining the plants, combing the roots with her fingers. Just a few seconds before, she had been observing tiny insects, fascinated by their activity. A honeyeater called from the old apple tree. 'Oh!' she had said softly, replying to its fanfare. She loved its yellow-tipped wings. But the shriek of her mother's voice cut into the sweet sound of the honeyeater.

The song ceased. What had she done wrong? She was perplexed. Fenella thought her mother would be pleased with her gardening. Hadn't she been told many times about 'deserving' the good things her father gave her? Hadn't the garden been given to the whole family? Fenella did not understand. She felt a flush, a rush of shame, but she didn't know what her shame was. She started to make her way up the garden, her mother repeating the exclamation appropriate to the behaviour of girls: 'How dare you!' But how had she dared? She could not answer. She returned to the house to do as she was told, to help with the dishes. Fenella would not go to the garden again without the shame that she had been given, the shame that had shocked her feelings. And anyhow, her mother reminded her, following her into the kitchen with a wagging finger, a proper gardener had been hired. Under no circumstances was she to dig plants. As she had no experience, she could not possibly know what she was doing. But Fenella did know what she was doing. And deep within, my mother knew she knew.

Indeed, my father had hired a gardener as a part of his scheme to improve Belvedere. He had at first consulted him about pruning the fruit trees and treating the apple for codling moth. The young man who came in answer to his advertisement in *The Mercury* was not really a gardener, my father said. He was a labourer, an Italian immigrant, probably no older than eighteen, but he was keen to work, even though he spoke very little English. He indicated to my father that he could prune fruit trees and do anything that was required. My father said he would pay him five pounds a day. It was agreed. So Felici came every Saturday and proved to be true to his word. He pruned the fruit trees and treated the apple for codling moth. He began work before breakfast and maintained a steady pace all through the day, breaking for coffee in the early afternoon. Even though we were forbidden to go near him because he was an Italian, and 'just a labourer' I now had an excitement that was entirely mine.

On Saturdays, I liked to wake early so that I could watch Felici's arrival from my bedroom window. And at seven o'clock precisely, he would enter the garden carrying a canvas haversack and a gardening fork. For as long as I could, I followed his every move. I observed him digging the Italian way, thinking his Italian thoughts. I watched him, this swarthy young man with the name that meant 'happy'. If only I could speak his language! At first, it was his name that I loved. How wonderful that a man could be called 'happy'! Was there ever such a name in English? I thought not. And after finding joy in a foreign name, it was so easy to fall in love with him. He was Italian. Had he not been born 'overseas', in the north, the place of origins and of art? Did he not know? I wanted to speak a few words of Italian to him, but the only phrase I knew, *La ci darem la mano*, came from Mozart's *Don Giovanni*. I knew nothing of Eros in Mozart. To me, it was simply romance and music. Didn't everyone love Mozart? Listening to my father's record, I rehearsed the moment. My heart pounded. I pictured myself greeting him under the mulberry tree, the perfect place for a tryst, where in myth the lovers Pyramus and Thisbe met in death, their mingling blood staining the white fruit of the mulberry red. But how could I summon the courage to say to the Italian gardener, 'May I have your hand?'

At the far end of the garden, I watched Felici drop his haversack. Plunging the fork into the soil he then walked around the garden at a leisurely pace, his sensitive fingers feeling the leaves, just as Fenella did. He liked the garden and everything in it. He looked at the fruit trees, the apple, pear, nectarine and peach, as if he were at home. Although he was 'just an illiterate from southern Italy', he had a sure touch, a gentle touch. And after hours of turning the soil with his fork, lifting and separating the plants as Fenella had done, he would stop work and sit down on the grassy verge, wiping his brow with a handkerchief. Peeping through the jasmine on the veranda, I watched Felici draw a flask from his haversack and pour himself a mug of coffee. He drank the coffee slowly. Sometimes he would disappear under the mulberry tree, concealing himself within its moist shadows. He was there, in the mythical meeting place, the place where things happened, where the despotism of fate might become the blessing of destiny. I was unhappy that I could not see him. What was he doing? Perhaps he was dreaming of old Italian orchards, inhaling the soft scent of orange blossom.

With the inrush of first love, with the coming of wild feelings, I forgot about Fenella and the Aboriginal treasures. The ritual finished and the dance over, I no longer saw the tragic face of Truganini. She belonged to an earlier age, and to the darkness of forgetting. What had become of the shells? I had lost sight of them. They were in another form, hanging in torn remnants from twigs and leaves, hidden from sight, deep in their secret activity, bright still in their primal lucidity. I did not see, nor was I able to hear. The time of my awakening had not come, nor could it happen in the *locus* where my journey began. I did not see, nor was I able to hear. Unknown even to the happy gardener Felici and unknown to anyone, the ears of the sea listened; they listened at the mouth of the bee.

Under the auspices of crystals, images of Colleen O'Hara bring to mind two beautiful associations. The first, from ballet, is a series of preparatory steps. These tiny steps, known as a *soubresaut sur les pointes*, or a *sous-sus*, that is, a little jolt that enables the dancer to balance herself before making a display *en pointe*, are some of the prettiest devised in an art that uses the body in its entirety. The dancer, assisted from behind by her partner, springs onto her toes, travelling forward a little, her legs close together one before the other. She comes to a sudden halt and then immediately, upon an inhalation of the breath begins her decorative turns, ending in a grand attitude. This brief arrest, this sharp focus before an elaborate flourish, fixes the movement for the viewer, making it memorable, its pattern unforgettable. The *sous-sus* is a choreographic device that enhances seeing and refines the theatre-eye in exactly the same way that an ornament graces the note in music and repetition delineates compositional form. It is in itself, a discriminating finger that says, 'Look! See what is about to be revealed! Do not forget the vision!'

The second beautiful association that belongs to the image of Miss O'Hara is the wand, a tool of transformation, made from any earthy material and used by healers. The most favoured instrument is the crystal wand. It comes in many different shapes and sizes. Some wands are decorated for specific purposes and bear the mark of their maker's intention. They may be bound with silver and studded with extra stones. But the simplest wands are the most inspiring, the naturally elongated elements lifted from the matrix, just as they are. They too, emerging from earth without pride or self-regard, point to something specific. In their primal simplicity, they transform negative energy and bring about change. And the most effective and affecting of all such tools is the amethyst wand, the sight of which produces a flutter in the hearts of crystal healers, especially if the crystal is seen to contain refracted light. True healers know the value of the amethyst wand, for amethyst itself is the energy that brings serenity and order. And to behold a wand, in that manner, and to feel its transforming potential, is a sacred thing. The ancient Romans knew it as *amethustos*, 'not intoxicated', by which was meant the unclouded intellect, the integration of all knowledge, true balance. Amethyst was worn in order to 'stay sober'. 'Speak to me of amethyst wands,' I say to those who know. And crystal healers, in an altered voice, speak from an amethyst experience that participates in the power and transformation of the gods. 'It is like this,' they say. 'It is art.'

When Colleen came into my life, the dancer and her *sous-sus*, the amethyst wand and her transformations, she entered the drawing room in order to display her gifts. Although I could not know it then, in the scheme of things beneath, she came for the specific purpose of change, complying with fate and alteration in all its subtleties. She entered the drawing room with her husband-to-be following close upon her heels, the living shadow of a man. Though jealous and possessive of her beauty, Angus Drummond permitted, but grudgingly, the display of her talents. He was not a music lover. Even then, I felt sure he pursued her with dark intent. Indeed, my father too was aware of something disturbing.

My father took satisfaction in observing his 'complete ignorance' before the gifts of his wife-to-be. What could he possibly know? He was a mere salesman, selling shirts behind the men's counter at Myer's Department Store in Liverpool Street. He knew nothing. Why was she to marry a man such as he? The dour Mr Drummond sat in an armchair, his hands clasped tightly beneath his chin. He was a narrow-faced man with a thin ginger moustache. At first, he said little. In a rather uncouth way, he accepted the hospitality offered by my parents and was only enlivened by alcohol and cigarettes. When two drinking and smoking men get together, no matter what the social gap, a bond is formed. Mr Drummond and my father met in their dubious rituals. Soon, they laughed. My mother, who had striven to look her best and so wore her hair up, chatted nervously to the woman who had appeared to glow in the eyes of her husband. In her desire to impress, she had spent the whole morning making almond petits fours. My mother presented her French delicacies on fine china plates, sitting in frilled paper patty-pans. She offered china tea to Miss O'Hara, while my father poured Johnny Walker whisky into his best crystal tumblers. Scrutiny and display were in the air; my father looking at his guests, formulating his judgements, my mother looking at Miss O'Hara, formulating hers; Fenella and I outside the circle, waiting. And as the occasion was for the making of good women, for which we were to be grateful, neither Edgar nor Horace was present. The moment Colleen O'Hara rose from her chair, at my father's invitation and moved towards the German instrument, awkwardness began to dissolve. She was there at the pianoforte, her hands hovering over the ivory keys, in the rare and beautiful breath of anticipation. The spotlight fell upon the artist and her little halt, her delicate *sous-sus*. Something was about to happen. The energy of transformation was seen to move like this: Colleen O'Hara played Debussy's prelude, *La Cathédrale engloutie*, after which she sang, to her own accompaniment, *Solveig's Song* by Grieg. She tested and proved my father's Lipp; she elaborated her musical virtues, decorating the air as if she herself was an amethyst wand. She displayed her gifts, just as a virtuosic dancer displays the art she serves.

    I think my father expected her to play something that was familiar to him and to sing something he knew. Priding himself on his musical education and his receptive ear, he was quite unprepared for an encounter with French impressionism and Norwegian romance. He had never been exposed to the *fântome* of Debussy, apart from the ghostly *Clair de lune* that his mother had played with a precision that came from an inherent correction of excesses. In the Lyric Suites of Grieg, she failed to raise Nordic mystery. Of course, under the circumstances, locked into the shock of new hearing, my father could say nothing. He was undoubtedly affected by what he heard. I saw the look on his face, the way in which he stubbed out his half-smoked cigarette, slowly. More than that, he was struck by the expressiveness of his guest, whose presence at the piano was so very different from that of his mother. Whereas his mother exemplified the straight back of German discipline and might have taken instruction from Clara Schumann, Colleen O'Hara's natural gifts had flowered under French and Italian influences. She was altogether more rhapsodic, given to fluttering, the perfect interpreter of the moodiness of Debussy and the crystallisation of his fantasies into sounds. Her small hands managed to encompass the octave and travel up and down the keyboard with the greatest ease. Enchanting to watch, her neat foot in black patent sandals touched the pedals, each depression producing watery overtones, dampening the dry summer air with dreams of the sea. From fathoms below a bell tolled mournfully.

The piece, so short in duration, a prelude without a fugue, seemed so vast, as if the preparatory *sous-sus* were the complete work of art, tiny steps running forward, coming to a halt over and over again. And yet there was everything. There was the vision. Although I did not understand the legend concerning the cathedral of Ys, sunk as a punishment for the sins of an impious population, the music produced such a tissue of fugitive impressions, I remember nothing but a hearing that carried me far beyond what I had imagined music could be. In this respect, I followed my father. I watched Miss O'Hara's body move. Bursting with desire, I longed to play the piano as she did. And so deep was she in her work of transformation, she remained unaffected by the eyes of my father. Miss O'Hara played without a score, raising the eroding ghost of *La Cathédrale engloutie* from the waters of memory. Immersed in art, she looked beautiful. Her summer skirt fell in folds across the piano stool, an accidental happening that was itself a cataract of beauty. And as the music rest was bare, the light from the standard lamp changed the shiny lacquer surface into an enchanting obsidian mirror, reflecting her face and her arms. Her image shimmered.

Of course my father saw this and fell in love with her. He loved her because she was 'art'. How could he resist the incarnate divine in her act of creation? As he watched her, even though she had her back to him, I saw his entire expression change. He too had seen a vision, her glowing face reflected in the surface of the German pianoforte, all through the medium of hearing. And by this time, hearing for my father had entered its difficulties. Already afflicted with incipient deafness, at church he cupped a hand behind his ear in order to catch every word, every nuance of the minister's sermon. My mother often repeated what she said. We were exhorted to 'speak up'. 'Speak up for your father!' I felt frightened of what might come, not from my music teacher, but from my father. There was a warning in the air.

And then there was the song. Oh, the song! It was the young girl Solveig, longing for the springtime return of her demon lover, Peer Gynt, an utterance from the heart, the very personification of Northern night; a deep melancholy that changes into a wild, unconstrained gaiety. Miss O'Hara's high, agile voice was the perfect instrument for Grieg. My father thought that he had never heard anything quite so tender, so intense. He installed Grieg as one of the great composers of the nineteenth century. His music was easy to understand, especially as Colleen presented him, through Solveig's longing. And although he would like to have embraced Debussy, my father found obstacles to an impressionistic hearing. Where was the foundation for this new art? Where was the structure? There was none. There was no intellectual to grip, so to speak, no mind. It was all water; all feeling. Debussy had drowned the only form he knew, the classical sonata. But what my father could not understand was just how careful Debussy is with his emotions, how specific he is with feeling. For my father, sonata form invoked reverberations of the First Principle, a kind of *Quicunque vult* of music, an Athanasian accuracy. Once upon a time, he had both a vehicle of truth and a creed. Now he had neither. As his former hearing became dilute, he was left with nothing but an elaborating absence, a shapeless stain beneath the beautiful impression of Miss O'Hara. And it was her image that remained indelible.

I pause here to consider what I have written. In the service of memory and understanding, it occurs to me now that my father might have suffered from an affliction that the Danish existentialist, Søren Kierkegaard, called an *exacerbatio cerebri*, an 'excitement of the brain' on seeing Colleen O'Hara. I can even hear him quoting the philosopher, diagnosing this condition in someone else, but never in himself. Oh no. Having been provided with an intellect that resisted self-revelation, he was quite unable to observe his own psychic life. He was trained to diagnose others. But I have to say that with the appearance of Colleen O'Hara, his agitation and his tendency to drink increased. He became altogether more severe. It was not only the music and the manner in which Colleen O'Hara conducted herself; it was also because she was, as he liked to say, 'a devout Catholic', and 'the soul of music'. Spiritually, she was in possession of all that he had been forbidden to know from experience, all that was to him, heresy. She had seen the awful anathema that condemned her belief as error; 'a thing devoted' that had become to Calvinists 'an accursed thing'. And according to his preaching father, a man of 'the true word', if heresy was damnable, which it was, it was also vile. And as the damnable vileness of heresy appeared in the feminine form of music, someone so physically appealing, bound by his Hippocratic oath as much as to his own morality, my father suffered an impossible entrapment. Colleen O'Hara, the Irish girl, became untouchable, in every sense of the word, even as his patient.

It is the clarity of amethyst that brings me to these insights, it is the beauty of crystal *amethustos*, crystal sobriety. And I am bound to say that it was not until, in the presence of amethyst, I happened upon Stendhal's description of his own panic, his terrible fear on leaving the Sante Croce Church in Florence that I began to make sense of my father's behaviour. And I remembered my own experience beneath Giotto's ultramarine blue. In 1817, the year of his grand tour, the French novelist fell ill with a strange psychic disturbance, the anathema that comes with seeing. 'I felt a pulsating in my heart', he wrote. 'Life was draining out of me, while I walked fearing a fall.' If my father had read Stendhal's words, he too might have said the same, that the novelist had indeed suffered an attack of *exacerbatio cerebri* in the presence of art, seduced by the intensity of colour and beauty of form. But he probably would have added the rider that it surely was an inherent instability in the man, a sign of mental weakness that prevented the proper working of his faculties, an alien to 'normality'. And with respect to Debussy, my father judged the absence of audible architecture in his small prelude, a lack of academic discipline, as if he too were 'out of control', a composer suffering from an attack of *exacerbatio cerebri*, or what psychiatrists now more commonly call Stendhal's Syndrome. It was clear that he had been overwhelmed by the torrent of his own genius and that creativity had inherent dangers. Where might it lead, but to moral confusion?

In the weeks following her invitation to Belvedere, my father talked about Colleen O'Hara constantly, discussing her life, her gifts, her training 'overseas'. My mother grew weary of his words of praise. At the same time, encouraged by my mother, and in an unconscious attempt to balance the excess of feeling in him, he searched for 'faults' in her life. And he found such faults in her forthcoming marriage. 'Angus Drummond is such a queer fish,' he said. He was an ignoramus. He was beneath her. What did she see in him? I listened to my parents speculating on the nature of her engagement. Surely, a woman such as she who could have anyone she so desired must be marrying him 'on the rebound'. It could be the only explanation. Something had happened to her. What an odd alliance! It was also the greatest interest to both my father and my mother that Miss O'Hara appeared to be older than Angus Drummond. 'Oh, much older,' my mother said, with a little twist of her body. In which case, she would not be able to wear white on her wedding day. Nor would she be able to wear a veil. Why hadn't she married sooner, at a more conventional age? Of course, she was a Roman Catholic, my father said. It was religion. That surely had something to do with it.

But drawing upon her knowledge of literature, my mother thought that while she was in Italy she had been disappointed in love and had been forced to return to Tasmania. In her state of dejection, Angus Drummond had pursued her. For some unknown reason, she had to marry him. My father nodded. He discounted a necessity to marry. It was not a 'shot gun' wedding. Certainly not that. No, he thought there must be something else going on. My mother insisted it was 'the past', that something was hidden. And Angus was not a Catholic. My father could tell. He was nothing in particular, just a nominal Protestant. For this reason alone, she would be refused a Nuptial Mass and a Papal Blessing, an indulgence that all good Catholics desired. It was 'most odd'. As for Angus, he couldn't possibly be interested in art or religion, nor could he ever appreciate Colleen. He was 'hopelessly uneducated'. It was 'such a waste'.

Hearing this interpretation of things, I found my own reason for Colleen O'Hara's disappointment and her engagement to Mr Drummond. Perhaps it was really like this: while she was living in Milan, singing at La Scala, the beautiful Colleen O'Hara had fallen in love with an Italian. They had appeared together in Mozart's *Don Giovanni*, she playing Zerlina; he the Don. It was he, her deceiving lover, who had sung the ravishing words '*La ci darem la mano*'. She was the shy Zerlina just as Tamara Karsavina was the unhappy Giselle. It was an irresistible parallel. Such are the transformations of art. And then came the tragedy. After the conquest, her Italian lover forgot his promise and abandoned her for another. In love's fickle game, he treated her he treated as all his victims, as a means to an end. Did she suffer the madness of Giselle? I wondered. Was her desire to play the piano in the face of her husband's ignorance an act of revenge for abandonment by her former lover? Perhaps he too possessed a sinister power of seduction. Surely this was how her life came to imitate the art she served in such an exemplary manner, and the sole reason for her return to Tasmania, just as my father had said in the beginning.

This was her tragic story. Although I would never know the truth, many years later, and long after I had ceased to play the piano, a former pupil who was a contemporary, visited me in England and told me of Colleen O'Hara's fate. Her husband, Mr Drummond, was a persistent drinker. I was shocked. Why hadn't I seen it? He became the worst kind of alcoholic, she said, the very worst. And what was that? I asked. 'An absinthe drinker.' Absinthe? For a moment I was puzzled. I had to think about absinthe. Could it be true? He brewed his own concoction from wormwood, a plant imported from Europe by the first settlers. And under the influence of this bitter northern brew, bearing the beautiful name Artemisia, Queen of the Arcadian night, twin sister of Apollo, divine exemplar of the arts, the repulsive Mr Drummond used to hit her. The possessive shadow became a surly monster who rose to acts of extreme violence. Stinking of drink, lurching towards her, gripping her small waist with one hand, he raised her body from the floor, pressing her against the wall so that she could hardly breathe. He slapped her face sharply. He bruised her. True to the repeating pattern of violence, he hit her over and over again. Having raised her on high as a mere trophy, glittering but despicable, he then dropped her in an unhappy heap. Because of his cruelty and his addiction, and because of the fear she felt in his presence, deep shame forced her to hide the awful reality from her family. She left him on a number of occasions, but just as she always left him, she always returned. Her marriage was childless. In time, she became the shadow, he the substance. Music her only escape, she wept as she played the piano. She devoted her life to teaching at the Convent of the Sacred Heart, near the unspoken compassion of nuns, close to her art and her faith.

Whatever Colleen's earlier story happened to be, it was never revealed to me directly. It was merely the speculation of my parents. By the time I began music lessons, Colleen was married. She and her husband now rented a bed-sitting room above McCann's Furniture Store in Liverpool Street. My father disapproved of this, describing it as 'unsuitable'. But after I had climbed the concrete stairs and had entered her small apartment, everything seemed entirely right. It was peaceful and neat. The interior was furnished with her elegant walnut antiques, the curtains and armchairs in matching floral chintz, with a crisp, new finish. Upon the walls were scenic pictures of Italy, and a tinted print of the grand auditorium of La Scala, reminding me of Hobart's beautiful Theatre Royal. The apartment was light an airy. From the window of her kitchenette were views of city buildings with red roofs and high winding fire escapes. As the room contained all her worldly possessions, her marriage bed, covered in a smooth white candlewick bedspread, was in full view.

Colleen O'Hara was not ashamed to show me the first home of her wedded life. On a low table beside the bed was an icon of Our Lady of Perpetual Succour, in front of which was a little pile of beads. Seeing my curiosity, Colleen picked them up. She held them over my hand. They trickled into my open palm. Did I know what they were? I shook my head. She explained. It was all to do with the 'Holy Mother', the sorrows and joys of the Virgin Mary. How could I not love them now, with the little crucifix beneath? They were beautiful. They were hers. Recalling the crystal feeling of the rosary, I like to think they were made of amethyst, but I have no idea what they were. But the pride of her apartment was her upright pianoforte, an imposing Victorian instrument, also made of walnut. It bore the name John Broadwood and Sons Ltd, London. After all my father's talk of German pianos and his insistence on their superiority, I had to consider the virtues of an English instrument. And when she told me that Chopin himself had played a Broadwood in England, I almost believed her English Broadwood to be better than my father's German Lipp. She offered a living connection with Chopin, with music that inspired the visions of *Les Sylphides*. And it was this powerful connection that spoke to me. It was so easy to love her and to open myself to all her artistic insights. And whenever Miss O'Hara greeted me, she would wrap her arm around my shoulders, drawing me to her, smoothing my hair with her hand. She called me by her special pet name, the only pet name I was ever given. She called me 'Snowie'.

Although Fenella's piano lessons began well, after barely a year, she wanted to give them up. It was scarcely a conscious decision; listening to music uncovered a sense of wonder not accessible to her in any other way. She found herself drifting into a purely pictorial world, the surprising riches of its imagery stimulated by vibration, then expanded by dabs of paint. It was the music she heard at home that changed things. It altered her by nurturing her capacity to see. She moved more instinctively towards the visual arts, the practising of her skills reconciling her to a life not just for the moment but for ever. Because of my father's increasing deafness, it was impossible not to hear the music he played on his gramophone. Belvedere shook with the obsidian depth of Beethoven's pronouncements, his calling to the cosmos shattering the old and summoning the new. With the volume so high, the house itself assumed the primary function of an ear. On Saturday mornings, my father liked to rise early for the joy of listening to his new records alone and undisturbed. Our sleep first interrupted by the sonata *Appassionata* rising from the drawing room beneath, soon the mournful reveille of Tchaikovsky's Fifth Symphony invaded our dreams, hauling us reluctantly into the day.

After attending a concert given by the Tasmanian Symphony Orchestra, my father fell under the spell of the Greek Dimitri Mitropoulos and his interpretation of Russian romance. The image of the stern conductor on the record sleeve commanded his attention as much as the work itself, so nervous and violent, inspired him. Playing Tchaikovsky over and over again, my father began to live through a more sensitive and altered hearing. And as it was the only Russian symphony that he would know intimately, repeated performances brought the composer's 'resignation before Fate' to us all. It was a double hearing, the priestly conductor and his god Tchaikovsky created as one in 'the inscrutable decrees of Providence'; the first secret of the universe pouring into the portals of his ear as a healing elixir into a crystal chalice. Through the gifts of Mitropoulos the priest, my father loved what he heard. And as he loved, he fell in adoration before the altar of his beloved art. Most particularly, the powerful voice of the symphony called Fenella towards her own separate destiny. Instinctively she knew that she could please her father by playing the piano. She could not serve music. She had other work to do.

There were difficulties for Fenella. My father noticed her reluctance to practise. More than disappointment in her, he felt a shocking blow to his pride, as if she had insulted him. Biblical ideas of daughters who adorned were precious to him. And then Miss O'Hara rang one evening to make a kind enquiry after Fenella. Was she not well? She hadn't attended the last two lessons. For a moment, my father was dumbfounded, holding the receiver just away from his ear, listening to Miss O'Hara in utter disbelief. He would tackle her, he said. He would get to the root of the matter. Fenella's behaviour confounded him. He apologised and hung up. Summoning her from her bedroom, he told her that he knew what was happening and that she was guilty of deception. Her pretence at having attended lessons was an outrageous lie. What did she think she was doing? What was her *game*? She was deceitful and wilful. She had humiliated him before Miss O'Hara. She had disobeyed. It must be a conspiracy between sisters. Was it? Terror struck me. The inquisitor was at work, penetrating pretence to get to the truth. Was I a party to deception? Did I know? I did not. And it was true. We took our lessons separately. I had no idea.

That night, my parents talked about Fenella, her name spoken over and over again. My mother listened intently. Yes, yes. She could see his point. My father said Fenella should be made to play the piano, and that she should practise for an hour every day after school, under supervision. My father insisted. But Fenella found her own subtle form of disobedience. She went to the piano as she was told, my mother ushering her into the room, saying 'You will do it for your father.' The door closed. Fenella carried out her exercises in a perfunctory manner, avoiding anything like hard work. Playing the piano was easy, and it bored her. She peeled off her practice pieces, the left hand pumping away at the Alberti bass, the right hand bouncing the melody through its configurations until there was nothing left to play and no interest whatsoever in learning anything else. She would then crash the piano lid shut, and as she flew from the room she slammed the door, leaving the air wild and disturbed. She went to the garden to dream under the mulberry tree or upstairs to the balcony, to her painting and drawing. With great attention to detail, she copied faces and figures in famous masterpieces. She thought about the secret ingredients of light. Adoring colour, she pored over prints from the Louvre and the National Gallery. In her sketchbook was page after page of anatomical studies. She preferred the intricacies of anatomy to the monotony of music practice. And as Fenella's instinct was to protect her secrets, I don't think my father knew that she had such an accurate eye, a sure hand. The pictures piling up one upon the other under the bed he never saw. And if she hadn't fallen dangerously ill, learning to play the pianoforte under duress would have continued indefinitely.

It was my father's habit to attend to our ills. As my mother was always reminding us, he was a doctor. It never once occurred to me that we needed anyone else. Indeed, I felt sorry for those who did not have a doctor-father, as they would have to be treated by someone they did not know. My mother said we were extremely fortunate. My father administered our vaccinations, as well as prescribing anything we might need when we fell ill. The medicine cupboard under the stairs was the home pharmacy, containing pills for every fault of body and mind. My father also fulfilled the offices of a kind of polymedic, diagnosing the conditions of all creatures within his sphere of concern, becoming a vet when necessary. As my father thought it was a waste of money paying another for something he could do himself, he neutered our cat Tommy at home. By doing so he said he was giving us a valuable lesson in biology. I hated it. It was impossible not to cry for the pains and struggles of the cat. He protested with all his might, but his resistance was overcome. Knocked unconscious by two Nembutal capsules pushed down his throat, he lay sprawled on the kitchen table. My father extracted two tiny seed-like things from his hidden regions and displayed them on his hand. He poked them with the tip of the scalpel. They had a name, but I had no idea what they really were. What was going to happen to poor Tommy? Something vital had been taken from him. I cried for the cat and dreaded anything else that might have to be done to him. As for our vaccinations, my father kept a screw-top jar of needles in methylated spirits on the back shelf of the car. He thought it best to give injections when we were asleep, as we were less likely to resist. But the fright of being awakened in the middle of the night to a bright light, the chill of spirits upon skin, the pain in the buttock, these experiences were far worse than receiving the injection in a state of preparedness. My father was the doctor, the 'consultant'. It was essential to do things his way.

When Fenella complained of stomach pains one evening, my mother said she should go to bed and rest. She said that her father would 'look at her' when he came home. But it was late that night when my father examined her, and he was irritable. Yes, he heard what my mother had said. There was something wrong with Fenella. All right. He would look at her. It was probably nothing but a bad mood. He strode into the bedroom, my mother following close behind, his sudden entry bringing with it the familiar thin smell of whisky. Sitting on the edge of her bed, moving with that diagnostic authority to which there could be no resistance, he pulled up her nightie in order to examine her. He covered her stomach with his cold hands, his strong fingers pressing her warm flesh. He pushed here and there, while Fenella, closing her eyes, winced and bit her lip, suffering the pain without a sound. Just as he thought, he could feel nothing. It was 'imagination'. His manner was brusque. She was pretending. In his considered opinion, her age and the nature of her sex caused the pain. She was a girl. Yes, she was feverish, her abdomen was tender, but the origins of the problem lay elsewhere. My mother was puzzled. She asked him what he meant. My father was convinced that the condition was nothing exceptional. Fenella was now an adolescent. There was no prescription for this 'state' except routine and discipline. 'Oh?' My mother did not understand. My father continued. Aberrant physical events, especially abdominal disturbances for which there were no obvious reasons, were common in girls. Were they? He got up and went out of the room. As he descended the stairs, he said, in his summary, that he had already suspected some kind of peculiarity in her. He had been waiting for it. My mother hurried behind him, twitching his sleeve. What did he mean? Yes, there was no doubt about it, he said. It was a matter of 'sexual excitement'. My mother said 'Oh' again. Her voice fell. She had not thought of anything like that. What exactly did he mean, 'sexual excitement'? Could it be? Yes, yes. Possibly yes. She was beginning to understand. But she wasn't really sure. Nothing like that had ever happened to her when she was Fenella's age. She was a healthy country girl. She said so. My father made a gesture of dismissal. She must take it from him. He knew. My mother did not know what to do. She reflected on his words. She had doubted for a moment, but the words she heard entered her with a particular stress, an uncomfortable heaviness. Perhaps he was right. Surely he was right. He was her husband. She wanted to believe him.

The next day found Fenella much the same. It was worrying because although my father told Fenella she must get up for breakfast, the pain prevented her from doing so. Now the fever was worse. She was retching over the bed. My mother stood beside her. She watched Fenella tossing in the ruffled sheets, and as she watched, she began to feel the niggling unease that she had felt when Edgar was a baby. The pain in her heart had never gone away. But the feeling was not quite the same, because, as her husband so often said, Fenella was a girl. She must remember that. She must never forget it. At the same time, she was forced to admit to herself that she was not happy. Because of the fever and the dry retching, she knew there must be something wrong with Fenella. But what? It was Saturday morning. Ought she to call another doctor, one of his colleagues? She dare not. Merton would be furious. What should she do? She bent over Fenella and placed her cool hand on her hot forehead. She must wait for her husband to return. She hoped he would come soon. She hoped he was not drinking at the Tasmanian Club. She just hoped. She didn't know, but while she waited, she thought she would put a wet towel on her forehead to help lower her temperature. It was all she could do. And when at last my father did come home, unsteady on his feet, my mother insisted he go immediately to see Fenella. This time, it was different. She had his attention from the moment he entered the house. He examined her again. Yes, he had to admit that Fenella was ill. He said he would take her to hospital. In his opinion, she was suffering from acute appendicitis. He would ring one of his colleagues. She would need surgery immediately.

I have to say that I envied Fenella her trip to Calvary Hospital, the dramatic car journey, wrapped in blankets. My father's colleague, Mr Alec Fry, who performed the operation, said her condition was very serious, that the appendix was much more than inflamed. She had developed peritonitis. Mr Fry exercised a certain restraint in questioning his senior colleague, nevertheless, in handing over Fenella to his care, my father was obliged to accept his findings. It was true. Fenella was suffering from shock. She would take a long time to recover. And since my father had identified the troubling affliction of 'sexual excitement' in the midst of peritonitis, since something fearful and dreadful had been summoned, we were bound to acknowledge the presence of an uncertainty, a haunting fear of the future. What could this possibly mean? It seemed that the inoperable and untreatable condition of being female was far, far worse.

Such a dark pronouncement was a warning to us both. There were awful things to come. And they would come, because we were girls. My father pointed to us, his daughters, as if we were intent upon deceiving him. Were we true or were we false? Most particularly, as Fenella was the elder daughter, in whom so much was invested, whatever befell her might become the augury of my own fate. My mother told us not to make our father unhappy. To that end, it was imperative to please him, to be faithful to him. I hoped to curb fatal tendencies by staying close to him and by believing in him, just as my mother did. My first response was to immerse myself in music. In this manner I would please my father, by loving everything he loved. Although the desire had already occurred to me, it came afresh and with particular force one Sunday, sitting next to him at church. Lowering his head towards me, he asked what the minister was saying. I repeated the minister's words directly into his ear, speaking in whispered speech, my hand cupped over my mouth. I was shaken. If he could not hear words preached from the pulpit, what would it be like not to hear the voice of Tchaikovsky? Surely a world of distorted hearing, of no hearing at all, would be torture. What could I do to help him? I must play the piano. I must play, not as his mother did, but as Miss O'Hara did. She was 'the soul of music'. By imitating her, I would assure my father's good hearing. I believed that the answer to his deafness and his drinking lay in the power of music to heal every affliction. And there was something even deeper. Hidden within Miss O'Hara's musical gifts were the secret operations of religion and unseen rituals. And although my father said the teaching of Rome was a Jesuitical conspiracy, and that the Papacy was to be deplored, I knew that he considered Miss O'Hara's Catholic piety exceptional, a state of grace that came in spite of inherent error. To my way of thinking, and contrary to my father's rigid religious convictions, there was a beauty, a true aesthetic that saved her. She was a paragon. She was an even greater exception than his mother. Miss O'Hara had overcome the otherwise fatal handicap of Catholicism. It was all to do with how she lived her life of art according to the highest faculties of hearing.

After recovering from her operation, Fenella's music lessons ceased. Nothing more was said. She had made her exit. The yielding presence of Colleen O'Hara playing *La Cathédrale engloutie* was still in the drawing room, her watery image impossible to dismiss. My father paced the room drinking, watching and listening as I practised a Mozart minuet. He saw me as Colleen O'Hara, the Catholic exemplar of the arts. He saw her sitting there at his German Lipp, a picture of music. His response was to enshrine the musical soul of my teacher within his own. In the strict analysis of his gaze, listening intently as I repeated a difficult phrase, I fell short of the ideal and made mistakes. Discord and the ruination of form caused panic in me. I would surely fail. But one day, while my father stood beside me, it occurred to him that the time had come to commission my portrait. Yes, he said, interrupting me, he liked to see a daughter sitting at the piano. I made a pretty picture. He would find another artist. And without there being any perceptible bridge from one event to the next, my father sent me off to have my portrait painted by Miss Florence Rodway. My father had seen an exhibition of her work at the Tasmanian Museum and Art Gallery. His conversion to her clear way of seeing was instant.

Among Tasmania's artists, Florence Rodway was admired for her delicate pastel technique. She was renowned for her portraits of a number of Australia's most famous illuminati. More remarkably, the artist was a woman, an exceptional woman whose natural modesty hid her away. She shunned celebrity. My father's voice leapt with excitement when he told my mother about his discovery. In his search for art, her description harmonised with the archetypal feminine, the model that kept cropping up in his mind, correcting, with the exception of Miss O'Hara and nuns, the inadequate reality that he believed surrounded him on all sides. From his enquiries at the Museum and Art Gallery, he learnt that she had painted a portrait of Australia's greatest singer, Dame Nellie Melba. Apart from liking the manner of her painting, an academic discipline that gave way to a sense of freedom in a unique combination of pastels and watercolours, this fact alone was the strongest recommendation to my father.

Miss Rodway's works of art were a continual succession of 'reformed' seeing, as if, for her own salvation as much as for the salvation of the seer, she employed the muted palette of Protestant theology. In her clarified eye, she secured the supremacy of hierarchical order. It was the delineation in her perception and her elevated sense of containment that satisfied him. Her gaze being so steady, her brush so very sure, she cast nothing out of the picture. My father saw her work as an exalted form of redemption in which there could be no uncomfortable residue, no suggestion of darkness. In his opinion, so much art accelerated ruin. As for me, I felt excited at the prospect of having my portrait painted. I was catching up with Fenella, entering a sphere of parental regard. Moreover, with the assistance of the secret ingredient of favouritism, I might even secure the desired place of honour before my father, superseding my younger brother. Although I knew I could not compete with my sister, for there was something that my father saw in her that he did not see in me, I knew his scrutiny was shifting. My mother told Fenella repeatedly that she was a 'disappointment', by which I understood that he now found fault with her painting as well as feeling affronted by her refusal to play the piano. I dared to hope that my father looked less critically at me. And because I was about to be captured by art, I believed at long last that I was ascending his ladder of perfection.

This brief but significant episode concerning the portrait and Miss Rodway brings me directly to the healing of malachite: an eye-catching bright-green mineral susceptible to a high polish. Under the auspices of crystals, I observe sensual impressions arrive one after another, breaking in frothy green waves upon a shore. The distinctive undulating layers and vortices of this ornamental stone are known to geologists as 'wheal leisure' or to crystal healers as 'the beauty of wounds'. Malachite commonly occurs in the presence of copper and water. It encourages the freedom of emotional release, of weeping. Atmospheric agents induce swirling green impressions so entrancing to the eye that one could be forgiven for believing malachite to have emerged from the absence of life in an Archaean age. But its history and its mythology belong to nearer antiquity. Holding a swelling lump of malachite in one hand, a branch of bay in the other, the auspex speaks. As a rhapsodist in a Greek tragedy, she moves centre stage. Awaiting the moment of insight, the crystal telling, she closes her eyes. Upon a long exhalation, in middle-pitched *Sprechgesang*, she declaims, 'Listen to the viridian voice!' I listen. The cadence of her repeating message, 'Come to me, come to me', falls in rhythmic dactyls. What does the viridian voice say? What is it to feel copper greening over aeons in subterranean seas? Indeed, in the episodic nature of my narrative, the crystal speaker is becoming even more refined and rhapsodic. The forces of art and nature are at work, intruding into the psyche as a crystal druse intrudes into cavities in the earth's mantle. And although Pliny first observed the soft origins of the mineral naming it malachite, 'mallow-like', beneath all linguistic layers, the voice of this stone is Russian. From vast mines in the Urals, the tsars obtained blocks of raw malachite weighing more than twenty tons. Bare sheets of polished malachite dressed the length and breadth of palace walls, fulfilling the function of pictures, turning every space into a temple to the colour green. Such was Slavic seeing. Drawn to the beauty of the stone, Russian princesses cloaked their throats in polished beads. Entering the body at that most sensitive location, the energy of malachite penetrated the atria of the heart, pushing healing through layers of tissue. And in the service of medieval art, malachite was crushed and washed, the extracted pigment mixed with linseed oil yielding varying shades of mineral green. The therapeutic nature of malachite imitates patterns of change in numberless ages of geological formation. Green turns repeatedly in the beauty of circles, meeting at the beginning. It flows.

At this point, I find myself revisiting my original place of entry, earthed to the colour that began my work with crystals. It is the green circle with its 'peacock's eye', the punctuation mark of malachite that heals wounds and protects the wearer from unregenerate energy. I have heard the crystal practitioner of the twenty-first century refer to malachite as 'poky'. How can something mallow-soft, tending to liquid, 'poke'? I ask. 'It is the viridian finger,' she says. The life force penetrates. And just as water intrudes through every opening, so does malachite, assisted by copper and its erecting strength. Acting with the determination of a vector, it possesses both direction and magnitude; it penetrates the soft foramen and floods cavities, the climax of its ritual being ecstasy. Malachite dyes all the senses with the heat of its pigment, alleviating pain. And in my experience of crystals, malachite is wholly present in the romantic music of Tchaikovsky. It is the healing of pure malachite that my father heard in his passionate Fifth Symphony; the composer prostrate before the operations of fate, submitting to the viridian voice of the auspex.

On the first day of my sitting, my mother chose the clothes she wanted me to wear, mindful of how she wished the artist to see me. I was to look neat and unostentatious. My father decided that I should wear my hair loose instead of plaited, with a red ribbon tied in a bow sitting on the top of my head. I objected to the nylon ribbon because when it was tied, it flopped over to one side. But my mother insisted. I was to dress exactly as I was told in my red jumper, my blue tartan skirt, with the obligatory red hair ribbon tied in its floppy bow. In pictures I loved, Russian ballerinas wore earrings and necklaces. And there was the icon of Truganini and her gleaming shells. Even the tiniest jewels enhanced seeing, lifting the picture in the mirror mind of the viewer. Plucking up courage, I asked my mother. Couldn't I please borrow her pearl necklace, just for my portrait? Oh please? My mother's reply was immediate. Certainly not, she said. I was far too young for jewellery. I was a girl, not a grown woman. The pearl necklace was hers. My mother was irritable with me because once more, she was required to give way to her husband's wishes. I knew from her manner that she did not want me to have my portrait painted. I was a daughter in the eye of her husband, to the exclusion of herself and sons. At the first sign of excitement in her husband's voice, talking about the portrait, she felt an unpleasant sensation, a wound opening in the wall of her abdomen, a seeping thing. This strange sickness turned from confusion to envy. Yes, her daughters were attractive young girls and would soon grow into attractive young women. But her husband had already warned of something in Fenella.

And now there was this. Perhaps it was all because of Miss O'Hara. She didn't know. Girls were difficult. Her husband said so. She tried to please her husband and to follow his instructions, but his attention was often elsewhere, preoccupied with work, drinking with colleagues, obsessed with ideas. He never mentioned a portrait of her. Was she not attractive to him? She remembered how he had neglected her when Fenella's portrait was painted. This neglect of her womanly feelings made her pine for the lost joys of their union, the wonderful time before the war. How she regretted the interruption to her marriage, the absence of 'affection'. He no longer wanted her in that way. She didn't know why, but he had become overly strict and overly religious, correcting her for wearing too much lipstick and powder. He brought her into line. He told her to wipe the 'war paint' off her face. She had felt such shame sitting before the mirror dabbing her mouth with cotton wool, weeping to herself. But why should she feel shame? And what was 'too much lipstick and powder' in this undisclosed war? She hid her gold lipstick with its cinnabar tongue in the bottom drawer of her dressing table. But surely she was a woman, not a child. Her husband was oblivious to makeup on other women when there was something else to praise. My mother was thinking of Miss O'Hara and her scented elegance. Miss O'Hara was from a world that had nothing to do with her, and for Miss O'Hara, everything was different. Merton kept reminding her that she was a Roman Catholic. Had Catholicism and music cast a spell over him? What was all this spending on art? Here he was again insisting on portraits of daughters. My mother decided, in that moment when her insecurities felt acute, when the pain seared her, that her husband was absurd in his pursuits. She would blame him for hurting her, for neglecting her needs. She did not understand him. She did not. But in her heart of hearts, she really didn't know what to think.

In the wake of my mother's complaints and in the presence of malachite, it is not possible to describe the portrait painted by Florence Rodway, except by using words of allusion. The picture retains an intrinsic meaning. The intinction of green pigment becomes knowledge that can only be experienced through seeing, just as crystals retain their knowledge through feeling. I choose the word 'through' with the best linguistic intentions. In portraiture, seeing through, feeling through and acting through operate as rituals working within the desire of the artist. The process begins and ends with the eye. The artist creates a 'sight' worthy of contemplation, an icon. Acting upon this seeing through, in harmony with the will of the intellect, produces the *objet d' art*, 'a thing of beauty'. As portraiture is an art in pursuit of a telling image, an inherent truth, I cannot be sure that there is not, at the same time, an immense and overwhelming absence at work. Absence applies to the work in question painted by Miss Rodway. The portrait was as most of her portraits, elusive. Something was not there. My father liked what he saw, his daughter sitting at the mere suggestion of a piano with a red bow on her head. He liked the merging of chalk and water, the hands disappearing at the edge of the picture in a scribbled smudge. He liked the background, the screen marked with swirls in blue and green, suggesting the decorative strokes of the ornamental arabesque. And I looked away from the ghostly piano, through space limited by the frame, out into the uncharted distance.

But what was the preoccupation of my seeing during the period that Miss Rodway was intent upon seeing me? I did not know how to participate, except that I was to imitate art by immersing myself in images that I already knew. I was to participate by wandering through my feelings until I reached the highest point. What that point was I was unable to grasp, as it kept moving out of reach. The finished product that Miss Rodway titled 'Decorative Portrait' for an exhibition of her work, was merely the impression of the impression I made upon the artist, the subtle absence that offered my father an affecting and illusory immediacy. I did not think I was really there in the picture at all.

And I can hardly recall the studio. All I remember of the sittings was the scratchy sound of pastel on paper, the smell of paint and her voice commanding me to 'sit up straight'. But what pleased me immensely and made me think that this seemingly fictitious image and its substitute name was a true picture of myself, but in an ethereal location, was the transformation effected by the eye of the artist. The red bow on my head, though blurred and chalky, instead of being thin and floppy, was fulsome and upright. From nylon red, it changed to a powdery vermilion. I liked it that way because it was a correction of my unhappy feelings at the time. And instead of seeing dense red in my jumper, Miss Rodway saw the pale green that appears in the last washing of malachite. Better still, there was the suggestion of graduated green beads around my neck, an impression that had not been there at all. Whereas my mother would deny their existence, not only did Miss Rodway see green beads, she depicted them. She told their story in the metathesis of colour, an alteration that occurred through-and-through the nuances of observation. She recognised my ardent wishes. She dyed me in malachite just I dyed myself in imaginings. More than anything else about the portrait, I believed that the transformation in her seeing transformed the seeing of myself. I felt better. Even the absence of my name did not disappoint me. To be called 'decorative' was the very best I could desire, the charm that would henceforth protect me from fear. Was I not now 'decorative' and 'art' to my father?

It is certainly true that my father became overly strict and overly religious, but the ecstatic climax to his fervour did not occur until after Fenella's fall from grace, when everything decadent was attributed to her. In the years before his diagnostic eye had seized her, my father encouraged Fenella's experimentation with art. It gave him pleasure to see her painting so freely, and to observe her read with astonishing speed. He felt proud of her. But as soon as her 'true nature' emerged and distorted what my father believed to be her 'proper development', he became prey to the assaults of a puritanical conscience that he himself had so sorely neglected. Desperate to subdue such disturbances, his prompting emerged as judgements, not upon himself, but upon the weakness of the flesh which flourished in women. The time for a religious reformation had arrived, for the destruction of monasteries and the burning of errors. In part recognition of the more disagreeable restrictions of his boyhood, he had not imposed upon his offspring the rigid training that he had received as son of the manse. Although we attended church every Sunday, he did not ask us to recite chapters of the Bible. In his busy life, it was not possible to follow the example of his parents and begin each day with scripture readings at the breakfast table. Besides, he was a man of the world, and although he had the greatest respect for his parents, he believed he was in the vanguard of the modern age, and in the supremacy of the Protestant faith was the intincture of reason. If he pointed the way, we would follow. He approved of the reinforcement of this teaching with physical punishment, because correction was enshrined in the Bible.

As a child, he too had been punished. He had been corrected for swearing. Without the slightest understanding of what he was saying, his mother heard him utter the disgraceful profanity, 'Jesus bloody Christ'. He liked 'bloody' because of its colour. It was easy to insert the slippery red word garnered from school between two rigid religious ones. The tongue-touch excited him. His astounded mother told his father. His father left his study immediately to thrash him with a leather strap. Confined to his room for three days, Merton was henceforth forbidden all 'corrupting' friendships. Because no one in the irreligious world could be trusted, he had no friends at all, except for his older sisters and his cats. And as corporal punishment came to be regarded as essential to the formation of a puritan, the greater danger, that of losing oneself altogether, came to pass in complete silence, as if it were nothing whatsoever. If he had suffered an accident and lost a limb, it would have been noticed. Throughout his life, my father was scarcely aware of the seriousness of his own situation, the limitation that had been forced upon him and that he in turn used against his own children. The severity of this early affliction prevented him from questioning the judgement of his parents. They were right.

The efficacy of punishment his conviction, it was a modern paterfamilias who permitted our freedom of expression, our painting and writing. This was an easy state of affairs, but only under the beneficent reign of the Belvedere Apollo when there were no storms within the sanctuary. By my father's example alone, we were encouraged to believe that there was something special about the arts. As Belvedere filled with books, authors and artists held sway over religious reformers. Only the highest intellects wrote books, only the best talent painted pictures. Fenella had certainly been singled out as belonging to the elite in their internal literary and artistic world. The advent of Miss O'Hara, and Tchaikovsky began the change. First there was the ecstasy, then there was despair. And even in the despair, there was an imaginative agitation, an *exacerbatio cerebri* that leapt from the troubled heart of my father.

Although as I have already said, my father was not in the habit of reading the Bible to us, after Fenella had been found guilty, formal readings of the King James Bible were instituted in the limbo hours of Sunday afternoons, when music practice was over and time died. And in the reading of the gospels, my father's voice rasping upon the ear, there were occasions when emotion so overcame the very reasonableness of the word that he collapsed over the Bible, sobbing uncontrollably while the thin white pages disintegrated under the weight of his passion. Such was the Raising of Lazarus one winter afternoon in the drawing room with the fire crackling. The episode in St John being particularly long, wishing myself anywhere else but trapped in language that made me tremble, I heard nothing of the story until my father reached the passage, 'They said unto him, Lord, come and see.' At that moment, entering the closet of the most ancient and grave divine, he spoke in the altered tone that is the response to extrasensory hearing. It was an alteration I feared. With an emphasis that caused all eyes to shift to him, raising his head in ecstasy he reiterated, 'Lord, come and see.' Then he fell silent. It was the word 'see' that was so powerful. I looked at my mother sitting anxiously beside him. I looked at my father in the silence he had summoned. After a pause that seemed interminable, he read the next verse, famous for its brevity. In a quavering voice he said, 'Jesus wept.' My father's head went down upon his lap, strands of dark hair falling forward, neck and shoulders quivering in rigors of grief. Fixed in repeated gasps, and so violent his movements, I thought he would surely suffocate. Over and over again, he said 'Jesus wept, Jesus wept,' until in his heaving paroxysms, my mother stretched out her hand and touched him.

This puzzling episode opened yet another door into the tormented spiritual life of my father. After the golden sun of Apollo had been banished, my father chose to confide in me the secrets of his Christian clairvoyance, secrets I had the greatest difficulty in recognising, except that the power emanating from the telling kept me in thrall, making the event unforgettable. He told me that he had 'seen'. His manner was confidential. I took this to mean that his seeing was extraordinary and that it had taken place in an extraordinary location. But what had he seen? I did not think that there had been an extraordinary appearance in St John's Presbyterian Church, or for that matter, in any Protestant church. Everything happening around the pulpit being dependent upon hearing, there was nothing beyond the ritual weight of language. But my father had dared to see this sacred something in a forbidden place, a Roman Catholic Church. It was England. Was this a confession, something that he could not tell my mother? I believed it was. Although I listened, my lack of experience could not summon the image from the language he used. With all the emotion and passion of his 'Jesus wept,' my father confided in me that he had seen 'the Major Elevation of the Host'. He had stood alone in the narthex, a place reserved for public penitents and catechumens, waiting to behold. And instead of leaving before the beginning of the Mass of the Faithful, he had remained there, his attention focused upon the High Altar. He had 'seen' a robed priest, 'embroidered with phylacteries'. His arms raised, the priest held something white above his head. Ah, that was it. My father had seen the heretical act of Transubstantiation. Language described the mystery, incomprehensible language. It was Miss O'Hara's secret, the divine anathema. It was the Great Silence. Standing in front of the fireplace, his back to the burnished *fleur-de-lys*, my father raised his arms. 'It was like this,' he said, lifting up his eyes, his face in momentary transfiguration. 'The Oblation', he said. 'The Victim. The

Spotless Lamb.' And then he fell upon his knees and clasped his head. 'Oh, awful,' he said. '*Awful.*'

A hot tremor passed through me. Although I could see Jesus weeping just like my father, the words that evoked the sacred thing, the cause of his collapse on the floor, brought nothing to mind. The space above his head was empty. My father said 'a host' had been 'elevated'. He said it was like 'this'. And it was 'awful'. It was silent. But what was so silent that could only be seen? What was so holy that could not be heard? There was nothing 'major' before me, nothing held high. I thought it might have had something to do with the Raising of Lazarus. Christ unravelled the layers of the grave; he unveiled the dead to reveal the living. This revelation was only for those who wished to see. Was there the same lifting in a Catholic Church? As I could not even imagine the ritual of the mass, I thought this 'major elevation' that had so transfixed my father must have more than one manifestation. Perhaps it appeared everywhere. Perhaps it penetrated everything. Had I not seen it too? Ah yes, it was surely height that my father saw; it was silent height that he had adored. It was the dance that Fenella and I loved, the dance of Truganini's shells that brought forth feminine beauty in the language of 'the mere girl'. Lifting was the ritual display that delighted the eye and soothed the ear, tearing away the veil of darkness. It was the 'major elevation' of dancing Giselle, her tiny wings in the middle of her back. Ah yes, now I could see the shafts of the goddess Artemis. It was this that he thought was 'awful'. And was not 'the host' the ghostly vision of the virgin daughter, the spotless lamb in her airy *augoeides*, travelling through the moonlit night for all to see?

It was difficult for my mother to accept my father's fixation on Catholic matters, his impassioned preaching against it and then his spurious pursuit of it through my education. She didn't want me to attend the Convent of the Sacred Heart and to be influenced by nuns. It was enough that Miss O'Hara taught me the piano. Although my mother had no reason to distrust the morality of her good husband, she was more than a bit suspicious of the Catholic religion, especially when Catholicism was as gifted as Colleen O'Hara. Rome was full of secrets, and her Protestant sensibilities rose up in revolt against the so-called 'Mother Church'. Had not her Scottish ancestors died for the Protestant Reformation? As for my Catholic education, my mother was worried about having to explain such a departure to the Rev. Nithsdale, the minister at St John's. But my father was insistent. He knew what he was doing. And in religious matters as in all else, my mother could do nothing but accept. I did not tell my mother about my father and the Major Elevation of the Host, anymore than she was able to offer an explanation to us, her children, as to our father's collapse over the Bible. My relationship with her did not lend itself to telling her anything. I was obliged to listen, just as Fenella was obliged to listen. But Fenella's listening had entered a deeper, more demanding level. She was forced to hear things that I never did, and far worse than visionary disclosures. And in the shame that her behaviour was supposed to have brought upon the whole family, listening and hearing changed. We were always on our guard, watching first our father, then ourselves. Our brothers were instructed to watch us, the sisters, and more importantly, to 'watch out' for us, as we had become 'dangerous'.

It was just before my sister's fall that my mother, in her morning telling, related a significant story from the golden days of newly wedded life. She spoke through her mirror image, before the altar of the dressing table. One night in the first flowering of their union, when she, the bride, was sleeping peacefully beside her husband, she was awakened by his voice. She opened her eyes. There he was sitting bolt upright beside her. He shouted, 'I do not believe in the resurrection of the dead!' She could hardly take in the meaning of his words. It was such a shock. She did not understand. Here was her husband, the son of a minister and a Calvinist from the cradle, denying the fundamental truth of the Christian faith, and in such an unexpected place, their matrimonial bed. Well, as she was a young bride and 'a mere girl', she didn't know what to do. She had never questioned the resurrection. Never. Why should he, of all people, sit up in the middle of the night and shout out loud 'I do not believe'? Was it a bad dream? In the wake of aroused feelings, my mother paused. Strengthening herself for the next sentence, she picked up her bottle of Milk of Roses. Unscrewing the top, holding it for a moment under her nose, she sniffed quickly. She then closed her eyes for the terrible utterance. My mother was ashamed to say that her bridegroom followed his denial of the resurrection by uttering the most shocking blasphemy. She couldn't repeat what he said, not to anyone. What she heard was so terrible she could hardly repeat it to herself. More than an offence to her, it was an offence to her father. He had never said anything like that. Nothing profane passed his lips. The comparison troubled her. She reminded herself that she was so young and unworldly then; so young. Hearing such words from her husband and not knowing what to do, my mother did nothing. She waited. And just as suddenly as he had sat upright, he flung himself back on the bed. For a while, she watched him sleeping, the episode, like some strange epileptic fit, finished. Thank God it was finished. Of course, she never told him. She couldn't bring herself to mention it.

Her memory now immersed in pretty things, my mother didn't say anymore. She patted her face lightly with her fingertips, observing her reflected emotions, enjoying her image. Then pressing a hand upon her breast and tilting her head to one side, she studied herself in the long cheval mirror. She thought she would put her hair up today. And she would wear a little makeup, just a touch. We watched her. She did not have to tell us what our father had cried out in the night when she was a bride. We knew. We had heard it ourselves, many times. Over and over again, we heard his profanities, his secret agitation, his *exacerbatio cerebri*, exploding under the influence of alcohol or some other stupefaction of the senses, rendering him unapproachable. And although I never heard my father denying the resurrection of the dead, when he was drinking in the drawing room all alone, or taking a shower, in the steam and heat of the inexplicable fearful, some devilish memory, bursting into the weird glossolalia of the inebriate, he would cry out 'Jesus bloody Christ!' 'Jesus bloody wept!'

Part III

The Inextinguishable Myth

Although our separation had already begun, for a few short weeks in late summer, Fenella and I came together to write and to paint. In a sudden gift of freedom, she moved her easel and all her painting paraphernalia to the upstairs balcony. Belvedere's rear balcony was an ideal space for painting, its elevation above the ridged roofs below being adjacent to the steep pitch of the newer structure, from which it jutted. Across the narrow strip of land down at the rear, with my mother's sagging clothesline, was the wild garden belonging to our next door neighbours, the three maiden sisters known as the Misses White. As we had never met or even glimpsed the Misses White, they seemed more legendary than real, while their garden, full of ornamental trees and bird song, remained as they did, untouched by human hand. Through the rotting wooden fence that separated their pristine enclosure from our own, a lean fig protruded, offering its hard and bitter fruit. But the taste of a softer and sweeter seeing was always from above. Looking down into their tangled paradise, we observed all the moodily beautiful modulations of southern seasons. We loved the upstairs balcony for many reasons, not least for a perspective that differed from the falling slopes of the front.

In the great renovations, the balcony which I describe as L shaped, had been partitioned creating a small room with high glass panes. A door in the partition opened upon a larger area, made entirely of wood and partly exposed to the elements. My mother strung another clothesline diagonally from one corner to the other for winter use. Here Fenella and I folded the freshly laundered linen, grasping the ends, stepping back along the length of the balcony, pulling the sheets until the edges were even. Behind the partition, in the glazed room with Venetian blinds, there was a divan bed and a small table for the use of visitors. My father hung a detail of Botticelli's *Birth of Venus* on the partition wall. Although we always referred to the picture as 'Venus coming out of a shell', her naked image had been reduced to a maidenly gaze. There was only this to see, roped hair lifted by the wind and sheared by the frame. After Our Lady of Perpetual Succour, I found the blonde goddess a more appealing icon. In the very beauty of her origins, airy elements deemed her worthy of their attendance. We studied the larger picture, along with many others, in our father's book, *The Colour Library of European Art*. Fenella and I leafed through the images, in long and short pauses, lingering over some, skipping over others. Some were beautiful and some were ugly. All were puzzling. The painting that was to be avoided and never ever seen, was Goya's masterpiece of horror, *The 3rd. May 1808*: The Execution of the Defenders of Madrid. I hated it. As the date happened to be my birthday, I thought Goya's depiction of violent death particularly ominous. Did the scene hold a message for me? The victim's arms flung above his head, his popping eyes and muted scream, the sickly yellow glow radiating from his body brought a horrible reality. Over and over again the rifles fired. Over and over again the bodies fell. I hated the picture and its pool of crimson blood so much I covered my eyes and turned away whenever we came to it.

But the balcony was not for such fears. It was essentially undesignated space, an area that had little to do with the life of our parents or our brothers. Eventually, the partitioned section was to become my bedroom. For the time being, it was a place Fenella and I enjoyed, providing an escape, a haven away from the main part of the house. And although we were never free to do as we pleased, the relatively unguarded life of the balcony suggested the same wholly innocent abandonment as the front garden. Sitting side by side on the divan, we read to each other; we composed verses, stories and amusing monologues. Without asking permission, we seized an old typewriter, its sticky fingers wielding our words, flinging them letter by letter onto Fenella's art paper. And during that special time of exploration, I began *Black Agatha*, the story of a dark woman. She flew in rhyming couplets for a while and then just as airily, she dropped to earth and disappeared, her power exhausted. A few teachers came under our scrutiny, a few idiosyncratic accents were imitated, particularly if they happened to be English, but apart from mild parodies and satirical verses, no reputations died and no scurrilous pamphlets were written. Our observations were innocuous, laughable. There was no conscious desire to rebel. If our parents had silenced us or if we had been disturbed by their midnight quarrels, such happenings were never discussed and never committed to paper. The balcony, in its fairness, resolved all uncomfortable feelings. Downstairs, there was the confinement of music practice and the perpetual watchfulness of uncertainty. Reaching out to the freedom of the seasons, we discovered an ideal space for stimulating risks that adhere to innate creativity. And succumbing to the power of instant print and mischief one afternoon Fenella sat down and typed an imitative funeral notice, following the format that she had seen in *The Mercury*. Commanding words to appear upon the page, she invited 'all friends' to 'respectfully attend' a service at St John's Presbyterian Church on such and such a date. Laughing, she ran downstairs to the drawing room and propped up her mock product on the mantle piece in front of the French carriage clock, her notice of the next to die. It looked so neat, so authentic sitting there, impishly announcing her demise.

Fenella was the adept. With her flair for recitation, her speech delighted me. Inspired by literature, by people and events in our narrow lives, we leant against the invisible perimeter and allowed it to give way, just a little. Without any acquired understanding of what we were seeing, we familiarised ourselves with the great sights of European history, religion and myth. We read colour and chiaroscuro in all its variant forms. Every sensation was to be found between the black covers of my father's art book, heavy with its burden of truth and beauty. Fenella turned to the Impressionists. Studying Manet's *Le Déjeuner sur l'herbe*, she thought about how she might copy it. She liked the dishevelled picnic on the grass, the enclosure of soft-leafed trees and the formality of dressed men, the arresting nudity of the woman sitting seemingly unconcerned in the midst of visual mystery. She saw herself, not as the naked woman in the foreground whose clothes littered the grass next to the spilled picnic, she saw herself more truthfully as the woman beyond, at the very peak of seeing. The distant image was the vision, while the outward gaze of nudity became the painterly trick to entice the viewer to enter the scene. Both images were beautiful, and in the presence of men, both were troubling. What was the truth of this seeing? The lesser gesture of a woman stepping from a woodland bath in white drapes was the mystical image that seduced the eye. Once more it was water and the story of Venus, her emergence from the sea, a woman in her origins. It was the shell and Truganini, the black Aphrodite of Aboriginality, the unimaginable image whose face cried out to be covered for the shame of what had been done to her. Was not Truganini born from the ocean, carried on a shell, driven to her southern shore in the might of the Roaring Forties? Was she not naked and raised to agony in a world of dressed men? However fantastic and inapplicable the idea, we believed it. Fenella was thinking deeply. She stared at the picture, waiting to paint *Le Déjeuner*. In it she saw incarnate form. And from gazing at *Le Déjeuner*, she inclined to the colour green, the pleasure-garden of antiquity. Raising her head from the page, she listened attentively to the voice of the auspex, the air around her a viridian vibrato.

At the easel, Fenella practised her skills. Moving from one medium to another, she took up chalk, charcoal, pastels, pencils and watercolours. Now she painted in oils, recreating earthy dyes upon the matrix of her palette, mixing and squeezing, releasing their secret recipes. In chromatic *études*, she laid out the chemistry of pigment upon white canvas. In nature's fantasy palace there are countless interconnecting rooms. She liked to recite the names of these inner rooms, crimson lake, cerulean blue, emerald green, and alizarin as loose lines of poetry. Sight and sound carrying her forward along the path strewn with colour, she visited each sanctuary one by one, absorbing the sovereignty of light. She loved alizarin. Before painting *Le Déjeuner*, she painted herself as a woman in a dress the colour of freshly pressed pomegranate, her body lifting from an arid and ashen landscape, an alizarin phoenix amid leafless, spear-like trees. To this day, I remember the alizarin woman covered in crimson. Her eyes were closed. Unlike Manet's naked woman embraced by green, she turned her gaze inwards. She fell backwards, into the picture.

Fenella worked rapidly. Paintings finished and unfinished pealed from her easel as dry bark exfoliates in the summer sun. Her colours carpeted the wooden floor. And during that amazing time when books arrived in periodic waves, when the supremacy of literature was reinforced with every parcel from England, I read to her. In a tangled paradise where all senses are interdependent, the words of Coleridge brought more impressions to mind. From 'caverns measureless to man', the fountain of the poet's opium-induced trance imaginings flung pictures into her painterly seeing. With quick wet strokes Fenella brought forth the Abyssinian maid, the 'damsel with a dulcimer', singing of Mount Abora in a land of cerulean blue.

The good effects of the upstairs balcony, our 'sunny dome built in air', were destined to end. As it turned out, they ended so abruptly and so cruelly that my retrospective impression of Fenella at her easel is imbued with the gauzy aura of perfection, an apotheosis that pursues the death of a loved one when reality is too painful to accept. And Fenella did die then, even though she lived until her mid-thirties. She died a death lingering in guilt and wavering in uncertainty, asking the question, what misfortune has befallen me? And yet I know full well that she came to accept her fate, securing for herself the loftier status of destiny. After she died, time crystallised her image. She became my icon. The myth is simple: Fenella paints her pictures; a sorcerer kills her; the auspex restores her. The crystal uncovers the symbolic meaning lying beneath history. But the auspex who uses crystals as her tools concedes nothing to false memory. Earth speaks her truth. The experience that first bound us together and at the same time separated us from the opaque world downstairs reaching to the foundations of Belvedere was conceived in this way. Beginning as it did so naturally, and according to a prompting arising from the ancient philosophy that the work of art is a reminder and something to be understood, we knew nothing else but a poetic life. The fragile perfection of this brief Eden was never to be repeated, except in the falling leaves of this crystal treatise. In the events that followed, every movement we made, every thought in our heads would come under our father's influence. We examined ourselves with an implanted eye of reason. Inevitably, a neurotic anxiety frayed the edges of our thinly woven stability. We became dissatisfied and horribly self-conscious. In dissecting the feminine, something unclean had been uncovered. But what had been uncovered? My father pointed to origins, to the tragedy of disobedience and the ethic of righteous punishment. He reminded us of the Bible, the shadowy land of the other school of remembrance. With forensic authority Fenella was stripped to reveal the hideous blemish. She alone was identified as the originator, the inciter and the destroyer. And worse than Eve in the myth of the beginning, she was the usurper Lilith, the Mesopotamian goddess of desolation who for her dark deeds was banished to the howling desert.

Now that we were growing up, Fenella and I began to feel the magnetism of adulthood and to desire its illusory liberties. Fenella was restless. Beyond the enclosed pleasure-gardens of the imagination was the real world, a thriving metropolis. Hobart had streets, shops, hurrying people and traffic. It had history, ships and a deep blue harbour. From our bedroom window, we watched all kinds of oceangoing vessels making their way up the River Derwent to Hobart's docks, to a harbour so deep and intimate with the city that huge ships were able to drop anchor within a short distance of the Town Hall. Because Tasmania was a small island lying in the southern parallels of latitude, everything sparkling came from lands far beyond our own. Of necessity, the needle pointed north. From Europe came foreigners called 'new Australians', their colourful customs and produce imported to our door. Italians arrived with Gaggia machines and opened coffee shops; Greeks bore tantalising varieties of Mediterranean treats and set up their delicatessens. Although we had hurried past Italian coffee bars on our way to and from school, we were often seized by the temptation to linger at open doors. Standing on the threshold, we peered and listened. In the dim interior, the sound of happy chatter, the smell of roasting beans and the hiss of steam pricked the senses. The finger beckoned, 'Come in, come in. Exotic strangers are within.' The invitation suggested a ritual with more than social niceties. It suggested an initiation into the mystery of men, darkly beautiful Italian men. The Mediterranean sacrament was the frothy cappuccino, emerging hot, soft and cinnamon-scented from the gleaming instrument operated by one chosen Italian. The priest of the machine conducted the ceremony with a flourish of arms and a clatter of metal utensils. As he enacted the rite, converting coffee beans into a rich beverage, he chanted to those around him in the musical cadences of his native tongue. And romantically, I remembered the first love of my life, the gardener, Felici. Was it his laughter I heard? I thought I saw him, but it was only the fibril of a dream. Oh, we knew great changes were taking place. We longed for the freedom of the city, waiting to participate in the meeting and the making, no matter how dangerous this might be. We wanted our very own experience of tasting in both the new and the ancient ritual. We longed for this just as much as we longed for the dominion of myth and our own creativity.

Quite properly, there were many prohibitions upon the freedom of the city. Adults could come and go, but adolescent girls could not. I refer to Fenella and myself as adolescents because my father always used this word, and with a medical emphasis, rather than the modern American word 'teenager' that was then in use. He deplored girls in gingham or seersucker. He did not like the category that trivialised and in some sense exempted the years between childhood and adulthood from the danger that inhered, making the transition period into a jaunty, carefree celebration. It was never that. Fenella and I had entered the dangerous years of puberty; we were beginning to develop sexually. And this burgeoning reproductive maturity being the accursed harbinger of the downfall of humankind, we learnt to observe both our bodies and our minds nervously. Yes, these were the words he favoured, adolescence and puberty. My father recited case histories from his surgery of girls 'in trouble'. Mothers brought him their 'difficult' daughters, whose social disgrace had begun by wandering the city streets and who, as a consequence, had become 'immoral'. But what was 'the trouble' that came with being female? What had it to do with the city? According to my father, colonial Hobart from its foundation to the present day was just the same as any city anywhere else in the world. In his opinion, because if the immigrant population, Hobart was every bit as dangerous as Naples. It was 'a city of erroneous conceptions'. As I had no idea of the dangers of Naples, the comparison puzzled me.

Even so, Fenella's journeys to and from school took her through the city, and naturally the streets assumed a sinuous influence within her. Walking upon stone pavements, she was struck by a compulsion to linger, to press herself into the feeling that rose in palpitating fountains from the soles of her feet. Just as it had happened in painting, she need only stretch out her hand to touch. It was all to do with location and the inevitable incursions of new images, a light flightiness that cancelled any semblance of composure. She knew that she was on the brink of disobedience, but she could do nothing about it. And because Fenella was now at Hobart High School and had a different routine, she disappeared into her own milieu, chasing after the vacillating fancies that flitted and thrilled like insects on the wing. In the upheaval, I lost sight of her. She was not in her bedroom, neither was she on the upstairs balcony. She had fled our usual places of distraction. Although she was nowhere to be found, wherever she had been was marked by colour, a *vultus sanctus* as indelible as the impression on St Veronica's handkerchief, an indent as physical as the thumbprint on a convict brick. I looked at the stained pots, the jumble of brushes. Scattered over the floor, as innumerable as leaves in autumn, her paintings basked in the afternoon sun. Such brittle things, I began to pick them up, looking at them one by one. Sitting upon the easel was *Le Déjeuner sur l'herbe*, an exercise in remembering in which she entered the theatre-eye of Manet. A reclining man in a black tasselled hat gestures to the woman who has cast off her clothes. The reclining man surveys her nakedness, yet we do not know what he is thinking. Born into the keeping of men, she gazes beyond the boundary of her incarnate space. Fenella copied the *Le Déjeuner* spontaneously, just as it appeared to her, lifting a problematic perception and a difficult technique into her unique seeing. It was still wet, its flesh tints applied with meticulous care, the dappled *vert de terre* finished with transparent strokes. Without any conscious awareness, by imitating *Le Déjeuner*, she was in effect practising an essential watchfulness in the presence of captors. She was learning to be a woman. From now on she would be compelled to survey everything she is and everything she does as it first appeared to her father, and then as it appeared to others. Her father will gesture to her nakedness. His eye will judge and punish. She could not know it then but he was about to show her sights beyond her youthful comprehension. *Le Déjeuner sur l'herbe* marked the point of departure, a sanctuary of transubstantiation to which she would never be able to return. Just as soon as Fenella completed the work, adding tiny touches here and there, she flung down her brushes. She was content. With the experience of the picture and its vivid colour pharmacy fresh within her, she flew to the new temptations of the city.

This is how it came to be that without any warning, Fenella exchanged Belvedere for the streets. On the way home from school, she linked arms with Coral, wandering in and out of Myers Department Store, avoiding the men's counter where Mr Drummond sold shirts. He was the narrow-eyed man she did not wish to see, nor did she wish to be seen by him. The city was now the *dramatis persona* in the making of her myth. For as long as they dared Fenella and Coral extended the time allotted for travelling to and from school. They extended it to its very limit. Oblivious to consequences, they lingered in the city, gazing at the latest fashions. Shops held their fascination, the windows so different from Manet's viridian *mise-en-scène*. Pop-eyed models with pert expressions thrust their hips forward, tilting at air with stiff limbs. Propped up in disconnected groups, necks in an unnatural twist, they leant away from each other, their empty gestures lit by electricity. But the new shade for senseless torsos was taupe, a French discovery that had not yet appeared on her palette. In Fenella, taupe aroused fur-stroking feelings, as if her hand rested upon a small animal. She loved the colour, just as she loved the striking window displays and the latest fashions. She wanted a soft angora cardigan in taupe with matching pearl buttons, just like the one in the window. But how would that be achieved? She was never given any money. Her mother would say taupe was 'too old' for her. Because everything desirable was, as her mother pronounced, either 'too old' or 'frivolous', wanting was frustrating. She had already asked for a pair of *Beau Monde* stockings in russet sirocco. Her mother said 'no'. Even if she did wear them to church, the answer was still 'no'. Nylon stockings were not suitable for 'immature' girls. They were ridiculously flimsy and they were certainly frivolous. Grey lisle was strong and sensible. To the question, 'When will I wear nylon stockings?' my mother made no reply.

Fenella and Coral drifted into city scenes and city dreams. Attired in their hearts' desire snatched from the windows of Myers, they might do anything they liked. In sheer sirocco stockings and angora taupe cardigans they might dance through the enchanted streets, seductive goddesses of the Beau Monde. In the madness of imaginative love, such finely threaded investiture would surely empower their nascent eroticism. They draped their nakedness in bands of loose, translucent colour. Without a trace of hesitation, they would say 'come hither' to young men, just as young men with predatory intent would say 'come hither' to them. Even though reality dressed them in dark blue uniforms, Italians were wont to gaze at them with rapacious eyes. They saw young girls as postulants of carnal knowledge, brimming with promise. Although it did not matter to them what they wore, school uniforms intensified the treasury of budding sexuality. And it was certainly true, as I have already said that Italian men populated the streets of Hobart. They moved in fluctuating clusters, exuding an exotic masculine charisma. In the flamboyant exhibition of a foreign language and its alien body gestures, Italian men were magnetic. Fenella watched them parading about, gathering at the kerbside smoking Turkish cigarettes, showing off their stovepipe pants and their shiny leather pumps. She saw them swagger. By lingering and looking, she invited them to veer towards her. Every day she saw them and they saw her, she instilled within herself further scenes, instigating the fates of meeting. She did not know it, in her developing sexuality and in her newness she was already 'a sight' to be desired, a sight stronger and more predatory in its power to set on fire than her seeing of them. And without any conscious knowledge of what was happening to her, she participated in a ritual, a primal order of courtship from which, sitting within the institute of her father's Calvinistic reason, she could not yield even a modicum of profit. The consequences of the encounter would cancel her existence. Intoxicated by sensation, she offered no resistance to the 'come hither', the tiny, sly wink. As the girls passed by, the Italian language translated itself into graceless English. 'Hey, hey,' gesticulated the young men, their eyes following supple movements. 'You are beautiful. Come please, talk to us? Yes?' Awkwardly, the invitation was offered. Day after day, it was offered, each offering upholding the ritual, becoming more confidential, more intimate until at last a slight veer, a mere hint was all that was needed. One afternoon, Fenella and Coral dared each other to walk into the Domino coffee bar in Elizabeth Street. As they did so, two dark-eyed Italian men followed them.

Perhaps it is not surprising that at first Fenella's absence went unnoticed. Now that she and Edgar were in their secondary years, it was expected that they should arrive home later than usual. The school day was longer; the workload had increased. Hobart High, on the other side of Argyle Street, was quite a trek from Belvedere. Not wishing to be seen with his younger sister, Edgar decided to be independent and to make his own way. Fenella said she preferred to walk, even though she could travel both ways by tram. Nevertheless, she was given money for the journey. So Fenella made an ideal arrangement for herself. As she had to pass Coral's house at the bottom of Forest Road, she would call for her so that they could walk together. My mother had some reservations about Coral. She didn't know; she wasn't sure. She thought Coral an odd sort of girl. My mother said, after only the briefest meeting one Saturday when Coral had called unexpectedly, that she was 'badly spoken'. But Coral was Fenella's friend. She liked her. Fenella tried to make Coral more acceptable by saying that Mrs Kemble was very nice. In fact, she was 'lovely'. My mother reacted with her characteristic body twist, the subtle mannerism that came with disapproval, particularly her disapproval of other women. She didn't know Mrs Kemble. And as Fenella had no experience of life, how could she possibly judge who was nice and who was not? But it was true. Coral's mother was extremely nice, extremely friendly. She liked talking to Fenella, and Fenella liked talking to her. From the moment she first met her daughter's new friend, Mrs Kemble responded warmly.

Mrs Kemble was completely different from my mother. She was a big woman, and rather unkempt, far too busy looking after her five children to look after her own appearance. Undoubtedly, my father would have called her 'fat'. If she had been his patient he would have prescribed a strict reducing diet. My father, who disliked having to examine and to operate on fat women, criticised them. He said adipose tissue was yellow, revoltingly yellow, the morbid colour of jaundice. Mindful of his censure, from time to time my mother went without breakfast, secretly. And although my father did not know Mrs Kemble, Fenella knew what his judgement would be. Mrs Kemble however, was not ashamed of her size. She hadn't a trace of vanity and may never have looked in a mirror. She didn't seem to care about coming to the door in her dressing gown and slippers, a faded apron bound around her large stomach. If Fenella arrived early, she would greet her with a little start of delight. 'Ah!' she would say, throwing up her hands. 'It's Fenella Grey!' She would then invite her in, offer her a chair at the kitchen table and pour her a cup of tea. It was all so easy. Mrs Kemble chatted to Fenella while Coral, who was invariably late, cleaned her teeth in the downstairs bathroom. Without annoyance or impatience in her voice, Mrs Kemble called along the corridor to Coral. Did she now Fenella was waiting? Mrs Kemble was glad that Coral had a nice friend, a doctor's daughter from such a well-mannered family. It was an association she wished to encourage. And she was interested in Fenella's painting. She had seen some of her 'beautiful work' in the art room at Hobart High. Her pictures were 'wonderful' and 'the pride of the school'. No pupil painted as well as she did. She didn't think the art teacher could be any better. Why, if it were so, he'd have to be a genius! She wouldn't be surprised if he couldn't paint at all. She'd never seen any of his work. Mrs Kemble laughed. Her praise made Fenella very happy. 'You keep going, my dear,' she said. 'One day, you'll be famous. Your paintings will grace Australia.' And with that she leant across the kitchen table and squeezed her shoulder gently. Fenella blushed. To Fenella, she was indeed 'lovely'. And Fenella liked Coral. She liked her a lot. Though Coral's father had died some years ago, nothing seemed to worry her. Everything about the Kemble family contrasted with her own. If disorder could be happy and without awful consequences, then the untidy Kembles with Mrs Kemble in her dressing gown and apron at the kitchen table surely exemplified it. And the reason I speak so knowledgeably about Mrs Kemble derives from my friendship with Coral's younger sister, Pam, and the manner in which she welcomed me. I sat next to Pam in Grade Six at the Goulburn Street State School. As for wandering through the city streets after school, window shopping on the way home, to Mrs Kemble, this was surely what young girls were meant to do.

On more than one occasion, Fenella was asked why she was so late. Sometimes it was after six that she turned up on the doorstep, exhausted by walking. My mother, who struggled to keep her own day even, reproaching herself one minute and then her husband the next, had no awareness of her daughter's secret life, or indeed that secrets were necessary, except for the primacy of her own secret myth. She had parted from her daughter long ago. All she did know was that Fenella was now an adolescent and that she was 'difficult'. Fenella said that she and Coral were working on a project at the library. And it might have been true, had she something to research for school. It was either the library, which to my mother aroused no suspicion, or an urgent need to buy more art material. The latter was more likely than the former because my father did not approve of borrowing books. He bought them. His latest acquisition was a set of *Encyclopaedia Britannica*, whose vast volumes now occupied a large space on the drawing room bookshelf. Everything required for homework, and much more besides, was at our fingertips. When Fenella astonished my father with her capacity for painting picture after picture, he gave her permission to call upon Walsh and Sons, the stationers in Macquarie Street, in order to buy whatever she required. He told the manager that she could use his account.

At the time he granted her the privilege of entering the city unaccompanied, my father was in the throes of constructing his lettered life. He was riding on a wave, harvesting his European heritage, accumulating all the accoutrements of culture. And for the short while that distrust was in abeyance, there seemed to be a coalition between Readers Union books and reams of paper upon which Fenella would work her magic. Approving of her then, he was the civilised man, the man of the world. He relished himself aesthetically. And above all, as a father of four children, he regarded himself as fair. Strict, yes, he would allow that, but he was certainly fair. Bearing in mind his own childhood restrictions, he likened his attitude to progress and reason. But after Fenella's hospitalisation and the doubts her condition raised in his mind, and certainly after she refused to play the piano, Fenella could no longer be sure of her father's confidence in her. Although she was perplexed, she could do nothing to modify her changing behaviour. The fact that she had read *Adam Bede* from cover to cover, and more than once, did not help her understand herself. How could it? She had read it because she was told to. It was only afterwards that she read it because she wanted to. Its meaning remained unreachable, hidden in the dense prose of nineteenth-century evangelical Christianity. But Fenella and Hetty were both girls. Set within the context of crime and punishment, of transportation to the colonies, the reference is clear. Early Belvedere and the barred room lay beneath. Having been told so many times that she couldn't possibly know about sinister intent in human behaviour, except that it was imperative to know her own, what could she glean from moralistic reading? What could she know of anything at all, apart from the shining sovereignty of light? Now that the city had intervened, it was necessary for her to become secretive about that which she did know. And what had art to do with this? I believe it had everything to do with the metamorphosis that was taking place within her, just as listening to Tchaikovsky had influenced her creativity by rarefying her seeing. It was music that moved her.

After painting *Le Déjeuner*, Fenella assumed a silence. Her noticeable withdrawal, while still in the midst of the family, made her larger than life. My father saw her. As if beginning a surgical operation, he incised her with his scalpel-eye. Art was fated to become her trial, her great ordeal. And I cannot do justice to my sister's memory unless I reach out and raise the gossamer veil that covered her secrecy, her power. When a young girl solemnly promises herself to beauty as an ideal, Kierkegaard muses, when she appears before witnesses wearing a sacrificial chaplet upon her brow, she becomes a bride. Art transforms her. She stands in the narthex adorned with her votive garland, waiting for the ascent to the sanctuary of seeing. At that precious moment, the dancer and her *sous-sus*, the auspex and her amethyst wand, unblemished, untouched by any man, she presents herself, the bride, ready to be elevated. And without any knowledge of the transforming force about to penetrate her being, she gives herself wholly to the sacrifice. At first Fenella was not even aware that she was being secretive. All she wanted was to enter the inner experience, the extension of her intrinsic hearing and seeing. Alas, the dramatic narrative flows more easily than the higher meaning can be extracted.

It was a Saturday afternoon that Fenella's absence was first taken seriously. My father was out on calls, my mother in the kitchen baking rock cakes, filling the biscuit tins, while my brothers must have been somewhere about the house, occupied with their boyish concerns. I hadn't finished my music practice, but my mother was impatient for help with the washing up. She came to the drawing room door, a crumpled tea towel slung over her shoulder. Would I please cease playing the piano and fetch Fenella from the balcony, or the garden, or wherever she might be? Would I do it now? Immediately I stood up, my heart skipped a beat. I bit my lip. Fenella had already told me that she was 'going out' and that I was not to say anything to anyone. At the time she told me, we were finishing the lunch dishes, tidying the benches and swilling the sink. 'Where are you going?' I said, hoping against hope that she would invite me too. Fenella lowered her voice. 'I am going to see Coral,' she said. And then she put her fingers to her lips, indicating that there was something else about her going out that she did not want me to know. She said she would be back in an hour and that what she had to do was terribly important. I don't remember saying anything in reply. I might have been surprised by her little secret, but I really cannot recall. I might have been wary, but I did not feel any imminent danger. She wanted to see Coral. She always wanted to see Coral. And she hadn't asked me to lie. She had asked me to remain silent. Looking back, I could not have been thinking straight. Or perhaps I was still in the vitreous hearing of Beethoven and the piano, asleep in a dream, picking up splinters of obsidian. So when my mother asked me to find Fenella, having quite forgotten what she had told me, I heard myself saying that she was out. As soon as I uttered the words, I covered my mouth with my hand. My mother noticed. 'Out?' she said. Her look was severe. 'Out?' she repeated in disbelief, spitting the consonant. I knew then that I had made a dreadful mistake. The truth now astray, I began to fear for myself and for Fenella. A hateful fate would make me lie. My heart pounded. 'Wherever she is,' my mother said, pulling the tea towel from her shoulder with a snap, 'your father will want to know.' And just before she made her exit from the room she added with painful irony, 'And if you are a party to deceit, your father will also want to know.'

It was well after seven when my father returned. I heard him enter the hall, a familiar and fearful uncertainty in his step, the slamming door reverberating to the dark foundations of Belvedere, to measureless cavities in the earth's mantle. There was a delay before he appeared on the threshold of the kitchen, the spirituous film of whisky dimming his vision. On the way home, he had called at the Club. As he negotiated his entry, he veered towards the dresser, correcting himself immediately. He muttered a profanity. The baking over and the washing up done, my mother was now preparing the evening meal. With my head down, I busied myself stringing beans, shrinking to a model of obedience. My mother ignored my father's demeanour. In pre-emptive attack, she wasted no time telling him of Fenella's absence. Speaking in an incredulous tone, as if their daughter had streaked naked into the ether and had disappeared, she said that she was 'nowhere to be found', that she had 'gone out'. My father stared at her. 'Fenella has been out for five hours,' she said with stark stress upon each word. My father, who seemed not to hear, cupped a hand to his ear. What was that? 'Out,' my mother repeated, enunciating the adverb, using her mouth dramatically. Then followed a pause. A moment's soberness returned to my father. 'Out?' The moment my father echoed my mother's word, I sensed that the world was about to be reversed. From now on everything would be different. 'Out' was 'beyond the bounds'. So ominous was the feeling, such foreboding came over me, I might have believed that the intelligible realm of beauty was about to be pealed back to reveal nothing but the mechanics of a cheap trick, that truth was on the brink of extinction. It was indeed as if a key had been turned in a lock, the master key of my father who alone controlled the power to open the remote rooms in the meaning of meaning; sights and sounds that would induce fear and trembling, an unending sickness unto death.

When Fenella opened the front door, she found her father waiting for her in the hall, her mother standing beside him. It was dark outside. Across the veranda, the city lights twinkled in the distance. Surprised by a reception, Fenella halted on the threshold, her hand resting on the doorknob. In the momentary confrontation, and in a sudden awareness of impending catastrophe, she inhaled sharply. She stood there, looking at them. Apart from the unusually late hour of her arrival, there was nothing different in her demeanour, nothing suspicious, except that her long black hair was undone, made untidy by hurrying. She wore her dirndl skirt, the one covered in stencilled leaves that she kept for church, and her high buttoned white blouse. In a rare kind of simplicity, in nature's apron, she stood before her parents as if she were posing for a portrait. She might have lingered there indefinitely, framed by the glistening city, had not my father hastened to destroy the delicate pause in which an attitude is captured and a picture conceived. For my father saw her quite differently. He saw her through the kaleidoscope of his own intricate difficulty. To his manner of seeing, she was much more than a young girl wearing a simple summer skirt. Even before she appeared in the doorway, ready to enter into catastrophe, his worst fears were coming to fruition. Seeing her confirmed his darkest premonitions. Her legs were bare and sinewy. She wore sandals with straps that tied at the ankles. How dare she. How dare she appear as 'another'. He recognised her, 'this other', the barelegged Jezebel, the lifted thing. He knew she existed. He had observed her birth. He had seen the forbidden ritual in which she was raised. In a rare error of judgement, he had overlooked the connection. What a fool he had been. He might have prevented it sooner, but here she was displayed before him, a sight for all to see.

Grabbing her arm, he pulled her into the hall. The door slammed behind her. Fenella shrank into the space she was forced to occupy, her feet upon the doormat. She looked at her father. How odd, she thought, that his mouth should thin. 'Where have you been?' he demanded. 'Speak,' he said. 'Speak the truth.' What words would she choose for the truth? In the ferocity of his utterance, Fenella knew that something terrible was upon her. Though confused and afraid, the sign of outward defiance was remarkable. She wore her mother's lipstick, applied from its golden container: a creamy, viscous red called *Cinnabar Sweet*. There were traces of tincture upon her lips, a faint lingering stain. She shouldn't have taken it. But she could not hang her head in shame. It was the beauty hidden in earth she loved so much and to which she responded; the transforming alchemy of vermilion, the mysterious vitriol of Venus. Cinnabar was sweet. It was paint. And why shouldn't she colour her lips? Wasn't she too a woman? Fenella had already made up her mind to say nothing. She would protect her secret, the palpitating instant that had happened in the city, innocent as it was. It was everything to her. She was about to admit her guilt about the lipstick and to tell the lie of being with Coral when my father wrecked her attempt to speak. He delivered the first great shock. He saw the stain upon her lips, suggestive red in crevices of her skin. He saw it and hated it, just as he hated the anatomy of her mouth. And his hatred of colour lain upon her, his daughter, his wilful, difficult daughter, caused such anger to rise in him that he hit her. Exercising his rightful power, he slapped her across the face. He covered her painted mouth with his hand, her orifice of lustful intent. He blotted the despicable stain. The force of his blow pushed her back against the door. And once he started hitting, it was impossible to stop.

In the kinetic momentum, seizing her arm, he dragged her the few yards along the hallway to their bedroom. Pulling her through the doorway, he flung her upon the bed, among folds of the bulbous pink eiderdown. 'Where have you been?' he demanded. 'What have you done?' In despair, he turned away from her momentarily, his hands gripping his head. And then pointing his finger repeatedly, jabbing at her face, he shouted, 'You will tell me.' Awful thoughts fractured his voice. 'You will speak.' But Fenella was shocked and unable to speak. He hit her again across the mouth. Infuriated by her silence, my father picked up his shoe and levelled blows to her shoulders and then all over her body, up and down her thighs and then once more to her shoulders. Sudden shock and the sound of punishment paralysed her instinct to shield herself. She lay there. 'Answer me, you…' His teeth clenched. And then he said it. 'Answer me, you harlot.' He slapped her face again. What did he say? What was the word? But Fenella knew the word. The impetus impacted upon her channels of hearing. It was the Bible. It was everything that she had already received. And so her father opened the ancient dictionary of degradation; the shame that was woman's own. She was to be trampled. With an intensity nearer relish than disgust, he initiated the awful seeing and the terrible hearing. Fenella turned her face into the eiderdown. My father threw the shoe on the floor. The flesh of his hand was better. As it stung him, it stung her. In such manner, in the authority of the father, he would shatter her intransigence. He would break her 'dumb insolence'. 'Where have you been?' Fenella said nothing. Her silence confounded him. Lowering himself over the bed where she lay askew, his face so close to hers that she could smell the chemistry of breath and decaying alcohol, in an auspicious tone, and with a peculiar halt in his voice, he said, 'What do you *know*?' And then, as if Fenella herself were the sole oracle of forbidden experience, the words hanging at her lips, he urged, 'Tell me. Tell me, you harlot.' Collapsing on the bed beside her, my father began to sob.

My mother, observing her husband's distress, angry with her daughter for causing his pain, tried to placate him. She clutched her throat with her hands. 'Merton, Merton,' she said, quavering. But her husband would not tolerate interference. He had to get to the truth. And he needed to do his paternal duty alone.

It took only three days to overturn the world in which we lived, to destroy it and erect a different cosmos from the inside. I need not replicate the scenes. The form above, the unforgettable sight, was the model from which subsequent daily and nightly variations derived. My father talked openly of crushing Fenella, of breaking her spirit. He gave full vent to his obsession. Every conversation between my parents was infected with the name, Fenella. He knew it. He knew it. Oh, how he knew it! Fenella was born like this. Corrupt in herself, she was responsible for my corruption and no doubt the corruption of her friend, Coral. The pinioned prey of a butcher-bird, it seemed as if my sister were impaled between branches for a continuous picking. Belvedere, of beautiful seeing, hung with her supposed sins, dispiriting pictures upon dispirited walls. For those who saw this from the edge of the event complicity was necessary; complicity that issues from fear. And so my mother and my brothers were inveigled into powerful entanglements of a distorted theology, just as I was. I became the principle witness. For some peculiar reason, Edgar was invited not only to observe, but also to participate in the degradation of the sister, by repeating my father's accusations verbatim, while Horace, who was the youngest and endowed with a special inheritance, was exempt. Perhaps he was too good to be spoilt by such gross seeing. Nevertheless, it proved impossible to escape implication. Such was the atmosphere 'under the ban' that the whole house gave itself up to a fatal hearing, assisted by history, myth and the porosity of bricks. All my father's persecutions of Fenella contained a strong moral teaching. And in the establishing of the new order of things, freeing himself from a fatal enslavement to a dark daughter, corporal punishment was the best method.

As I have already explained, my father never questioned its efficacy. I can only equate his actions with the most startling examples of overweening power. All ruthless dictators advocate extreme punishment as an integral part of upholding their ideologies. Stalin too said, 'Beat them, beat them. It's the worst you can do to them.' Stalin was never able to recover from regular childhood beatings administered by his own father. There is also the belief that military might conquers the unequal inheritance of evil in the world. In truth, it shatters the centre. Nothing could be more reinforcing of the virtues of physical punishment than a mechanised war in which my father participated. In response to the threat to Western democracy, my father endorsed the operational hierarchy of force. Though never called to arms as a fighting soldier, he prided himself on his military experience, considering himself the equal of Montgomery. He too was a strategist. Likewise, as a father, it was his responsibility to act forcefully when necessary, to instil a respect for authority and instruct his offspring in Judeo-Christian morality. Christianity was first and foremost a war against sin. He would begin with Fenella and the lie of silence. But there was much more to Fenella's punishment than correction of her 'dumb insolence'. Insolence itself was seen as the sin, and tendencies towards it needed to be cut out at the root, cauterised like a cancer. The tendency, which was surrounded by irresistible fear, was somehow worse than the sin itself. In my father's analysis of human nature, if there was a tendency to one kind of evil, the tendency to all manner of evil was also there. Especially was it there in a girl. And by deceiving her father, Fenella intended to deceive God. He was furious with her because she thwarted his need to hear with his own ears, to hear precisely what she had done. As the lie is embedded in language, he insisted on words. Deafness exacerbated his frustration. Deprived of vital hearing, believing the worst, my father lost control of himself. He wanted her to confirm what he already knew, he wanted her to 'come clean', as he so frequently expressed it, so that her reconstitution could begin. He loved her. Oh, how he loved her! And because she remained silent and refused to speak, he resolved to punish her fully and completely.

Strict confinement was added to sporadic hitting. She would be limited to the house, locked away, deprived of all social contact. He would remove her from school. He would prevent her from painting. He would write the word 'degradation' upon the walls of her being. And above all, he would beat language out of her. Inevitably and to this end, hitting assumed a ghastly regularity. He hit her because she was mute. He wounded her because she was mute and tumultuous. And as silence too is incarnate, he could not stand it.

As for myself, experiencing a similar beating on the night of Fenella's shattering, her *Kristallnacht*, her *Verklärte Nacht*, I became the very daughter of obedience. I reacted differently. Whereas

Fenella maintained a stoic reserve, I panicked and screamed. In a display of involuntary supplication, I fell to my knees, begging for forgiveness, saying over and over again how much I loved my father. I lay prostrate at his feet. Whatever happened to her under his powerful hand, Fenella appeared to remain upright. She retained her bodily integrity. Regrettably, I was never able to do so. Even into my adult life, the authoritative force of my father's voice, his pointing, discriminating finger still had the power to cause my bladder to collapse. The night of Fenella's beating, sent back to bed after witnessing the institution of daughterly shame, I was too shaken to change my pyjamas. Fenella's bed next to mine was empty, but the sounds of her punishment continued until the small hours of the morning. Underneath, my father shouted and hit. Every now and then, my mother offered her hesitant interjections.

For the rest of the summer, my father gave up indulgence in despair for a lightning strike upon all occasions of sin, anything at all that might contribute to further corruption. But it was belief, religious belief that bound him to ultimate meaning and to the idea of a favourable outcome, a goal that he was determined to reach. Though he still visited the Club, he was seen to modify his drinking, to walk in a straight line, as if by punishing his daughter, he was in some way rectifying a tendency to excess in himself. He came home earlier to preside over his newly ordered household, to watch over his daughter and to enforce the law. And during this period of correction, my parents enjoyed an exceptional connection with one another. In the fall of their daughter they found themselves miraculously united. At first shocked by the violence of my father's reactions, by now my mother was inured to the method of the man, her husband. She had no wish to oppose him. After all, he was the head of the household, a person whose opinions were respected. She loved him. She wished it could be different, but what could she do? Fenella was a wilful, difficult girl. As for physical punishment, it was impossible to stay his hand. She had tried, oh, she had tied many times, but he was determined to assert his authority. Just as with Edgar, he insisted on his 'right' to do so. She had to agree with him. So it was in a mood of collusion that my parents came together to talk about

Fenella. In my father's irrefutable finalities nothing could be discussed. And because he was a projector of views, a preacher no less, and my mother a natural follower, during Fenella's years of enforced isolation, a new concordat on the facts that mattered most to both seemed to appear. There was little inspiration in any of this. It was a just an alarming development of the trend.

My mother followed blindly. We all did. And as I said at the very beginning of this long journey, I could not accept that my sister was 'a bad girl', I gave every appearance of accepting it. Pitiful are the words, shaming are the words, 'What else could I do?' But my father was intent upon her reformation, a process that, out of necessity, was also his. History was his teacher. It was his passion for intellectual justifications that sent him straight to literature, reviving and nourishing his obsession with the printed word. He pulled more books from the shelf. He recited lines of poetry. He quoted verses from the Bible. And if I am to be truthful in my observation of the inner conditions that possessed my father, I am bound to say that he strove against despair in himself, because he saw it as a sign of weakness. In an agony worthy of Kierkegaard, he would also say that despair was both defect and merit. To be able to despair brought him to the darkness, the fatal flaw, from which salvation sprang. He was duty-bound to pursue the 'eternally firm', to keep Satan and his peers behind him. Constructing an impenetrable edifice, which was really all for himself and had nothing to do with Fenella whatsoever, he locked his whole family into a rigid framework that would prove almost impossible for its members to modify without feeling shameful betrayal and impending punishment. Intellectually, he recreated himself a Puritan, but with a justifiable getaway. He reconstructed his deity in the manner in which he felt he needed it; a supra-eye with a searing sword to whom he presented himself as a faithful servant. Even so, I think my father struggled with a sense of unworthiness before the complex, fearful deity that was his God.

One of his first tasks was to cancel Fenella's outside life. Her formal education ended there and then. It seems astonishing now that he carried out such a strategy. No one protested. The following Monday lunchtime, my father drove Fenella to school for the removal of all her belongings and for the termination of her attendance. The event was so unprecedented in the annals of the Education Department that it was somehow allowed to happen. Fenella gathered her textbooks from her locker. She removed her paintings from the art room wall and placed them in her portfolio. He then took her back home. Apart from her books, which she would need for a correspondence course to be supervised by my mother, she was denied the freedom and the privilege to paint. Oh, he knew it was her gift. He knew that all too well, but he had come to see this so-called freedom as an unnecessary if not dangerous excursion into the unknown. He staunched all his ardour of the arts while he took a good look at the circumstances that had brought her to perdition. He must analyse everything. He ordered Fenella to put all her paintings and drawings, every one of them, out of sight. He didn't care what she did with them as long as they were nowhere to be seen. With the exception of one work, still wet on her easel, she gathered them up and stacked them under her bed with her other things. She did it obediently.

His next task was to call on the Kemble family and announce the severance of Fenella's friendship with Coral. He wanted to make it quite plain to Mrs Kemble that her daughter was not welcome at his home, and that she was never to see her again. Mrs Kemble, surprised to see the doctor on her doorstep, was about to invite him in when she saw Mr Grey was not making a social call. Captivated by his astonishing story about Coral and Fenella, she was soon rendered speechless with embarrassment. Her heart pounded. What he said was so terrible to hear. She recovered her presence of mind to say she knew nothing, absolutely nothing about their being late home last Saturday night. Coral was here. She did not go out. And what did they do in the city after school? Meet men? What men? Yes, she would look into it. She was terribly sorry. She had no idea. She placed her hand on her breast. Was Fenella all right? She would miss her. And so would Coral. But my father did not hear her. He presented his case for severance and then left. When he returned, he told my mother that Fenella's association with the Kemble family was over. They were 'unsuitable' people. My mother agreed. Of course, she had had her suspicions. My father made much of Mrs Kemble's particular kind of unsuitability. As a man of the world, he knew what he was talking about. He referred to her gross size and her 'lack of education'.

It was at this critical juncture that my father approached the acting Mother Superior of the Convent of the Sacred Heart in New Town, Sister Mary Dominic, to accept me as a pupil. He approached Sister Dominic in his authority as a surgeon, rather than from the weaker position as a Protestant father asking for his daughter to receive a Catholic education. Everyone knew his work over the way at Calvary Hospital. Although Sister Dominic was happy to educate non-Catholic girls, and she was very welcoming of the doctor and his daughter, it was the policy of the Catholic Church to be strictly inclusive when it came to other religions. In matters of faith, the school made no concessions. But my father insisted on my removal from lessons in catechism. He forbade my attending mass in St Joseph's Church or my presence at any Catholic gathering. He said that he did not wish me to see or hear anything that contradicted my Protestant upbringing. See? Hear? Sister Dominic considered the matter. Though his request was unusual, she wanted to help. The school needed pupils. Most generously, Mr Grey had offered a substantial donation to their new building fund. It was difficult for her to refuse. She ventured a gentle suggestion. Would Mr Grey be happy for his daughter to attend the weekly service of the Benediction of the Blessed Sacrament? It was a blessing anyone could receive, anyone at all. And it was a beautiful service. But my father would not be happy. No, he would rather I did not. And because he had no idea that prayers were said every hour of the school day, he did not mention the rosary or the offices of the Virgin Mary. He did not know that Catholic piety demanded a whole body immersion as incarnate as dance. Even though the gabled shape of Giotto's *Ognissanti Madonna*, looked down on him from Sister Dominic's wall, in the chastity of lapis, he would not have me 'see'. I would continue my music lessons with Miss Colleen O'Hara; I would study the curriculum and I would obey all school rules. I was there to receive good instruction from nuns and to learn how to conduct myself in a ladylike manner. And to explain his reason for wanting me to be educated at a convent, he mentioned the problem of his elder daughter. Tragically, she had fallen into bad ways and had come to moral harm. It had been necessary to remove her from school so that she could be closely supervised at home. Sister Dominic listened sympathetically, but as she was speaking to a Protestant man, she didn't really understand. She was not a natural disciplinarian. She did not like punishing girls. She left such punishment as was necessary to those nuns who had no compunction in using the cane.

At home, the new structures were in place. Fenella began her penitential term, her ever-extending penitential term, living a life of confinement, forbidden even to go to the garden. As she had made a habit of deception, saying that she was 'at the library' when she was in fact wandering the streets with Coral, she could no longer be trusted. From now on, her day to day life would be regulated. Every book she read, every image she looked at would be subject to my father's censorship. More than ever, he would direct her education. Addicted to logical disputations, his dialectics were quite without any acknowledgement of beauty and its formation. Very soon, music too would be removed from her hearing, heralding the death of Tchaikovsky's Fifth Symphony, the one work he knew by which he came to judge not only the man but also his spiritual destiny. By so doing, my father secured for himself a kind of submissiveness from all who approached him, a willingness to be scrutinised. In the domination of my sister, I was forbidden to speak to her, unless I was given express permission. So very afraid of my father, obeying him was easy. I gathered my belongings from our shared bedroom with the bay windows and took them to the balcony. For the following years I slept there under the benign eyes of the Botticelli's Venus, while at school I sat under the flat, slanted gaze of Our Lady of Perpetual Succour.

Over months, Fenella's reformation took shape, each day beginning with an accusation followed by an inquisition. What had she done? What did she know? Constant verbal attack and frequent beating wore her down. Fenella began to change. Although the prohibition on speaking to her did not apply to my mother, and my brothers were under a separate directive to treat her as a minion, my mother's manner towards her was straightened and without the faintest flutter of sympathy. She issued instructions, listing tasks she must carry out, her voice haughty. She said, 'Now you will peel the potatoes.' 'Now you will set the table.' To all intents and purposes, Fenella was the halted servant and slave of the home. This being the new arrangement, my father announced that Mrs Hussey should be dismissed. He said Fenella should do the washing and the ironing. So in circumstances that puzzled the faithful Mrs Hussey, she left. Fenella took over her duties, and much more besides. My mother supervised her, urging her to hurry, hurry when she could not, complaining about the way in which she dragged herself through the chores. Fenella irritated her. Clapping her hands, she said, 'Come on, Fenella. Jump to.' It was a depressed Fenella who piled clothes into the whirring washing machine in the kitchen; it was a reluctant Fenella who lugged creaking baskets to the sagging line at the back. She did not have the will to 'jump to'. Slowly, slowly, she cleaned and dusted and then slowly, slowly she returned to the kitchen table and her books. My mother stood behind her, directing her eye to the exercise before her, reminding her of Pythagoras and his theorem. 'Think, think,' she said. 'Please do think.' And then pointing to the text with a ruler, she said, 'It is not that, Fenella. It is *this*.'

But my mother's slight aptitude for teaching was no match for the challenges she met when it came to her daughter. Her memory under hourly attack, she seemed to have forgotten everything. My mother didn't know what to do for the best. And after Mrs Hussey's dismissal, it was a strain teaching Fenella, supervising everything. Fenella was resistant, difficult. My mother was concerned that she appeared to show 'no emotion'. She hadn't cried. Was this normal? It was impossible to know what was going on in her. She had never needed such discipline when she was a girl. She didn't have a secretive bone in her body. What could Merton do for the best? My mother did not know. She hoped restricting her was the right thing. Sometimes she believed in it; sometimes she did not. She just did not know. I observed my mother's moments of uncertainty, moments when she dared question the severity with which her husband treated Fenella. But because her husband now needed her, and the problem of Fenella brought them closer, she looked into her mirror, wavered momentarily, and then called the whole episode 'a pity' and 'a misunderstanding'. She wept a little. It was regrettable, very regrettable. It was always 'such a pity'. And it was awful for the boys, awful. She hadn't said so before, but she thought Merton had indulged Fenella with her painting. In that respect, he had paid her too much attention. And far too much money and time had been wasted on paints and painting. If she wanted to paint, she could do it when she was older. She had all the time in the world for painting, if that was what she really wanted to do. Of course it wouldn't lead anywhere. How could it? She agreed with her husband that art and 'artiness' were partly responsible for her present trouble.

And there was the other matter of her writing. Both girls had been composing the most questionable, far-fetched nonsense up on the balcony. She had read what she believed to be Fenella's gothic oddity, *Black Agatha*. Who but Fenella would write such a thing? It was surely her dark side, the destructive power in her. She didn't like it. Not only was this writing 'peculiar', it was dangerous. She might turn it upon them. Her two daughters exhibited the most worrying tendencies. What sinister urge, what malign motive had led Fenella to compose her own funeral notice? How could she do such a thing? My mother did not understand. When she found the piece of paper in front of the carriage clock, neatly typed and finished with a row of asterisks, she took it straight to my father. He seized it immediately. 'Ah!' he said as he read it, a little expletive upon the breath. This was the 'hoodwink'. This was the evidence he had been looking for. This, a 'hoodwink'? According to my father, for some reason Fenella was determined to 'throw dust in their eyes'. What did he mean? I did not understand the language he used, nor did I understand his obsession with certain words and expressions.

After we had both gone to bed, I heard my parents mulling over the probable and peculiar either/ors of Fenella's behaviour, their voices joined, gnashing into the pitch-black night, undulant agony distressing the air. Invoking the age of Blake, quoting the poet's fragmenting madness, my father said, 'Truly, my Satan, thou art a dunce/ And dost thou know the garment from the man/ Every harlot was a virgin once/ Nor canst thou ever change Kate into Nan'. The case against Fenella was hopeless. She was now the poet's harlot, Kate. Was he, like William Blake, speaking 'To the Accuser who is God of the World?' Hearing the eternal inquisition, the man of the woman, in a passion, my father flung himself from the bed. He could bear it no longer. He must make her 'come clean'.

Ascending the stairs in a rush, he passed the door to my balcony bedroom like a red-hot arrow, his racing pace followed by the lighter sound of my mother scuttling behind him, her voice of faint restraint saying, 'Merton, Merton. Do you think you ought to do this?' But Merton said he had a right to get to the truth. Fenella must get up for questioning. So Fenella got up to be questioned yet again. She was questioned and beaten, at any time of the day or at any time of the night, and anywhere in the house. He dragged her body everywhere. What did my father want to know? What did he want to hear? He wanted the truth, the awful truth. He questioned her about her knowledge of men, about her appetite for lust. He wanted to know what it was like to experience such a blatant, despicable desire. He wanted the substance of lust, the hearing of her lasciviousness, the lasciviousness of his daughter, to seep like a poison into the portals of his ears.

Stealing the words of Ben Jonson, he said, 'Queen and huntress, chaste and fair', and then distorting the meaning in a play upon the ear, instead of 'queen and huntress', with utmost satisfaction he said, 'Diana huntress, *chased* but not *chaste*.' Did she hear? He threatened her with his finger. But Fenella did not hear. This vision of depravity, her hunted unchastity, the irony that he had discovered in language, made him break down and sob. That she would not hear infuriated him. He hit her across the face. He told her that he had never looked at a woman 'in that way'. In himself, he had never known the state of unchastity. Though men had consorted with prostitutes during the war, he had always kept himself pure. He had remained a man apart. Fenella became distressed. What did he mean? The coupling of the words 'lust' and 'pure' confused her; the play upon 'chaste' she did not understand. At her father's insistence her reticence gave way to a few wavering words. Yes, she and Coral had skipped school. And what else? *Come on! Come on!* Yes, they had made friends with two young men. Ah! Now he was getting somewhere! This much he did know: she and Coral had formed a dangerous liaison, not only with each other, but also with two Italians. Italians? Looming over her, he repeated the word. And then he said incredulously, 'You mean illiterate Italians from illiterate Italy?' What else was there to tell? And did these Italians come from the sinister south, from Eboli, where Christ had 'stopped', where he could go no further? Did they?

Fenella was in bed, lying on her side, her hand covering her mouth. The allusion was something to do with a book, but she did not understand why. Stricken with confusion and shattered, she could not think. Her tangled hair fell in fragmented strands over the yoke of her sprigged nightie and onto the pillow. Pulling herself up slowly, she began to speak. Yes, it was true that she had met a young man in the city. He came from Calabria, not Eboli. He was a good man, but his family was very poor. He had come to Tasmania to earn money for his sister's dowry. He worked hard. He worked very hard. His name was Luigi. In the astounded silence of my parents, she paused. And then summoning courage, she raised her head. His name was Luigi, she said. Luigi. And she had kissed him.

At the Convent of the Sacred Heart, the Sisters of St Joseph looked forward with great expectation to the canonisation of the latest Catholic saint. From heaven fell a new name, that of a twelve-year-old girl, Maria Goretti. Pope Pius XII said Maria Goretti was 'the saint of the century'. Even Mussolini had advocated her canonisation. The nuns, uplifted in spirit at the prospect of such a spotless lamb, spoke freely of Maria's martyrdom. It was a gift. It was a rare and beautiful gift. Maria Goretti, a mere girl, was surely the most perfect offering. One morning after the midday Angelus, Sister Carmel announced the news of the approaching canonisation and how the school would mark the event. She wanted us to be aware of the moment, the very instant at which Maria would become available to the faithful for intercessory prayers. We would all be taken to the State Theatre in North Hobart for a special showing of the Italian film, *Heaven over the Marshes*. And after witnessing this catechism of the cinema, the story of her life and death shot on location, we would return to the Church of St Joseph for a special service and an inaugural vigil. At the Benediction of the Blessed Sacrament, the blessing of the Lamb in unleavened bread, the child Maria would receive her first petitions, our very own prayers. What would we ask of her? Had we considered our supplications? Sister Carmel spoke in earnest, her hands clasped before her breast. She was excited. We should never forget that Maria had died a martyr's death. She had chosen agony after resisting the advances of a young man 'with impure intentions towards her,' a young man that under different circumstances she might have loved. And as she lay dying from fourteen stab wounds to her heart, she forgave the one who had lusted after her virginal purity. She didn't think of her own suffering. She thought only of her murderer and what she could do for his salvation. It was love, spiritual love that was to save him from eternal burning, as it had saved herself. Choosing as she did led to her glorification, bringing her a prize higher than salvation itself. Her earthly chastity was now made perfect in heaven, her body an oblation.

So touching was the story of Maria Goretti's short life, rising from the poverty of Italy's Pontine Marshes, that we were exhorted to follow her example and ask for her help in all circumstances. We needed her protection. With rubrical emphasis, Sister Carmel brought forth the living image of St Maria, encouraging our envy of the unenviable. Every girl, myself included, received a holy card, the likeness of the newborn saint in her raiment of predestination, embracing a palm frond and flanked by sumptuous white lilies; a child in a dream, dreaming that she was dreaming. Dare I love her? The holy card was now my most precious possession. In a minor miracle of the icon, tiny flecks of gold drifted from the fateful stamens to cling to the deckled edge of the picture. I treasured my Catholic gift, a little key to the inner world of Colleen O'Hara. But how could I possibly keep it? How could I tell my parents that we were to see a film about the life of a modern female saint, an Italian girl? When the lesson was over, while others were filing from the classroom, I waited for Sister Carmel. I would explain why it was impossible for me to go. She would understand. Sister Carmel looked at me, a 'non Catholic'. She did not understand. She had heard nothing about my being treated as an exception. 'The film will do you no harm,' she said. 'And Benediction is what it says, a blessing. No father could possibly object to that.' I had to go. I had to hide the truth. At the Convent of the Sacred Heart, religion was so apocryphal, so populated and so pious that I was powerless to insert a word. For the Sisters of St Joseph, the vaunted reforms that my parents gave voice to were wholly absent. They simply did not exist.

I had my secret life, my troubling secret life. But what was happening to Fenella? She had now reached the ultimate degree of metaphor, and having reached that most distant spot, her apogee, there was nothing more she could possibly carry. Her image began to collapse into its intimate intensity. Living a pathetic existence to which I had no access, what joy she ever had in art and in nature was now as futile as the longing of a moth for a star. She was accused of wildered looks, wily words and evil speech, when in truth she uttered nothing. The menial of the home, my father instituted certain rules of enslavement. As he could no longer trust her, he locked her in her bedroom. I heard him say repeatedly to my mother that she was bound to escape, bound to 'bolt into the night'. He lived in nervous expectation of her revolt. So it was my father who opened her bedroom door to the miseries of the early morning. It was my father who ordered her to rise and prepare the breakfast for the family. With the key in his possession, he could enter whenever he felt the urge to question her. And in the peculiarities of his reasoning, intent upon corrective measures, he ordered her to do his personal washing. Never mind the machine. She must do everything by hand. He required his white shirt, his underpants and his socks to be washed by Fenella and then hung up to dry over the bath. When he came home for lunch, he inspected her work, examining the collar and cuffs to see that she had done it properly. If not satisfied, he would fling his clothes on the floor and order her to do it again. Disorientation affected Fenella's vision and made it difficult for her to see what she was doing. Numb in my lack of understanding, I watched my sister's fading existence. Though fear prevented me from going in search of her, very occasionally, I came upon her. From time to time, I would see her as she really was. One afternoon, I walked into the drawing room to find Fenella sitting there, a sight. A look of self-rebuke upon her face, she sat stiffly in a chair, her hand tugging at strands of hair. She tugged at her hair until little patches of white appeared in her scalp. Over months of punishment, she picked her head until it bled. My father diagnosed signs of 'mental illness', of manic depression and possibly schizophrenia. Yes, that was it. There was something 'radically wrong' with her. He prescribed and administered drugs for her radical wrongfulness, standing over her while she swallowed them.

On other days, I watched her at the kitchen sink, dunking my father's underclothes in soapsuds like an automaton, but hardly able to lift her arms. She did not seem to know what she was doing, nor was she aware of my presence. Ostracised within the family, it was not long before Fenella turned into a spectre of her former self, a pitiful thing. So worn down, she was human in appearance only. Living as an eerie spirit, a simulacrum from under the house, it seemed as if she might vanish at the touch of a finger. At times she floated like an elemental with sickle wings, a fleeting *wili* of folklore with a back as hollow as a kneading board. And then in an instant she became a figure from hidden Belvedere forsaken of light, reduced to the heaviness of matter, a creature of ashes, smoke and darkness. She moved silently in her land of shadows, passive before its hazards, palpitating beneath a suffocating veil. If I had had any presence of mind, any active connection with the tragedy that was taking place before my very eyes, I might have called out to her from a great distance 'May Heaven help you!' or better still, 'May the agony of Maria Goretti help you!' It is to she, the virgin girl, that I should have addressed my first petition, for she was more alive to me than any azurite mother. To my eternal regret, I did not. Restrained then as I was by my father's arm, I turned away. Here, in the shedding leaves of memory and under the auspices of crystals, I am free to believe everything. Such are the uses of truth and beauty. For three intense years, as indeed for the rest of her short life, my sister suffered a form of excommunication. Because she had become a temptation to men, she was an anathema, a sight not to be seen. Having confused everything beautiful with everything ugly, recalling the English language to a baneful Babel, its work now complete, my father's words, or any words for that matter, had little power over her. She could not hear.

The consummation of my journey approaches. At my point of departure, I would like to believe that there is one supreme declaration in accordance with truth, one *oraculum ex veritate* to answer queries of existence and bring consolation, reassurance and certainty. But such a discovery would reduce the mystery of life to a question and an answer, when in reality there are as many questions and answers as there are seekers after the meaning of meaning. I happen to be captured by the language in which the question is asked, the images and influences that arise and the manner in which information, all information, is applied. Western civilisation offers the saving body of Christ, but more often than not his healing remains hidden in the stifling swaddling of doctrine, dogma and sacerdotal power, his precious relics fought over by rationalists as much as they are claimed by mystics to derive from divine revelation. Although I have referred to my writing as a thesis, my thoughts are nearer to those of an apologist's allegory than they are to any argument from reason, or anything inspired by theology, even though revelation is an integral part of my imagery. My language is that of the poet, and so with the poet, I defer to the mystery of creation and creativity, to the elements of the earth, and to the transforming inspiration of the philosopher's stone in order to nourish my existence. I revive intuition, *ab origine*. I elevate a shell. Immersed in life, I too am obsessed with incarnate form. But it is really formation, the very manner in which the artist works, just as much as it is an appreciation of the form itself that leads me along the artist's path.

For the manner in which I have written this treatise over the past winter months has constituted the healing that I sought right from the start. And into my hearing of 'the word' uttered in English, the only language I speak fluently, comes Western music, also in its unique form, an apotheosis of all human experience.

In truth, hearing also being an inner eye, giving rise to visions, and visions giving rise to feelings, it is impossible to elevate one sense above the other, though many say that hearing reigns above them all. I had every intention of answering the first question that came to me at the very beginning of my journey, 'What did my father hear?' I have entered crystals; I have touched upon many psychic mysteries in my desire to answer the question. Though no one answer has come, the intense energy of elements and the question itself have yielded something far more important. The dark path of enquiry has been illuminated, the boundaries separating inner and outer realities have been dissolved. I met my sister Fenella once more. Under the auspices of crystals, I restored her. In restoring her, I entered into the sacred remembering that is art. In that sacred remembering, I found ritual. But I am still far from knowing how music first inspired my father and then in a flash came to represent everything damnable. For the story of my hearing of Tchaikovsky belongs more to my own journey than it belongs to my father. We never discussed his music. As far as I am aware, after he condemned Tchaikovsky's Fifth Symphony, making it null and void, for the rest of his life he barred its influence from himself, even though the prohibition was initially for the family. And because he selected and condemned one composer and one work, the vexed question of how to judge the rest of the pantheon soon arose. Though convinced of his own critical reasoning, his behaviour was that of a dogmatist, a repeater of aphorisms. The works of the most reasoning of Western philosophers, Immanuel Kant, were not on his bookshelf. For in spite of my father's love of classical learning and the printed word, music was his real literature. Irrationally, he chose to keep Beethoven among the elect, simply because of his puritanical tendencies and sympathy for his deafness. He had read somewhere that Beethoven, the great bridge to Romanticism, had dismissed a maid for telling a lie. The servant had been dispensed with even though her lie was to spare Beethoven's feelings. My father quoted his words: 'Such a person cannot cook a clean soup,' he said with considerable satisfaction. And he wholeheartedly agreed with Beethoven's opinion of Mozart's *Don Giovanni*, in that 'the sacred art ought never permit itself to be degraded to the level of a foil for so scandalous a subject'. Even so, the sonata my father loved so much was also silenced, simply because of the name 'Appassionata'. After Fenella's disgrace, the work was too full of feeling to reason with. I don't think he ever listened to it again. And as much as he loved Colleen O'Hara, her presentation of *La Cathédrale engloutie* confounded him. He could not know then just how potent his teaching about hearing was, though at the time I do not believe that he had anything but perverse and destructive tendencies. Whatever he happened to hear in Tchaikovsky, I did not. And in the shock that Fenella received, she heard nothing but numbing accusations. So deep was the wound to her intuition, the absence of Tchaikovsky meant little to her.

Nevertheless, the condemnation of Romantic music required that I too obey orders. To that end, I banned Tchaikovsky from my own hearing. My lessons with Miss O'Hara continued after I left home and up to the year I departed for England. I practised with fluctuating commitment, and often in despair. I never achieved the high standard that I demanded of myself to rescue my father from his agonies. I did not impress him as his mother had, nor did I approach the exquisite gifts of my teacher. The very last pieces Miss O'Hara taught me were Schumann's *Bunte Blätter*, coloured leaves of autumn that fell from his troubled genius just before his final breakdown and the closing years of insanity. And having to bid farewell to my teacher, I relinquished my struggle with the instrument I loved so much, making a vow from then on to become a hearer, to assimilate the talents of the most discerning and discriminating devotee, to recreate myself as a receiving ear. I said to myself, is not hearing the noblest sense? How could a composer function without the subtle organ to which his art is given? And still I could not bring myself to listen to the music of Tchaikovsky. It was not until I arrived in England that the spell was finally broken. In Winchester where I happened to live for a time, a chance encounter with two college boys in the street one summer afternoon making la-la sounds to the final movement of Tchaikovsky's Fifth Symphony suddenly flung up the shutters that had covered my ears for more than ten years. Hearing them joyfully half sing and hum as they passed me, beating the air with their boaters and waving their arms in mock conducting, forced me to stop in my tracks, to catch my breath. I stared at them. They were young and free, enjoying the first fruits of hearing. They were singing Tchaikovsky! It was Tchaikovsky's Fifth Symphony! Had I come to the Northern Hemisphere just for an awakening, for the prompting of memory? I watched them walk by. I thought of my father. And as they continued on their way, their humming fading, the image of the priest of music, Dimitri Mitropoulos on the cover of my father's record sleeve raised itself before me, the icon of a man-god. The silence now over, the persecution of Tchaikovsky had come to an end. And does not the word recording derive from the Latin root *recordare*, meaning to bring to remembrance, to get by heart, to go over in one's mind? Hearing the symphony vocalised, spoken by young boys as *logos*, the beautiful assertion, was enough to prompt the wonder of my very first experience of music, the impact of the first word. How can I not be grateful to my father for his prohibition?

Elevation and iconoclasm are paired opposites. They work together. Following Sister Carmel's orders, saying nothing to my parents, it was with some fear that I went with the school to see the film, *Heaven over the Marshes*. Everything we had been told about the life of Maria was true. The Goretti family were poor. They were so very poor that their home was empty of all possessions except for the barest necessities. I was shocked to see Maria eat her meagre meal directly from a wooden table without either china plates or utensils. Every day, the hollow figure of Maria Goretti in thin clothing skimmed barefoot through the marshes to the whitewashed church. Approaching an image of the Virgin Mary, she prayed. Her hands clasped beneath her chin, she murmured her *aves*. At her first communion, she appeared as a blanched child bride clothed in a transitory robe, holding her rosary. Her hair was adorned with flowers. Kneeling before the altar, her eyes closed and her mouth open, the priest dropped the white disc onto her trembling tongue. Then followed the ritual of her martyrdom, the awful suggestion, the chase, the violent death. I looked away from the screen. A horrified gasp rose from the mesmerised audience. The nuns wept discreetly, dabbing their eyes with large white handkerchiefs.

Hurrying back to the Church of St Joseph for the Benediction of the Blessed Sacrament, not knowing what to expect, impeded by my ignorance in the midst of such familiarity, I entered the sanctuary of seeing cautiously. Catholic girls knew what to do. Their religion so well rehearsed, it was an easy dance with sure steps. Filing passed the glass stoup hanging on the wall beside the main door, dipped fingertips splashed a sign of the cross. Imitating their gestures, a water bead wet my forehead. The interior of the church was dim, a place where the perfume of old beeswax, encrusted frankincense and leather-bound missals was hoarded. As the girls genuflected before the High Altar, their shoes squeaked on the polished floor. Going immediately to their pews, they knelt on hassocks, and following the example of the devout, bowed their heads in silent prayer, waiting for the vision to appear. The High Altar was dressed in white linen and lace. In the centre, between ascending rows of burning candles, stood the hooded creature, the holy showing that we had come to behold. A priest robed in a gold cope paused before the altar. He genuflected deeply, his reverential expression heavy with the weight of brocade. Prompted by the priest, voices hurried through the Latin liturgy. Ascending the steps to the altar, swathed in hazy plumes of incense, slowly, slowly, and with sacerdotal authority, the priest removed the white linen hood. For a breathless moment, he fell before the spangled vision. Silver bells tinkled. Grasping the ornament by its golden stem, he raised the glittering victory on high; he elevated the spoil of earth, the reality of heaven. And then turning towards the congregation, in the abyss of an immense concave, he caused the stainless eye of maidenhood to pass over the assembly before him, its silent power descending to touch each solemn head. Radiance streaked the misty darkness. I could not lower my gaze. This, oh, this was the monocle of God, the lifted thing! This was the forbidden seeing, the feathered arabesque, the spotless disc living within her shimmering *augoeides*! I knelt in the narthex to see her flying veils and her dark tresses. I felt her quiver in the scented breeze. I came to see her sinewy legs, her cinnabar lips. This was the elevation of all elevations, the advent of the virgin girl.

My father was brooding over Fenella's 'Bohemian tendencies', her dark intentions, her lying. He never knew what she might do next, nor could he be sure what she was keeping from him. So he called her his 'artful Artemis with her poisoned darts', an expression that sprang from nowhere but gave him satisfaction to say. The poetry of these orphaned words struck him forcibly. He smarted under their power. He gave them his approval. But what did they mean? Although Fenella did not understand the origins of his contempt, the manner in which he called her 'Artemis' made her feel ashamed. She knew she had done something unforgivable. She knew. It was his look of hideous hints that distressed her, the accusations of his eye as much as his carefully selected words. He said she was 'lustful'. Having fashioned a fictitious quip about the goddess Artemis, about whom my father knew nothing except her appearance at Ephesus in the Acts of the Apostles, he repeated it over and over again, just as in weeks before he had discovered 'Diana huntress' and the play on 'chaste'. 'Get up, you artful Artemis,' he would say bursting into her bedroom in the morning, pulling the sheets from her sleeping form. And then breathing right into her ear with a sneer, 'Get up, you artful Artemis. Get up and face the day of your iniquity.' He would then heave her body roughly from the bed, ordering her stand upright before him. Hearing himself utter the word 'iniquity' called upon the familiar teaching of the scriptures. He saw an image of the immoral Jezebel on her most famous day, the day she was thrown to her death, her kohl-black eyes peering over the parapet. 'See yourself as Jezebel,' he said, slapping her face.

'I do.' And he would slap her again.

'You can take my word for it. I will declare your shame to the world.' He would then leave the bedroom just as abruptly as he had arrived.

So obsessed with Fenella was my father that he made a case of her behaviour to his colleagues at the Tasmanian Club. He told his drinking friends, or whomever he found to confide in, that he had a harlot in the family living under his very roof. He accounted for his part in it by saying what he, a responsible father, a professional man, was doing about it. 'Be sure of this,' he said. 'I am correcting her ways. I am directing her reformation.' He had it all worked out. Everything was under his control. He told his colleagues that in the course of her correction, which would continue indefinitely, he had given his daughter Flaubert's *Madame Bovary* to read. Although my father declared the story of Madame Bovary 'a tragedy', he chose Flaubert's masterpiece not because he identified with Emma, but because he saw himself as her long-suffering husband Charles, an honest country doctor duped by a 'flighty' wife and her hidden powers of destruction. His colleagues would understand what he meant. He intended that Fenella recognise the ruin Madame Bovary wrought not only upon her husband, but also upon herself. She used the escape of self-murder because she was 'out of control'. She swallowed white arsenic. Under the circumstances, what else could she do? It was as much theological predestination as it was pagan fate. So my father saw to it that when Fenella was not usefully employed around the house, or studying for her Schools Board certificate, she was learning the lessons of literature, the lessons that he judged to be necessary. However long it took, my father was determined to see the 'whole sorry business' of her reformation through to 'the bitter end'. He spoke about his paternal duty as if he were an executioner with a distasteful dawn assignment.

The brooding continued. The relentless stewing, sifting, and analysing went on day after day, night after night. A determination to destroy her art took hold of him. Now he was getting to the root of the matter. He returned to her bedroom to question her, to examine her possessions. Stacked under the bed he found all her sketches and miscellaneous works. Determined to inspect everything, and with his diagnostic eye to get to 'the nature of the trouble', he pulled them out and threw them across the floor. Fenella stood beside the bed, the floor sinking under her feet, the walls spinning and cracking apart. Light fell in pools of glassy blackness. She knew that if she spoke, she would go mad. But what was her father looking for? He was looking for signs of erroneous seeing. He was looking for the prodigious and scandalous use of colour, the mixing of inappropriate elements. 'What's this?' he said, pointing at the alizarin woman, picking at it repeatedly it with his finger. 'What ill omen have you produced here? Ah! You have painted yourself as a scarlet woman! Is this your art?' Fenella said nothing.

Her father was shocked to see her studies in anatomy. He leafed through them roughly, slapping the pages as he did so. 'Why this nudity?' he asked. 'Any men for your obscenities?' He was searching for shapes that might give clues to her inner workings, all the while looking at her with his hard eye. He lowered his voice dramatically. 'Any pictures of Luigi?' He was getting at her secret perversion, her 'carnal knowledge'. He wanted to see all of it, everything that she had ever painted. There was *Le Déjeuner*, the naked woman sitting on the grass with two fully dressed men. 'You will show me that French picture,' he said, stressing the adjective. 'I want to see the extent of your depravity.' Bowed in shame, Fenella followed her father to the balcony. The picture was still drying on the easel surrounded by her painting paraphernalia, just as she had left it before her fateful visit to the city. Her father hit the picture with his fist. 'Which one is the Italian, eh? Is it the one with the stick and the tassel on his hat? Is it the one ogling you?' Fenella looked away. 'Do you want Luigi to see you naked?' Oh the shame! And then lifting the picture roughly with both hands, her father held it high above his head. It was a moment of disgust. It was a vision of abhorrence. He then slammed it back on the easel, upside down. 'Look at it,' he said. 'Look at it now,' he said, pointing with his finger. 'This is the work of a pervert.'

It was all deplorably artificial to him, all fleshly vanity. He demanded that Fenella tell him more. But she could not. She did not know what 'pervert' meant. All she could see was how his fist smeared the paint, and by hanging the image upside down, everything that had once delighted her eye changed to an image she could never have imagined. Bodies remained suspended. All meaningful sense disappeared. The woman emerging from the woodland lake hung in the middle. Fenella felt ashamed of what she had done. She should never have copied Manet. All she could see were the imperfections, her failure to participate in the art she strove to serve. If she had been better, if she had painted the mulberry tree, her father would not have seen her work in the way he did. It was all her fault. She was not an artist. She was found to be lacking, oh, how she was found to be lacking! 'Look at your mind displayed before you,' he said, 'your twisted mind.' Fenella looked, but her seeing was impaired. 'You will destroy this,' he said. 'If you are artful, then I will make you artless. You will take all your work to the incinerator. You will take every single thing that you have made, you artless girl, and you will burn it. You will burn it now.'

There are deeds that have no form, sufferings that have no expression. After burning her paintings, watching the shimmering heat in the old incinerator lick and quicken the reduction of her art to ash, Fenella's inner self collapsed. This was the place where everything was burnt, a wasteland that received shed blood, a *locus sacer*. Her father stood on the veranda watching her, just as he used to stand on the veranda dreaming his distant dreams in the first days of Belvedere. When he was satisfied that she had incinerated all her work, the last painting, *Le Déjeuner*, flaring angrily into the air, he turned away from this *auto-da-fé* and went back into the house. Fenella remained where she was. Waterless and withered, she drifted. No birds sang. This was what her father had meant when he said he was going to 'wipe the slate clean'. She had read about madness; she had followed the declining life of Emma Bovary, but so great was her own misery, she could not identify with a character on a page, no matter how skilfully drawn. All she had was her own confusion, her own particular insanity. His persistence with the language of the damned made it all true; everything that she had done was her own fault. She only had herself to blame. And so she must be what he insisted, 'mad'. It was distressing for her because unlike the freedom of her former creativity, feeling the nearness of nature and nature's ways, now nothing moved. There were no seasons of change in her life. The garden did not exist. She had been told to erase Luigi from her mind. At first she dared to say that she loved him. The word 'love' upon her lips had brought a shout from her father, a shriek from her mother. The girl didn't know what she was talking about. What could she possibly know of such mature feelings? It wasn't possible for an adolescent girl to experience real love. It was silly nonsense, dangerously silly nonsense, if it were not perverse and depraved. And slight as her meeting with Luigi had been, brief her intimacy with him, he lingered painfully in her mind for a while until tender memory was overwhelmed by the unbearable weight of her father's authority. Fenella entered forgetting.

My mother knew that Merton had ordered Fenella to burn all her paintings. He had told her. He said it was a necessary step in bringing her under his control. She had to learn who was master in the house, and to whom she was responsible. My mother listened, but once more, she didn't know. Did it matter about her painting? Was her interest in art a factor in making her the kind of girl she was? My mother was not clear about the connection. All she knew was that Fenella was not responding. She was withdrawn. Was this normal? Although my father offered a variety of answers to her doubts about what to do with Fenella, my mother was concerned about her isolation. Perhaps Fenella would benefit from talking to another person, a good woman from the church. She hadn't been to church since Merton had confined her to the house. It was all very well to make Fenella stay at home to prepare the Sunday lunch, to lock her in, or to leave Edgar in charge, but this meant that she saw no one outside the family from one week to the next. If Fenella wouldn't 'come clean' to her father, perhaps she would be more forthcoming with a 'good woman', someone with a sympathetic nature and with experience of adolescent girls. My mother suggested that he invite Miss Cattermole from the church to talk to her, because she was a good woman, or even the minister. He ought to know about Fenella. He really ought to know. My father dismissed the idea of Rev. Nithsdale. His theology was poor and his preaching weak. Clearly, he had nothing to offer. Nevertheless, he agreed to invite Miss Cattermole to Belvedere. He had reached the end of his tether. Yes, he would be specific. He would tell Miss Cattermole that it was essential that Fenella 'own up' to what had taken place in the city. He would grant this one concession. But if she didn't get a confession out of her, he would have to take the matter into his own hands.

Miss Cattermole, a woman bearing a name of unknown origin, was a middle-aged spinster with a clean, washed face. She was one of the odourless in the ranks of Puritan women, and wore her greying hair tied in a small bun at the nape of her pale neck. She respected my father, as everyone did. And she was pleased to be invited to talk to his daughter, Fenella. The Elders of St John's often asked her to give instruction on Christian morality to the senior members of the Presbyterian Fellowship Association. She had developed a special way with girls. They liked her. So when Miss Cattermole arrived one Sunday afternoon to talk to Mr Grey's 'difficult' daughter, the one who had strayed from the straight and narrow, she thought it fitting to bring her Bible. And while she talked softly to the frightened child sitting opposite her, the girl with so little to say, she placed her Bible on her lap and rested one hand upon it, while the other rested upon her tightly bound bosom. In such manner she talked to Fenella about the proper way to conduct herself in the presence of young men. 'We woman must never give men any cause for concern,' she said. 'It is our Christian duty not to arouse their passions.' Fenella looked at her, and then she lowered her head. She believed now that she had done that. She had aroused 'passions'. Seeing Fenella change momentarily, Miss Cattermole ventured to ask the question she knew her parents wanted answered. 'Tell me, Fenella,' she said, leaning towards her confidentially. And then in an affectionate tone, her hand still on the Bible, 'Tell me honestly, Fenella *dear*. Tell me truthfully.' She paused. 'Are you pure?' Fenella looked up. She frowned. For a moment she was puzzled by the word. Why should Miss Cattermole ask her such a thing? What had the word 'pure' to do with anything that had happened to her? At last she could speak. She wanted to speak. Without any elaboration, she answered the question in its perfect form, speaking with an even emphasis on each syllable. In her terrible confusion, it was her only clear and unambiguous utterance.

'Yes, Miss Cattermole,' she said. 'I am pure.'

It was early next morning that my father entered Fenella's room. He hadn't locked the door the night before. He thought it no longer necessary. Apart from her obstinacy in confessing carnal knowledge, her rebellion was over. He had broken her spirit. And Miss Cattermole had failed to convince him. In spite of what she had reported to him after her visit, he felt sure his daughter was incapable of telling the difference between right and wrong. There was a part of her cerebral function that, to his trained mind, seemed to be absent. She was 'amoral'. In which case, it was his perfect and inalienable right as both doctor and father to examine her, just as he would any other patient, to determine, by physical enquiry, whether she was 'intact'. It was a matter of principle.

As soon as he came into the room, a frightened Tommy, who had spent the night curled up on the foot of Fenella's bed, woke suddenly and fled into the corridor. Fenella was still asleep. My father didn't disturb her. Just as it had been his habit to administer injections suddenly and swiftly in the night, he did the deed while she was dreaming fitfully. It was a simple procedure, a standard examination that he had performed hundreds of times. As he stripped away the bedcovers and pulled up her nightie, Fenella, who was sleeping on her side, breathed deeply and then turned onto her back. Sensing a vague presence, hearing the scampering noise of Tommy's claws on the wooden floor as he dashed from the room, she half-opened her eyes. When she became aware of her father leaning over her dressed in his pyjamas, she closed her eyes again tightly. Although she was not alarmed, she did not wish to see. Whatever was about to happen to her, she would endure it blind, in the opaque world of unknowing. Pushing her legs apart, he arranged her quickly. It was easily done. And then with his index finger, his naked discriminating finger, as a high priest of haruspicy, he penetrated the soft foramen of her sexual orifice; he pushed into the pearly shell, the very anima of her being. He touched the veil of Hymen. It felt like this, the maiden thing, the little disc. It felt like *This! This! This!* He withdrew his finger. His daughter was 'intact'. She was his.

My mother was dismayed. When my father told her that he had examined Fenella to reassure himself that she was untouched, and that, as far as he could tell, she had no carnal experience, she felt disturbed, uncomfortable. She could not understand why Fenella had allowed herself to be examined in such a manner. Why hadn't she protested? She would have protested if her father had done such a thing to her. Suddenly, the whole business about their daughter's virginity, her husband's obsession with it, had become 'trivial'. She was tired of it, sick to death of the worry. Rising up in anger, she questioned my father. Did he think he had done the right thing? Might she not tell someone? But my father insisted that he had acted responsibly. 'What else was I to do?' he said. 'I have to know. I am her father.' My mother had nothing to say to Fenella except that she was a foolish, foolish girl. She was vain, stupid, disobedient and reckless. She was responsible for complicating the whole sorry affair. She was *shallow*. Why hadn't she kicked and screamed? Had she no life in her? Why had she let her father do it?

I find myself back at the beginning, reaching the final day of feeling recall under the auspices of crystals, living the myth of the eternal return through repetition and participation. And throughout the long winter months of writing, nothing significant would have occurred without the creative assistance of the elements that surround me. My enquiry began in uninitiated time. I stood outside the temple, in the very meaning of the word 'profane', waiting for the moment, the very moment that I would be admitted. As I entered the sacred space, picking up one stone and then another, today holding a piece of rough-hewn rose quartz in my hand, in every step I affected the abolition of the profane and the recreation of the archetype. First I stood upon the threshold. Then I found myself standing in the narthex, my eye attracted by the distant activity, shrouded in mist. It was this that I had come to see. And although I would like to say that I ascended the steps to the sanctuary, I did not. The ascent belongs to Fenella. It was sufficient for the consummation of my understanding to stay precisely where I was and allow my senses to be activated by the element that I held or at other times laid upon my body. And immersed in religious memories, the call came from far deeper regions. The vision made itself plain. Because of the crystals I love so much, and in spite of the pain, the experience yielded something beautiful. The *mise-en-scène* was always mythological, the dance outside time, moving naturally and graciously within the eternal.

I remind myself that the deep secret of Eleusis, the *arrheton* as it was called, which having been seen may not be uttered, belonged to Persephone. Indeed it was Euripides who said she was the only one of all divine beings to be given the epithet *arrhetos koura*, the ineffable maiden. Buried in nature, she emerged in the sacred rights of Eleusis, one of the great mysteries of antiquity, just as Aphrodite, the foam-born goddess, became 'she who rises from the sea', to be adored by all who are drawn to water, and to the symbol of the shell. But it was Persephone about whom nothing could be determined. In all secrets, she was the secret. And in a very real sense, every maiden to whom something profound happens shares her mythology. It is to the ineffable, *ab origine*, that we return. In the history of my sister Fenella, I have only mythology to relate. For all these years, she has been my secret. Separated from her, I fretted for her. I did not know what to do. In England, I found myself saying, 'If Fenella were here, she would love the ash tree. If Fenella were here, she would identify the bird by its flight.' Repeating her name as often as I did, I came to hear myself say over and over again, 'If only Fenella were here,' by which I meant, if only she were here, then I would be healed of my pain.

Our separation being so complete, in the latter years of her life, I did not know where she was living, or if she was living at all. I do know that after leaving home, she entered a wandering, disconsolate life, a life without memory. And because she lived without memory, she lived precariously. She was seen, but only in glimpses, everywhere. From time to time, it was reported to me that she was in one place, and then, within a period that seemed absurd, impossible, I would hear that she was elsewhere. Such were her sightings. She lived like a bird on the wing, sheltering in trees, dropping a feather here and there to be picked up by those who collected such things. And when she disappeared from view, it was impossible to know where she was going or what was happening to her. She remained 'the ineffable maiden', flitting in and out of reality, attuned not only to the rhythm of the seasons but also to the high mysteries of creativity. No member of the family knew anything about her. In fact, out of necessity, the strangest stories abounded. Fenella 'went wild'. Life could not tame her. I know it was her destiny, as indeed it was her fate, to remain a child of nature, living an unfinished life, a life that would always be talked about; a confabulation in the absence of facts; Fenella, the unfinished poem, *Christabel*. Indeed, I know she lived precariously. Living precariously, living 'on the edge' as it is described, endangered her existence. Under strange circumstances, she died. As a bird drops from the sky, she died. I have never wanted to enquire into these dark circumstances. I never wanted to know. But the rediscovery of her origins has explained everything to me. I have traced the bird to its hatching, to its very nest. Though the nest is long abandoned, there is evidence of frantic activity, the urgent shedding of the eggshell. Now there is nothing more I need see; nothing more I need know. Fenella lives. Through the creatures of the imagination and through the creatures of nature, through everything that is incarnate and dear to her, through art, she has been brought to life.

Perhaps it is not without significance that I reached the consummation of my narrative just as Spring breaks in England, in Persephone's celebratory season, and in the town that witnessed the birth of the great Romantic poet, Coleridge. That the poet visited these pages at the beginning is significant, so perhaps it is not unsurprising to write the epilogue within his sphere of influence. This is a time when the colour green is most active, when the shout of resurrection is heard and in response to the cry, everything moves. I use the word 'perhaps' only as a literary device, for in truth there is no perhaps and no coincidence that cannot be touched. As I emerge form my inner world, I see my sister Fenella reborn here, in the place where I now live. And when I travel to Exeter, it is she that I see appearing from around the corner to greet me. She sits with me in a cappuccino bar. We chat happily, the Gaggia machine hissing merrily behind us. But however much I want her, she will not be captured. She cannot live here. Fenella belongs to Tasmania. Her mythology is truly, and sacredly, ineffable. It is secret. The secret is the real power that locates her where she belongs, and where she, for her own sake, needs to be.

When we were together as girls and then, very briefly, as young women, I observed her closely. I saw her responding to a distant call. The mysterious call came through the warring winds of alienation and separation, from the island lying south of the land, from Bruny Island. And as I summon the image of my sister now, I dance with her a dance of removal. We are together, weaving into the ocean wind, stepping lightly upon the white sands of Adventure Bay looking towards the threatening frozen unknown of the south. In the strength of the gale that silences everything but itself, we are raised. We enjoy the elevation. We are together, merging effortlessly with the transforming power of creativity, the gift that she was given. There is no suggestion of an Antarctic winter. The day is bright. Fenella is full of joy. When I came to England I brought Fenella with me. She remained asleep in my unconscious, wrapped in the winding-sheet of forgetting. Now profane time has come to an end. Having raised her life and her death to consciousness and having restored memory, both hers and mine, my custodial role is about to be transformed. Fenella will leave the England of these pages where she has been stored for so long, she will be lifted from this brief epitome, and she will return to Tasmania, to her place of origins. I am seeing her for the very last time. For this final ritual seeing, her apotheosis in the sanctuary of nature, she wears around her neck three strands of spiky shells, the tiny jewels from the southern sea that Aboriginal women have named 'maireeners'. She wears the relics that we found under the house at Belvedere, the ornament that is art, the once-forgotten rite of being. They are the shells we called 'Truganini's'. They exist in the myth of the 'ineffable maiden'. They are hers, these sea creatures left hanging in the mulberry tree. It is they who activate the rite. And as I dance with my sister along the shell-strewn way of Adventure Bay, she in her billowing apron of stencilled leaves, the wind carries her further from me. Fear of separation intervenes. She travels swiftly over tussocks and dunes, over glistening sands, far across waves that break as rapture on the southern shore. I call to her. With desperation in my voice I call to her, 'Fenella! Fenella! Please don't leave me!' But Fenella is far from my scene. Airborne, she skims and dips upon the swelling ocean like a cormorant, the pearly shells gleaming in myriad sea-eyes around her throat. Absorbed by the restorative energy of nature, she is intent upon her own destiny. The apotheosis of truth and beauty complete, Fenella disappears.

A crystal that has sustained an injury while being extracted from the earth needs special attention in order to arouse the healing power within it. I have in my possession one such stone that seems to have been dropped from a great height; a body flung from the parapet. All I can say in describing its condition is that it feels bruised. Whenever I see it, I inhale sharply, a bitter sting upon my lips. Although it is only a small piece of rough-hewn rose quartz, the injury to it is real. I hold it tenderly in my hand and wish the healer healed. I bathe its wounds in lavender water. This is a strange state of affairs, I say to myself, to find that which heals me in need of my healing. But it is true. I feel it. I see it in the flight of birds. At the end of my journey, waiting to begin another, I speak with the authority of an auspex. A mutuality exists between the healer, as an instrument of healing, and the recipient, be it animal, vegetable or mineral; a reciprocal energy that makes manifest the powers of nature latent in us; an immersion in earth's virtues that awakens us to origins and to our true, spiritual belonging.

In 1994, a former Tasmanian, now living in Devon, on a visit to the Royal Albert Memorial Museum in Exeter, sighted Truganini's shells in a display cabinet. Three years later, in November 1997, the necklace and bracelet were repatriated.